"This text provides an outline of how to incorporate the arts into literacy teaching and learning at the K–12 level. It is also a text that many teacher preparation programs will find valuable. What I find most compelling about the text is its ability to span what is often seen as two very different approaches to curriculum and pedagogy. That is, the teaching and learning advocated for in this text situates literacy as a social practice, an approach most often aligned with progressive education movements that run counter to current education reform as it is practiced at the school level. At the same time, the book provides smart examples of how the arts and literacy actually support and move forward some of these same reform agendas such as the Common Core State Standards and the edTPA in teacher education. We need more books like this that work across disciplines to make common cause in service to our students."
—*Professor Cindy Maguire, Adelphi University, USA*

"This scholarly and yet accessible exploration of arts literacies offers a valuable contribution to those with an interest in expanding the notion of arts education literacy practices within K–12 classrooms. You will find in these pages thought-provoking ideas and critical questions for guiding your own inquiry into the arts literacy practices necessary for engaging today's learners."
—*Dr. Susan O'Neill, Simon Fraser University, Canada*

Arts Education and Literacies

In a struggling global economy, education is focused on core subjects such as language arts and mathematics, and the development of technological and career-readiness skills. Prior to the development of National Core Arts Standards, arts education has not been a central focus of education reform movements in the United States, and none of the current education standards frameworks deeply address the processes, texts, and literacies that are inherent to arts disciplines. This lack of clarity poses a problem for state and district leaders who might be inclined to advocate for the arts in schools and classrooms across the country but cannot find adequate detail in their guiding frameworks.

This volume acknowledges the challenges that arts educators face and posits that authentic arts instruction and learning can benefit a young person's development both inside and outside of the classroom. It presents ways that arts teachers and literacy specialists can work together to help others understand the potential that arts learning has to enhance students' twenty-first-century learning skills.

Amy Petersen Jensen is professor and department chair in the Theatre and Media Arts Department at Brigham Young University, USA.

Roni Jo Draper is professor of teacher education at Brigham Young University, USA.

Routledge Research in Literacy

Edited by David Barton, Lancaster University, UK

1 **Women, Literacy and Development**
   Edited by Anna Robinson-Pant

2 **Literacy and Globalization**
   Reading and Writing in Times of Social and Cultural Change
   Uta Papen

3 **Popular Culture and Representations of Literacy**
   Bronwyn T. Williams and Amy A. Zenger

4 **Romani Writing**
   Literacy, Literature and Identity Politics
   Paola Toninato

5 **New Literacies around the Globe**
   Policy and Pedagogy
   Edited by Cathy Burnett, Julia Davies, Guy Merchant, and Jennifer Rowsell

6 **Arts Education and Literacies**
   Edited by Amy Petersen Jensen and Roni Jo Draper

Arts Education and Literacies

Edited by
Amy Petersen Jensen and
Roni Jo Draper

With

Daniel T. Barney
Paul Broomhead
Pamela S. Musil
Benjamin Thevenin
Jennifer J. Wimmer

LONDON AND NEW YORK

First published 2015 by Routledge

2 Park Square, Milton Park, Abingdon, Oxon OX14 4RN
711 Third Avenue, New York, NY 10017, USA

Routledge is an imprint of the Taylor & Francis Group, an informa business

First issued in paperback 2017

Copyright © 2015 Taylor & Francis

The right of the editors to be identified as the authors of the editorial material, and of the authors for their individual chapters, has been asserted in accordance with sections 77 and 78 of the Copyright, Designs and Patents Act 1988.

All rights reserved. No part of this book may be reprinted or reproduced or utilised in any form or by any electronic, mechanical, or other means, now known or hereafter invented, including photocopying and recording, or in any information storage or retrieval system, without permission in writing from the publishers.

Notice:

Product or corporate names may be trademarks or registered trademarks, and are used only for identification and explanation without intent to infringe.

Library of Congress Cataloging-in-Publication Data

CIP data has been applied for.

ISBN: 978-1-138-80697-9 (hbk)
ISBN: 978-1-138-08496-4 (pbk)

Typeset in Sabon
by Apex CoVantage, LLC

Because of
Evan, Quinlan, Bennett,
Lily and Lauren

Contents

Acknowledgements   xiii

Introduction: Arts Education and Literacy in Support of Conversation   1
AMY PETERSEN JENSEN AND RONI JO DRAPER

SECTION I
Creating

1 **Music: Creating**   13
PAUL BROOMHEAD

2 **Dance: Creating**   20
PAMELA S. MUSIL, AMY PETERSEN JENSEN, AND RONI JO DRAPER

3 **Media Arts: Creating**   29
BENJAMIN THEVENIN

4 **Theatre: Creating**   36
AMY PETERSEN JENSEN

5 **Visual Art: Creating**   43
DANIEL T. BARNEY

6 **Theatre in the Elementary Classroom: Creating**   52
JENNIFER J. WIMMER AND JULIA ASHWORTH

SECTION II
Performing

7 Music: Performing   61
   PAUL BROOMHEAD

8 Dance: Performing   69
   PAMELA S. MUSIL

9 Media Arts: Performing   76
   BENJAMIN THEVENIN

10 Theatre: Performing   83
   AMY PETERSEN JENSEN AND JULIA ASHWORTH

11 Visual Art: Performing/Presenting/Producing   91
   DANIEL T. BARNEY

12 Media Arts in the Elementary Classroom: Producing   99
   JENNIFER J. WIMMER AND BENJAMIN THEVENIN

SECTION III
Responding

13 Music: Responding   109
   PAUL BROOMHEAD

14 Dance: Responding   116
   PAMELA S. MUSIL

15 Media Arts: Responding   124
   BENJAMIN THEVENIN

16 Theatre: Responding   132
   AMY PETERSEN JENSEN

17 Visual Art: Responding   140
   DANIEL T. BARNEY

18 Visual Arts in the Elementary Classroom: Responding   148
   JENNIFER J. WIMMER AND DANIEL T. BARNEY

SECTION IV
Connecting

19	Music: Connecting PAUL BROOMHEAD	157
20	Dance: Connecting PAMELA S. MUSIL	165
21	Media Arts: Connecting BENJAMIN THEVENIN	174
22	Theatre: Connecting AMY PETERSEN JENSEN	181
23	Visual Art: Connecting DANIEL T. BARNEY	189
24	Dance in the Elementary Classroom: Connecting JENNIFER J. WIMMER AND KORI WAKAMATSU	198
25	Creating and Continuing the Conversation between Arts and Literacy Educators RONI JO DRAPER AND AMY PETERSEN JENSEN	206
	Contributors	213
	Index	217

Acknowledgements

Many of the ideas about literacies presented in this book were developed through collaborations with other members of the Brigham Young University (BYU) Literacy Study Group. We are grateful for our continued work with our colleagues Jeff Nokes, Sirpa Grierson, Stephen Shumway, and Daniel Siebert.

This book represents a collaborative effort between the various chapter authors. Arts educators, sometimes in collaboration with literacy educators, created drafts of each chapter and shared those drafts with members of the entire editorial team (Amy Petersen Jensen, Roni Jo Draper, Daniel T. Barney, Paul Broomhead, Pamela S. Musil, Benjamin Thevenin, and Jennifer J. Wimmer). The editorial team, who are also chapter authors, read and discussed each chapter at weekly meetings. These discussions provided chapter authors with opportunities to refine ideas, sharpen arguments, and ensure that the ideas presented across the chapters are coherent without being overly redundant.

Introduction
Arts Education and Literacy in Support of Conversation

Amy Petersen Jensen and Roni Jo Draper

Education, as Oakeshott (1959) put it, is "an initiation into the skill and partnership of [the human] conversation" (p. 11). While conversation may result in the exchange of information, inquiry, persuasion, discovery, or improvement of the human condition, it certainly needn't. Rather, conversation simply allows humans to acknowledge and enjoy one another. It is the conversation, Oakeshott suggests, that sets us apart as humans. Thus, to educate individuals is to prepare them with the intellectual and moral habits required to engage in the human conversation.

The purpose of this book on arts literacies is twofold. First, we wish to present ideas to help prepare young people to engage fully in the human conversation. Indeed, we understand that the arts are integral to making the human conversation possible. Second, we wish to invite arts and literacy educators to engage each other in conversation. As it stands now, arts educators and literacy educators may view their goals and purposes at odds. Perhaps that is because educators find themselves fighting for resources or because policy, curricula, and assessments seem to place emphasis on some literacies that seem unrelated to those needed to participate in arts settings.

Ultimately, we do not believe that educational reforms—either general reforms that privilege literacy and numeracy or arts reforms—are at odds with one another. Rather we see educational reforms in literacy and the arts as complementary. In this chapter we will discuss the complementary nature of school reforms, share our conception of literacy and its usefulness for the arts, and provide an overview of the book.

EDUCATIONAL REFORMS

Arts education has not been a central focus of key education reform movements in the United States. The No Child Left Behind Act of 2001 certainly includes the arts as a core subject (2008) but primarily addresses other subjects as academic indicators. Prominently produced education standards frameworks developed at the national level such as the Partnership for Twenty-first Century Skills (2012) and the Common Core State Standards

(2010) also refer to the arts as core subjects, but their inclusion is cursory and does not include the details or specifics of the other subjects. None of these documents addresses the texts, processes, and literacies that are central to arts disciplines.

This lack of clarity about the arts and their place in schools poses a problem for state and district leaders inclined to advocate for the arts in schools and classrooms across the country but who cannot find adequate descriptions of arts instruction in their guiding documents. Because educators, both at the local and state levels, work from standards documents adopted within their state systems when implementing education reform, they face two choices for arts education. First, educators simply can forgo further development of the arts in their school curricula by choosing to focus planning and resources on other core subjects or career and technical areas. The second course of action for educators working to support the arts is to work to fit arts curricula into standards developed for other key subject areas such as English language arts, science and technology, history, and mathematics, which provide tacit approval for arts programs without the resources or funding to back that support. The first choice results in schools where the arts are absent regardless of their inclusion in reform documents. The second attempt, while noble in many respects, identifies the arts as enhancement to curricula, thus the arts are valued as servants to what are deemed as other more central subject areas.

From outside the arts education community, either of these approaches might seem an acceptable way to address the pressures placed on schools to prepare young people for their futures. Core subject areas such as language arts, mathematics, science, and history are certainly important. Moreover, due to economic conditions, leading to increased class sizes and decreased budgets, educators have had to make difficult resources decisions within school systems. Many people have reasoned that competing in a struggling global economy requires schools to focus more intently on established core subjects as well as technology to support information literacies and career readiness skills (National Research Council, 2012).

Arts educators and advocates, however, argue that participation in the arts should be at the center of every educational environment. Arts educators argue that engaging in arts processes can provide children and youth with unique opportunities to imagine and create tangible products, focus on emotional expression, live with ambiguity, and make connections with others in collaborative environments (Davis, 2008), all attributes that will aid students in their immediate and future lives outside of school. Anyone who has participated in the development of a theatrical play or as a contributing member of an orchestra probably understands the value of the arts processes they experienced.

Thus, arts educators have engaged in educational reforms to strengthen arts education. Most recently, in 2014 the National Coalition for Core Arts Standards (a partnership of organizations that led the revision of the 1994

National Standards for Arts Education; from this point the organization will be referred to as NCCAS) established voluntary standards for arts edication. A key component of the most recent arts education framework was the decision to organize the standards to include artistic literacy. NCCAS defined artistic literacy as "the knowledge and understanding required to participate authentically in the arts. Fluency in the language(s) of the arts, or the ability to create, perform/produce/present, respond, and connect through symbolic and metaphoric forms that are unique to the arts, is embodied in specific philosophic foundations and life long goals" (NCCAS Framework, p. 17). Thus, NCCAS embraced and promoted the notion that all individuals should have access to participation in the arts.

The arts educators who worked together to create the arts standards uphold that the opportunities for individual development in the arts not only dovetail nicely with 21st Century learning practices such as "innovation, creativity, and communication," which are described by the Partnership for 21st Century Learning (see Arts map, 2010) but also enhance child development (The College Board, 2012). Certainly, the learning outcomes associated with engaging in arts processes provides opportunities for learners to develop technological and information literacies. Likewise, these opportunities hold the potential to allow young people to advance their career readiness in ways that other core disciplines may not. For example, a young media artist using tools acquired in the visual arts classroom becomes familiar with the same technological applications that are used in career and technology education courses. However, to create as an artist within the medium of her choice, she also engages in various creative artistic processes that require inquiry and critical thinking to make meaning. Moreover, *authentic* participation in arts learning—or learning experiences where teachers and students actively work together to create, perform or present, respond, and connect to works of art—builds unique literacies that potentially can address 21st Century goals for life and work such as those described by the National Research Council, including, "problem solving, critical thinking, communication, collaboration, and self-management" (Pellegrino, Hilton, & for the National Research Council, 2012, p. 1).

Like Pellegrino, we believe that arts educators, using the texts, processes, and literacies that are unique to each respective arts discipline can support intellectually and practically the deeper learning necessary to students' success in education, work, and all areas of life in ways that other disciplines cannot. Additionally, we believe that authentic arts instruction and learning can benefit a young person's development both inside and outside of the classroom setting. For instance, a young musician who understands the circle of fifths and can apply this knowledge in a musical setting might also recognize other relational patterns in the world around him. Similarly, a dancer engaged in the collaborative processes of creating a dance composition with other dancers will be able to use problem-solving skills developed in that arts setting when she encounters other interpersonal challenges at home or in the workplace. Moreover, we insist that the human conversation, as suggested by Oakeshott, is maintained by recognizing the diversities of expression available to support human relationships—including the expressive opportunities only made possible through the arts.

Regardless of the complementary nature of the various educational reforms, the difficulty for artists, arts educators, and arts programs is that they must continue to insert themselves into conversations about educating young people effectively. Currently arts educators may find themselves on the margins of what counts in education. Thus, we argue that for educational reforms like those associated with the adoption of the Common Core State Standards (2010) and the promotion of 21st Century skills (2009) to thrive, the arts must also thrive. Indeed, we have confidence that teachers and artists can be better advocates of arts learning as they attempt to enter into conversations with literacy specialists. These conversations are central to commencing to work together within schools and school systems to prepare young people to participate in their worlds outside of school.

CONCEPTIONS OF LITERACY

To begin the conversation, arts educators and literacy educators may find common ground in thinking about literacy. Literacy can be viewed as simply the ability to read and write traditional print texts—in which case, a conversation about literacy may offer little of interest to most arts educators looking to improve their work with young people. However, when one considers that all human interactions are mediated by texts (print and otherwise) that individuals create and imbue with meaning, the ability to create and negotiate those texts (literacy) becomes an important notion. Indeed, the very idea of the human conversation depends on the ability to create texts—utterances—that others can use to make meaning. It is this in the creation, sharing, and negation of texts that the human conversation takes place. Thus, literacy, defined broadly, is a notion to which all educators can contribute ideas. In fact, as mentioned in the previous section, the 2014 National Core Arts Standards are framed around artistic literacies. Rather than decide that artistic literacies vary drastically from literacies understood and valued by literacy specialists, we offer a conception of literacy that both arts and literacy educators may find useful.

The conception of literacy that we find most useful is *literacy as a social practice* (Barton, 1994; Gee, 1996; Street, 1995). We agree with Kelly, Luke, and Green (2008) when they state that "specific social groups, including discipline-based groups, create specialized discourse, signs and symbols, ways of representing knowledge, and ways of thinking and inquiring that come to count as knowledge in these groups over time." For us this means that instead of describing literacy as a set of proficiencies to be understood and mastered, we believe that literacies are socially constructed interactions among individuals and other people, spaces, and objects that they come into contact with in the various circles in which they move—both in school and out of school.

This is certainly true within artistic communities. Artists do not practice their craft in isolation; instead, they engage with others, utilizing common signs and symbols that are accepted within their field to make meaning or to create the "specialized discourse" that Kelly, Luke, and Green point to in their statement. Meaning making in these settings often has personal, social, cultural, political, and economic implications for the artists and those who interact with their work. This means that arts educators interested in helping young people acquire and practice arts literacies must be aware of, and intentionally expose their students to, the unique contexts in which artists practice their craft.

Framing discussions about arts literacy through the theoretical lens of literacy as a social practice (Barton & Hamilton, 2000; Gee, 2001, 2004; Street, 1995) provides educators a checklist of practices they can use to reflect on their teaching and the learning of their students (see Barton and Hamilton, 2010). This checklist includes the following notions:

- Literacy is best understood as a set of social practices; these can be inferred from events, which are mediated by texts [construed broadly].
- There are different literacies associated with different domains of life [or different areas of disciplinary study].
- Literacy practices are patterned by social institutions and power relationships, and some literacies are more dominant, visible, and influential than others.
- Literacy practices are purposeful and embedded in broader social goals and cultural practices.
- Literacy is historically situated.
- Literacy practices change and new ones are frequently acquired through processes of [formal and] informal learning and sense making. (p. 8)

The checklist may help arts educators to stop thinking of arts learning and literacy in a vacuum and begin to think purposefully about what is unique about each arts discipline and where the arts have common goals and cultural practices. Furthermore, the checklist should demonstrate how the goals of arts literacy meet with the broader social goals and cultural practices of the larger literacy community as well as the more dominant and visible goals of public schooling.

To engage in the human conversation, one's literacies matter. Moreover, as the technologies and tools available to humans continue to change, conceptions of texts and literacies also must change. Thus, the discussions of literacy have shifted away from traditional literacy (as the ability to read and write print texts) and toward discussions that address a broad range of social literacies (Gee, 1996; Street, 2003), digital media literacies (Alvermann,

2008; Boyd, 2007; Hobbs, 2007), and adolescents' literacies both in and out of school settings (Ito, 2010). Indeed, general literacy conversations have opened the door to exploring a more broad notion of *texts* and their accompanying *literacies* as they relate to digital and technological means or even to mathematic equations (Draper, Broomhead, Jensen, Nokes, & Siebert, 2010; Kress, 2000; Moje, 2008; Shanahan and Shanahan, 2008). As such, arts educators may enter the conversation by describing key arts texts such as the body, a stage, a canvas, or a musical instrument as text. They also may think about the various literacies required to make sense of these arts texts. Additionally, literacy educators are usually unfamiliar with arts processes—creating, performing/ presenting/producing, responding, and connecting—and the accompanying literacies that occur when arts educators and young people engage in those processes together. However, literacy educators have much to offer arts educators interested in understanding texts and literacies—especially when literacy educators enter those conversations with curiosity—because engaging the curiosities of literacy educators may be the perfect way for arts educators to understand their artistic literacies better.

The contributors to this book are interested in exploring the texts, processes, and literacies inherent to arts learning and are suited particularly to initiate a conversation about arts literacy. They are members of the Brigham Young University Literacy Study Group (BYU LSG), and many of the participants have been engaged in conversations surrounding disciplinary literacies (including the arts) for nearly a decade. Our previous work as the BYU LSG has focused on ways that literacy specialists and content area educators might work together to provide adolescents with more authentic experiences in the disciplines they study. Our goal has been to expand the notion of literacy to move beyond the reading and writing of print text with the purpose of helping teachers and young people engage in literacy events and activities that are essential to learning within individual content areas (Draper et al., 2010; Draper, Broomhead, Jensen, & Nokes, 2012). Our collaboration has been fruitful in that it has allowed for an unusual cross-curricular conversation that has enriched and broadened group participants' notions of texts and literacies. Additionally, as we have studied educational policy, theories, and practices together, our conversations surrounding this study have made us all more conscious of the affordances and limitations of the texts and literacies inherent in each of our disciplines.

These conversations certainly have helped literacy educators appreciate the texts and literacies associated with the arts. However, the conversation also has been useful for the arts educators who wish to improve the ways in which they might engage young people in the arts. As such, conversations around arts texts and literacies have allowed us to note the particular affordances and limitations essential to arts texts, literacies, and learning. For example, we have found that thinking about the body as a text, and then imagining the literacies associated with using the body to create a dance performance, has given us useful language for making arts processes more accessible to novice artists in educational settings.

As such, our conversations surrounding expanded notions of texts and literacies can be helpful to arts educators as they think about ways that texts and literacies are employed within arts disciplines. But this requires a degree of translation on the part of the arts educator, and translating general ideas about literacy into the particulars of an arts discipline often leaves something lost in the translation. In fact, leaving these translations to literacy educators who may have limited experience with or understanding of arts processes may only contribute to the difficulty of creating instruction that addresses the unique arts literacies needed to participate fully in the arts. Instead, arts educators need concrete arts examples that are developed by disciplinary specialists who understand the nuances of their art forms and are familiar with the discourse of arts education. This, of course, requires that arts educators and literacy educators engage in conversation. Indeed, our hope is that this book enables that conversation.

While there is substantive scholarship focused on the arts, literacy, and schooling (Birch, 2008; Davis, 2008; Duncum, 2004; Ryan & Healy, 2007), there are currently no scholarly discussions that directly address literacy and literacy instruction within the arts that are equal to those describing literacy and instruction in other areas of the education landscape, such as English, science, history, or mathematics. Specifically, there are no prominent pieces that discuss the potential for literacy instruction that is situated within the context of dance, media, music, theatre, and the visual arts. Our work in the sections that follow is an attempt to open the door to further conversation about the texts, processes, and literacies that are crucial to skills and knowledge building in each of the arts disciplines. Our intent, for this book, is to create a conversation about how the knowledge and understandings necessary to participate authentically in the arts, including the ability to create, perform/present/produce, respond, and connect might function practically in K–12 classrooms.

HOW THE BOOK SECTIONS ARE ORGANIZED—DISCIPLINARY CHAPTERS

To explore the various ways teachers might engage in literacy instruction with their students, we have organized the book into four sections. Each section focuses on one of the four artistic processes outlined earlier and identified in the NCCAS definition of arts literacy. These include the following:

- *Creating:* Conceiving and developing new artistic ideas and work.
- *Performing/Presenting/Producing:* Realizing and presenting artistic work.
- *Responding:* Understanding and evaluating how the arts convey meaning.

- *Connecting:* Relating artistic ideas and work with personal meaning and external context.

We understand that each of these processes is never really isolated. Rather, creating most necessarily involves connecting to meanings, whether they be personal, historical, or both. Additionally, responding to the work of another artist is often the impetus of creating. Thus, our discussion of these processes as separate is primarily for convenience as it reflects the work of the framers of the NCCAS.

Each of the process sections is comprised of short chapters from each of the five arts disciplines (visual arts, music, dance, theatre, and media) that are written by disciplinary specialists. Each of the authors describes the arts process and how arts educators might identify and improve on the arts literacy already occurring in their classrooms. At the center of each chapter, authors describe a *literacy event*, or an authentic arts learning activity where texts, processes, and literacies have roles[1]. According to Barton, Hamilton, and Ivanic (2000) literacy events generally are characterized as observable events in which texts (print or otherwise in arts classrooms) are central to the activity. The events arise from disciplinary processes and often are shaped by them. Additionally there should be talk and actions around those texts. Using the frame of the literacy event, our authors explore the texts, processes, and accompanying literacies that artists use to create, perform/present/produce, respond, and connect within their artistic domain(s). To be clear, the authors do not include these literacy events to suggest one way to engage students in the arts or to propose a limited view of texts and literacies for their disciplines. Instead, each author provides one concrete example from which arts and literacy educators can work to create arts instruction that promotes young people's full participation in the arts.

For the purposes of this book, we define artistic texts, processes, and literacies in the following way:

- *Arts Texts:* Our definition of texts requires that the traditional notion of text be expanded to include texts that are essential to each discipline. These texts may or may not be print texts but could include a lighting plot, the human body, digital images, a musical instrument, choreography, or paint applied to a canvas.
- *Artistic Processes*: These are the processes whereby something new is created as young people and teachers use imagination, investigation, construction, and reflection in arts environs.
- *Arts Literacies*: Arts literacies encompass the knowledge and skills essential to learning in the arts. Instructional ideas that build arts literacy should provide opportunities for students and teachers to participate in authentic disciplinary practices.

Additionally, in each short chapter we demonstrate how teachers and students can explore texts, literacies, and processes that are essential to arts learning and development within each given field of study as if they are artists working authentically within their disciplines. Ultimately, our goal is not promote arts classrooms as literacy spaces. Rather it is to illuminate how arts classrooms are locations in which young people confront and create arts texts as a natural part of engaging in the various arts processes. Thus, literacy instruction is a crucial part of a complete arts education. Moreover, arts education is a crucial part of a complete education. Welcome to the conversation.

NOTE

1. All names used are pseudonyms.

REFERENCES

Alvermann, D. (2008). Why bother theorizing adolescents' online literacies for classroom practice and research? *Journal of Adolescent and Adult Literacy, 52*(1), 8–19.
Barton, D. (1994). *Literacy: An introduction to the ecology of the written language.* London: Blackwell.
Barton, D., & Hamilton, M. (2000). Literacy practices. In D. Barton, M. Hamilton, & R. Ivanic (Eds.), *Situated literacies: Reading and writing in context* (pp. 7–15). New York: Routledge.
Barton, D., Hamilton M., & Ivanic, R. (2000). *Situated literacies: Reading and writing in context.* New York: Routledge.
Birch, J. (2008). Expanding literacy and integrating curricula through dance. *The Educational Forum, 64*(3), 223–228.
boyd, d. (2007). Why youth (heart) social network sites: The role of networked publics in teenage social life. In D. Buckingham (Ed.), *MacArthur Foundation Series on Digital Learning-Youth, Identity, and Digital Media* (pp. 1–26). Cambridge, MA: MIT Press.
The College Board. (Eds.). (2012). Child development and arts education: A review of recent research and best practices. New York, NY: Author.
Common Core State Standards. (2010). *Common core state standards.* Retrieved February 19, 2011, from http://www.corestandards.org
Davis, J. H. (2008). *Why our schools need the arts.* New York: Teachers College Press.
Draper, R.J., Broomhead, P., Jensen, A.P., & Nokes, J.D. (2012). (Re)imagining literacy and teacher preparation through collaboration. *Reading Psychology, 33*(4), 367–398.
Draper, R.J., Broomhead, P., Jensen, A.P., Nokes, J.D., & Siebert, D. (Eds.). (2010). *(Re)imagining content-area literacy instruction.* New York: Teachers College Press.
Duncum, P. (2004). Visual culture isn't just visual: Multiliteracy, multimodality, and meaning. *Studies in Art Education: A Journal of Issues and Research, 45*(3), 252–264.
Gee, J.P. (2001). Reading as situated language: A sociocognitive perspective. *Journal of Adolescent and Adult Literacy, 44*(8), 714–725.
Gee, J.P. (1996). *Social linguistics and literacies: Ideology in Discourses.* Second Edition. London: Taylor & Francis.
Gee, J. P. (2004). *Situated language and learning: A critique of traditional schooling.* New York: Routledge.

Hobbs, R. (2007). *Reading the media: Media literacy in high school English*. New York: Teachers College Press.

Ito, M., Baumer, S., Bittanti, M., boyd, d., Cody, R., Herr, B., . . . Trip, L. (2010). *Hanging out, messing around, and geeking out: Kids living and learning with new media*. The John D. and Catherine T. MacArthur Foundation Series on Digital Media and Learning. Massachusetts: MIT Press.

Kelly, G., Luke, A., & Green, J. (2008). What counts as knowledge in educational settings: Knowledge, assessment and curriculum. *Review of Research in Education, 32*(1), vii–x.

Kress, G. (2000). Multimodality. In B. Cope & M. Kalantizis (Eds.), *Multiliteracies: Literacy learning and the design of social futures* (pp. 182–202). London: Routledge.

Moje, E. B. (2008). Foregrounding the disciplines in secondary literacy teaching and learning: A call for change. *Journal of Adolescent and Adult Literacy, 52*, 96–107.

National Coalition for Core Arts. (2012). *Pre-K-12 Arts Learning. Foundations for Arts Literacy*. Retrieved from http://www.nccas.wikispaces.com

National Governors Association Center for Best Practices, Council of Chief State School Officers. (2010b). Common core state standards initiative. In *Common Core State Standards for English Language Arts & Literacy in History/Social Studies, Science, and Technical Subjects* (pp. 1–64). Retrieved from http://www.corestandards.org/assets/CCSSI_ELA%20Standards.pdf

National Research Council. (2012). *Education for life and work: Developing transferable knowledge and skills in the 21st century*. Committee on defining deeper learning and 21st century skills. Washington: National Academy of Sciences.

No Child Left Behind Act of 2001, 20 U.S.C. § 6319. (2008).

Oakeshott, M. (1959). *The voice of poetry in the conversation of mankind*. London, England: Bowes and Bowes.

Partnership for 21st Century Skills. (2009). *Professional development for the 21st century*. Retrieved from http://www.p21.org/documents/P21_Framework.pdf

Partnership for 21st Century Skills. (2010). *Arts skills map*. Retrieved from http://www.p21.org/documents/P21_arts_map_final.pdf

Pellegrino, J. A., Hilton, M., & for the National Research Council. (2012). *Education for life and work: Developing transferable knowledge and skills in the 21st century*. Committee on Defining Deeper Learning and 21st Century Skills. Retrieved from http://keyconet.eun.org/c/document_library/get_file?uuid=b4b7ca8f-bda7-4622-a8df-8f1eec3e1a13&groupId=11028

Ryan, M., & Healy, A. (2007). Artefacts of knowing: Multiliteracies and the arts. In A. Healy (Ed.), *Multiliteracies and diversity in education: New landscapes* (pp. 82–101). South Melbourne, Vic.: Oxford University Press.

Shanahan, T., & Shanahan, C. (2008). Teaching disciplinary literacy to adolescents: Rethinking content-area literacy. *Harvard Educational Review, 78*(1), 40–59.

Street, B. (1995). *Social literacies: Critical approaches to literacy in development*. New York: Longman.

Street, B. (2003). What's "new" in new literacy studies? Critical approaches to literacy in theory and practice. *Literacy, Education and Development, 5*(7), 1523–1615.

Section I
Creating

1 Music
Creating

Paul Broomhead

The National Core Music Standards (NCCAS, 2014, MU: Cr1,2,3-E) describe the music-creating process as involving four components: *to imagine* ("generate musical ideas for various purposes and contexts"), *to plan and make* ("select and develop musical ideas for defined purposes and contexts"), *to evaluate and refine* ("evaluate and refine selected musical ideas to create musical work that meets appropriate criteria"), and *to present* ("share creative musical work that conveys intent, demonstrates craftsmanship, and exhibits originality"). These may be considered the four basic stages of creating in music.

Thinking of creating in music might bring composing immediately to mind. Improvising may be included quickly as well. Indeed, music is produced in these central types of musical creating. However, one of the most important forms of creating is the act of embellishing music beyond corresponding notation for expressive purposes. For example, key-word emphasis typically is not marked in scores, nor are any fine nuances of rubato, accent, vibrato, decay, forward movement, and so forth. All of these types of embellishments (departures from notation) are necessary to produce a performance that is considered to be expressive. These actions may not immediately be seen as "creating" music but in terms of calling upon musical creativity that they be considered equal to composing and improvising.

The nature of music texts and literacies involved in music creativity is possibly the most difficult of all literacy processes to define. One reason for this is the conceptual complexity of applying the present operating definitions of texts and literacies to the act of creating musically. The definition refers to literacy acts as "negotiating and creating" texts (Draper & Siebert, 2010). So strictly speaking this chapter cannot be simply about creating texts; it must be about both *negotiating* and *creating* texts in the nurture of musical creativity. This notion twists the mind a bit but is exactly what literacy instruction requires in relation to creativity in music.

Another important introductory aspect of music literacy related to creating is its tendency to blur the lines between text and context. The act of creating usually involves being creative within parameters—either given or self-imposed. These parameters form context for creation and, indeed, involve negotiation during creation. For example, in a jazz quartet the members take turns improvising solos, while the others provide the harmonic and rhythmic context for the improvisation. This context must be treated as a text and must be carefully negotiated, while an improvised melody is created that will blend with and complement rhythms and harmonies provided by the ensemble. This blurring of the distinction between text and context does not alter the basic literacy processes when we see the negotiation of the context/text (sounds of the jazz ensemble) as an integral part of the creating process.

Bringing up these blurred lines is an attempt to recognize real-world complexity involved in musical creativity and to present the notion of negotiating and creating texts as applied to its nurture. Simply put, when individuals interact with something as a text (i.e., when they are negotiating and creating it in meaningful ways), it very simply *is a text*. Music instructors who take it upon themselves to address musical creativity can present appropriate and authentic musical texts and provide guidance in negotiating and creating them.

The following literacy instruction event includes several examples of such authentic texts. In the vignette students are presented with notation representing a phrase from a well-known song. Thus invoking the most common text in music, notation, the teacher asks them to creatively embellish the music beyond the notation to create an expressive phrase shape. Students will negotiate several other music texts as they act creatively upon the musical phrase; these include the parameters for creativity provided by the teacher, the musical modeling of the teacher, and their own musical imaginations—a somewhat hidden but very real type of text found within the creator him/herself.

Instead of the typical vocaleses, Mrs. Zorn, the high school choir teacher, begins class a little differently today. "I've got a new term for you." *She writes the term* speech prosody *on the board and explains that it refers to how words and phrases are spoken to effectively convey their meaning. She concludes her brief explanation saying,* "Some call this inflection."

Standing by her whiteboard with marker in hand, Mrs. Zorn asks (with exaggerated inflection), "What kinds of things do we vary in speech to create the emphasis and de-emphasis in expressive speech prosody?" *For the next 5 minutes of discussion, Mrs. Zorn cannot seem to say anything without a comically extreme demonstration of the concepts given by the students.*

"Pitch," *says one student.*

"Really?" *says Mrs. Zorn with a conspicuous rise in the pitch of her voice and a smile.*

"Volume," *responds another.*

"WHAT?" *Mrs. Zorn yells back, quickly followed by a very soft,* "Oh, I guess you're right." *Students are laughing now.*

"Tempo?" *asks another student.*

"Hmmmm," *responds Mrs. Zorn. Then, after a long, thoughtful pause, she speaks very quickly* "You know, I don't know," *followed by another pause.* "I guess tempo, or, the duration of the words . . . could . . . matter." *The last two words are spoken very slowly and deliberately.* "Any others?"

Mrs. Zorn validates a few other responses while waiting to hear something related to intensity. "You know," she says, "It doesn't always take loudness to create emphasis." She says this very softly but very earnestly.

Finally, Mrs. Zorn cries out emphatically, "Look at how complex this is. To enhance verbal communication, we incorporate all of these things in just the right amounts, and at just the right times, and in just the right combinations. Giving emphasis and de-emphasis to certain parts of a message can be done in several different ways—using pitch, volume, tempo, and intensity."

Then she asks, "Now, at what age do humans use speech prosody (or inflection) to communicate meaning?" The discussion results in two conclusions: (1) that inflection is used even before humans are good at using words and (2) that this is an almost universal set of skills because of the sheer amount of daily and hourly practice.

Mrs. Zorn then displays the notation of the first phrase from "Shenendoah" and solemnly delivers a charge to her students: "Your challenge is to apply your speech prosody skills to singing this phrase. First, speak the phrase with appropriate inflection." The students speak with reserved inflection.

"Do it again, this time as if you really mean it." This time the students speak with greater range of inflection.

"Not bad. This time, listen to others around you while you speak, and make sure that no one is surpassing your range of emphasis and de-emphasis." This time students are quite dramatic.

"There it is," says Mrs. Zorn. "This is the shape that I heard from you just now." She draws a rising and falling line representing the collective spoken emphases and de-emphases.

"That is the type of range in pitch, duration, volume, and intensity that a sung phrase needs. Now sing the musical phrase in your imaginations in a way that matches as closely as possible the way you just spoke it."

Mrs. Zorn watches facial expressions to make sure each person is thinking through the musical phrase and sees a few looking confused. "Try to hear the music in your head as you think through it." She sings the first two pitches then lets the sound fade, while her face and neck clearly show the tempo and the emphasized and de-emphasized syllables as she silently thinks through the rest of the phrase. "Now let's all think through the phrase silently." A pause enables them to do so.

"Now sing it." As with the spoken phrase, the students' first try is a little lackluster.

"This is the shape I just heard from you," Mrs. Zorn complains, while she draws on the board a line representing the uninteresting shape they just sang. "Look at this and compare it to the spoken shape. This is what I heard." Mrs. Zorn then sings the phrase as she heard it from the class collectively while tracing the line on the board.

"This is how I would sing this one." Mrs. Zorn sings the phrase with much greater emphasis and de-emphasis as she traces the spoken shape with her finger. "One of these shapes is interesting, and one is not. You can see that it will take a greater range of emphasis and de-emphasis to achieve this shape [pointing to the spoken phrase drawing]. "I'll give you another 15 seconds to achieve that in your imaginations." She pauses.

"Okay. Sing it." The students sing with improved inflection.

"Better. I would say that you came 70% of the way. Now imagine yourselves actually being more extreme than I was. I'll give you 10 seconds on this." There is a brief pause. "Go!" The students really go for it.

"Yes! Now that is a vivid and interesting shape." Mrs. Zorn gives them a satisfied smile and allows the sense of accomplishment to sink in.

"Okay. So now we have lots of emphasis and de-emphasis. But some of you could tell that it was still lacking a little bit of musicality because it didn't really go anywhere. That's because the syllables that were emphasized were all emphasized just about the same amount; the same is true with those that were de-emphasized. So now you need to make the emphasized syllables unequal to each other (and the same with de-emphasized syllables). Start by choosing which syllable in this first phrase should be emphasized the most. This is the phrase climax." She pauses. "Raise your hand when I get to the one you chose." Mrs. Zorn points to each of the emphasized syllables in turn.

"Oh. Nice! We actually had two that were chosen by a substantial number of you as the phrase climax. There are no wrong answers here. If the syllable Shen is the climax, the phrase could look like this." Mrs. Zorn draws yet another rising and falling phrase shape with Shen as its highest point. "Let's sing it." The students sing.

"See? That sounds more than interesting and vivid; that sounds quite musical as well."

"Now the majority of class chose see as the climax. This is what the phrase might look like with that climax." Mrs. Zorn draws a phrase shape with see as its high point. "Let's sing it." The class sings.

"Well, that's very musical too. You can see that there are different shapes that we can create that are musical. I'm just so impressed by your ability to come up with these shapes."

"Now, let's try the next phrase without any guidance from me. Remember, your job is to be creative in developing a musical phrase shape. You need to make sure that you are (1) using vivid and interesting speech prosody as your basis, (2) varying the emphases and de-emphases in creating a phrase climax, and (3) singing in such a way that your decisions can be heard clearly, while you are singing. I'll give you 40 seconds to come up with a phrase shape for the second phrase."

UNDERSTANDING THE MUSIC LITERACY EVENT

Understanding the texts and literacies that are in play in this literacy event requires application of the broad notions introduced in this book: that texts are anything imbued with meaning and that literacies are the abilities to negotiate and create those texts. What are the actual sources of content that these students negotiate and create as they develop creating literacies? And what is the instructor's role in guiding the students through the creative processes? Following are descriptions of the music texts Mrs. Zorn presents to students, the processes she uses, and the literacies she nurtures in the instructional event.

Texts

In this vignette students are required to negotiate and create three primary texts. After establishing the concepts involved in speech prosody, Mrs. Zorn presents them as parameters for musical creativity. These parameters must be considered texts (rather than contexts) in that they provide important content for the students to negotiate as they create phrase shapes. Students are free to interpret individually but are expected to do so using variations in pitch, volume, tempo, and intensity. Mrs. Zorn supports literacy in relation to this text by using the spoken performance as the guide for the sung performance and then by providing feedback using that comparison.

One of the most central texts is the musical model provided on numerous occasions by Mrs. Zorn, beginning with her vocal dramatics demonstrating the various aspects of speech prosody and including the representations both drawn and sung that she uses to demonstrate musical imagining and phrase shaping. This is the type of text with which she presents much of her feedback, which includes singing imitations of the students' performances and demonstrating preferred models of phrase shaping. After each negotiation of these texts, students immediately create models (texts) of their own.

I include a third text, though it may be somewhat controversial and more difficult to apprehend and define. The musical imaginations of the students do constitute a text as central to musical creativity as any others. By repeatedly directing students to think through their performances before singing, Mrs. Zorn presents them with repeated, meaningful interactions with this text made up of imagined sound. She nurtures literacy by watching their faces, by insisting that they try to hear the music inside their heads, and by demonstrating what the process looks like when she is doing it.

Processes

The four stages of creating in the National Core Music Standards are all apparent in this instruction.

- Imagining takes place as the students explicitly consult their musical imaginations on how they might emphasize and de-emphasize certain syllables while singing.
- Planning and making take place as students mentally construct a phrase shape that they plan to demonstrate while singing.

- Evaluating and refining are explicitly addressed as Mrs. Zorn offers feedback and allows students to revise their decisions.
- Presenting takes place repeatedly in a rehearsal loop of perform, evaluate, revise, and perform again.

As I discussed at the beginning of this chapter, students must both negotiate and create texts as musical creativity is nurtured. Although students in the vignette are negotiating all three of the texts described (and others), negotiation requires that they respond by creating texts—holding the creating process solidly in the foreground during this activity. Students simultaneously consider Mrs. Zorn's musical models and their own musical imaginations as they create/sing texts of their own. These created texts in response to negotiated texts, often referred to as *trials* in music, constitute the major aspect of any rehearsal-type activity in the music classroom. The performing process is, therefore, also prominent in this instruction in that each creative iteration is immediately subject to performance.

This vignette portrays a teacher attending to the individual creators while working with a group. It is important for students to be creative as individuals, although it often surprises us the extent to which they agree in their shaping interpretations. A next step will be to help students learn how to balance individual interpretations with the collective interpretations of the rest of the ensemble. Instruction surrounding this step in creating phrase shaping heavily invokes responding processes.

Literacies

When Mrs. Zorn starts the lesson with her exaggerated vocal inflections and continues her instruction by singing her feedback to the students, she is nurturing their ability to apprehend and replicate pertinent aspects of speech prosody. Eventually, she hopes students will be able to achieve a marriage of sorts between speech prosody and melodic line; the vignette shows her first step. Other literacies included the ability to apply creating parameters to the activity of shaping a line as well as the ability to activate and utilize one's creative imagination when shaping a phrase. In all three cases, these literacies are necessary to enable students to both negotiate the texts and respond by creating texts of their own.

CONCLUSIONS

As students learn to negotiate and create musical texts involved in musical creativity, they become more capable of meaningful interactions with music as music creators. As I described and discussed Mrs. Zorn's creativity-oriented literacy event, the need for brevity prevented me from attending to some important aspects of using speech prosody as a set of creating parameters. For example, because a previously composed piece is used, students aren't given opportunities to create emphasis and de-emphasis by varying pitch. However, this aspect certainly can come into play when students are writing their own melodies.

It is important to see creative literacy as attainable by all. Many music students may appear to be naturally creative or uncreative. While I have no intention of engaging here in the nature-versus-nurture argument, I do argue that creative literacies can and should be nurtured in all music students. I urge instructors to interpret some students' apparent lack of creativity as a lack of literacy rather than a lack of innate ability.

While the literacy event described in this chapter reveals the importance of creating texts and literacies, we need to recognize the infinite variety in ways to nurture music creativity and in types of musical creativity that may be nurtured. Other musical creativity instruction can be expected to look vastly different. This unit focuses on using speech prosody as a set of parameters for creating embellishments of written notation—specifically shaping a phrase. Instruction that nurtures improvisation or composition may seem to have no resemblance. But what all music-creating literacy instruction will have in common will be negotiating and creating authentic music texts in the nurture of musical creativity.

REFERENCES

Draper, R. J., & Siebert, D. (2010). Rethinking texts, literacies, and literacy across the curriculum. In R. J. Draper, P. Broomhead, A. P. Jensen, J. Nokes, & D. Siebert (Eds.), *(Re)imagining content-area literacy instruction* (pp. 20–39). New York, NY: Teachers College Press.

NCCAS. (2014). MU: Cr1,2,3-E. Retrieved from http://musiced.nafme.org/files/2014/06/Core-Music-Standards-Ensemble-Strand1.pdf

2 Dance
Creating

Pamela S. Musil, Amy Petersen Jensen, and Roni Jo Draper

Dance literacy involves negotiating and creating using the body as the primary focus (NYCDOE, 2005). Indeed, dancers create using the bodily experience as their origin of exploration and innovation. Ann Dils describes dance literacy as "a set of interconnected knowledges through which we understand the body and movement, how these operate in various dance traditions, and what meanings they might hold for us as individuals and societies" (2009, online). This definition reveals that the study of dance creation includes the integration of social, intellectual, and kinesthetic awareness *along with* the practice of dance technique (Hagood, 2000; Hong, 2000). This chapter explores the integration of the social, intellectual, and kinesthetic aspects of dance creation with the technical study of dance to contribute to the development of knowledge and skills students need to create authentically in dance environments. We also describe the processes and texts with which dancers engage while developing dance creation literacies.

When creating, dancers engage in the processes of imagining and experimenting, organizing and planning, and revising and refining as they develop works of art (NCCAS, 2014, DA: Cr1.1, 2.1, 3.1). Artists practicing in the field of dance master this set of knowledge and skills as they create. Dance educators invested in authentically preparing students for dance environments should acknowledge these processes; literacy educators will recognize these processes as literate activities. Therefore, a dance teacher engaged in literacy instruction will involve students in activities in which they create by imagining, planning, and presenting ideas for dance projects to their peers. Dance students participating in classrooms with a literacy emphasis will have time to ask questions, improvise, and problematize their ideas and movement. They also will work toward expressing artistic intent through their bodies (College Board, Dance, 2011). In literacy-based dance classrooms, teachers and students regularly will acknowledge the interchange that happens between performer and audience during creation. Time is taken for reflection and response that leads to ongoing revision of the work to achieve the goals of the artist.

The dance classroom that allows students opportunities to engage in these dance processes and develop a wide range of dance literacies necessarily will require students to learn more than simply the technical aspects of dance. Rather, it requires dancers to use a variety of texts as they participate in creating art. In addition to the body, they work to read or negotiate, other multimodal texts, including other bodies, physical space, music, lighting, costumes, props, and so on. Dancers also embrace traditional dance texts (e.g., choreography texts, writing about the history of dance, genre studies, or dance biographies) as well as signs and signifiers from other disciplines (photographs, newspapers, paintings, etc.) in preparation for creation. Dance educators who understand the importance of literacy will find opportunities to engage young people in the exploration of various types of text while providing the appropriate scaffolding for these texts to promote the development of understanding and artistic ability.

The following vignette describes one teacher's effort to help her students create using dance literacy strategies. Students in this classroom are enlisted as choreographers and are encouraged by the instructor to participate in authentic dance processes as they read dance texts and learn dance literacies to generate ideas for a dance project.

Ms. Greves and her advanced senior students are in the early stages of planning a project that eventually will result in a themed dance concert based on the works of the visual artist and former dancer, sculptor Heloise Crista. Ms. Greves invites her students to consider several photographs of Crista's sculptures that are placed around the dance studio. Audible murmurs of appreciation escape unchecked as students consider the photographs of Crista's motion-implied sculptures that are laid before them. Initially Ms. Greves' only instruction is to encourage students to look at the photos and identify sculptures that they feel have movement potential, which she describes as the shaping or inherent suggestion of motion within a particular sculpture or thematic content that could be developed and expanded into movement.

Students eagerly peruse the selection and quickly begin trading and wrangling over the various photographs that are offered as choreographic inspiration. Ms. Greves watches with satisfaction as the intensity and decibel level in room make a steady crescendo: participants animatedly converse and brainstorm about choreographic ideas that are already flowing.

In this moment Ms. Greves's role is to encourage, facilitate, and channel students' ideas. Because multiple student conversations are taking place at the same time, she constantly moves among conversations, giving feedback and suggestions that help students mine their nascent ideas for essential nuggets that could lead them to richer and more profound artistic expression. For example, Jenna chooses a sculpture of a woman that she is drawn to for its curved shaping, but beyond that observation, she can't articulate why she likes it or whether it has movement potential. Ms. Greves prompts her by asking, "Why do you think the sculptor may have chosen to represent the woman this way? More importantly, how do the shaping, facing, textural qualities, and other aspects of the sculpture impact you as an observer?"

Jenna responds with more information, saying, "I think the sculptor wanted the woman to appear isolated or alone; the sculpture's curved, inward shaping, its orientation with the woman's back to the observer, and the smooth, black marbled surface of the sculpture all suggest to me that that perhaps the woman is harboring some hurt or sorrow but that perhaps she also feels hope and inner strength." Ms. Greves nods encouragingly: "Okay, why do you imagine that she has hope and inner strength?" Jenna says, "Well, mainly because I see her face in profile, and it looks strong, like she is resolved to something." Ms. Greves probes even further: "Why are you drawn to these qualities?" Jenna thinks for a moment and responds, "Well, I can't say exactly—it's more of a feeling—but I think it's because at some level I think I can relate. I don't know—like I sort of get her—and like, she calls to me." Ms. Greves continues. "Really good thinking, Jenna! I'm impressed with your thoughtful analysis."

Speaking to the class, she says, "So now, your assignment is to write down as many qualitative words as you can think of that depict your sculpture." As students begin brainstorming, Ms. Greves cautions: "Students, ultimately this assignment requires movement rather than words—so be careful in your word selection. Which words have inherent movement potential, and which words do not?" With help from peers and the thesaurus on her smartphone, Jenna identifies words like smooth, stark, enclosing, protecting, lonely, introspective, inwardly resolved, and resolute.

After a few minutes of brainstorming, Ms. Greves asks Jenna and the rest of class to explore some of their words through movement and create one or two short dance motifs that would depict the qualities described by these words. Jenna soon recognizes that certain words have more movement potential than others. For example, she finds the word stark more difficult to convey in a single movement or body shape, but the words smooth, enclosing, and protecting are particularly suggestive of motion and body shaping. She finds that the word resolute might be suggested through careful bodily posturing and notes that even though the word stark is difficult to convey in movement, there might be ways to address it in staging.

Ms. Greves leads all of the students through this process of identifying observed sculptural qualities: describing them in language; identifying qualitative words with inherent movement potential; and encouraging them to use these words as springboards for developing movement. In the short class period that ensues, students share beginning impressions, explore and improvise with embryonic movement motifs, listen to and encouraged one another's ideas about how sculptures might inspire dance, speculate about how specific sculptures might first be interpreted and translated, and propose how that information could then be used as a springboard that would lead them to create their own choreographed works.

Ms. Greves charges the students to choose one sculpture and design a written and physical proposal articulating how they will develop a work of choreography based on the sculpture they have selected. The student *choreographers leave class with the assignment to verbally articulate their proposal before a panel of their peers and to perform approximately 1 minute of original movement based on their chosen sculpture. Ms. Greves hands out some questions to remind and guide their explorations: "How does one take the stillness of a sculpture and translate it or expand it into motion? How does its shape, texture, or other qualities inform one's movement choices? How can descriptive words help guide one's artistic process? How does one explore and create movement motifs that represent the essence of what one hopes to convey through movement?"*

Over the next few days the class begins a shared journey that leads them to consider these questions. Each student works to organize a proposal that clearly and dynamically communicates artistic intent. Sharing ideas with each other, they are able to begin answering the questions that Ms. Greves has posed to them. More importantly they experiment together with chorographic designs, exploring how their ideas might eventually translate into choreography that they would set on other members of the class.

A few short days after the initial brainstorming in class, the students present proposals for choreography inspired by specific sculptures. Some read poetry and other written texts that they feel help them better articulate and shape their ideas. Each student presents original movement that they have designed in response to ideas and impressions they feel their sculptures revealed. Ms. Greves leads a conversation in which each student is questioned about movement choices: how each had arrived at specific choices and what they feel these movement choices represent. She reminds the students that much like the process of writing where one searches for the most expressive yet simple words to convey meaning and richness in written text, the process of creating movement in dance requires similar probing and sifting. This happens through extensive improvisation, experimentation and revision.

Ms. Greves invites students to go deeper with their movement explorations, to seek to discover new layers of meaning that could be conveyed and interpreted in various ways, saying, "You've made a good beginning, but let's think about what we might refine for our work. Sierra, will you act as an example and describe what your next steps might be?" Sierra hesitantly responds, "Well, to be honest, I'm not exactly sure. In their critique of my work, Hannah and Samuel noticed that I chose some movement vocabulary that was based on my preferred way of moving instead of the sculpture I selected. They also said that some of my movement didn't seem to have a clear reason for being there, except as eye candy." Ms. Greves reminds Sierra and the other students of questions she has been asking them that might be helpful in considering new possibilities for refining their work: "Why did you choose that particular movement? What do you think the movement conveys? Does its stylization impact your ability to communicate what you want it to? Are there ways that you might communicate that particular idea differently or more effectively?"

Through this process of questioning and discussion Sierra begins to recognize that she hasn't really given thought to every single movement she has selected. "Oh, man, I get it—but I had such a hard time when I went into the dance studio to work. I felt I was trying to pull movement from thin air. It was so hard! So yeah, I might have stuck a few things in there that didn't belong just to fill up my minute." Ms. Greves acknowledges and validates this struggle: "In the creative moment, sometimes what initially comes forth is what feels comfortable to us; but what is comfortable and appealing to me personally doesn't necessarily represent what I'm trying to convey. Consequently, as an artist I eventually might discard those early movement choices as trivial or superficial. But through serious, persistent exploration, movement with more substantive meaning often begins to emerge. It IS hard work, Sierra. But it also can be playful and fun. Keep at it, and you'll find something that works—I know you will. Students, the process that was modeled in the class period where the project instructions were first shared works! Remember my initial instructions?"

- Articulate what you see as the essence of the sculpture.
- Brainstorm words to qualitatively describe it.
- Find the movement potential.
- Explore movement that represents a single word or contrasting words.
- Create a movement motif that can be developed into a full phrase, and build from there.

Using this reminder, Sierra's classmates help her recall and revisit the words she had chosen initially and suggest specific ways she might consider representing those words in movement. Sierra leaves class with a clearer sense of what she needs to work on to make the movement more authentic and impactful. Ms. Greves pulls her aside as class ends and tells her that she is sure that when Sierra returns to class, her movement material will reflect her answers to the questions that she and her peers have posed.

UNDERSTANDING THE LITERACY EVENT

In this vignette Ms. Greves and her class are creating together. As they create, Ms. Greves certainly is interested in developing technical skill and dance aptitudes in her students. However, she is far more interested in helping them to explore a holistic vision of dance. She espouses a teaching and learning philosophy similar to that of Tina Hong: "Learning in dance education is not to be undertaken in terms of a set of decontextualized skills and competencies to be mastered. Rather it should be understood as open-ended and evolving confluences of knowledge, skills, understandings, and dispositions that are socially constructed and contextualized within social events and practices" (2000, online). This philosophy of dance education guides Ms. Greves to introduce her students to essential texts, processes, and literacies within the field of dance.

Texts

Ms. Greves introduces her students to a variety of texts. First she asks the students to examine photographs depicting the work of the sculptor Heloise Crista. She supports their investigation of the still figures within the photos by requesting that they consider the works of art using a dance context. She specifically invites them to read the two-dimensional picture of the sculpture, looking for suggestions of motion or thematic content that appeal to their artistic sensibility. In this way she encourages students to honor a dance perspective when reading the photograph. By inviting the students to think as choreographers about chorographic principles while engaging with the photograph, she also establishes an authentic creative purpose for their reading of the photograph.

Ultimately, Ms. Greves provides opportunities for her students to use their own bodies as texts as they translate the meanings they create from their viewing of the photos to representations created with their own bodies. This act of creation is quite different than performing the interpretive and creative acts of another choreographer. It allows students to engage in the decision-making process that surrounds the technical aspects of dance. As such, Ms. Greves provides her students opportunities to develop important literacies as choreographers and as dancers.

Additionally, Ms. Greves provides opportunities for students to read each other's bodies as texts. Her lessons offer occasions for students to perform their movement ideas in front of their peers with the intent of receiving useful feedback as they revise and refine their work. Ms. Greves scaffolds the revision experience by carefully modeling questions that both performers and audience members might ask about the creative work in the development stage. By modeling and then asking students to use questioning techniques, she builds critical and analytical skills through which students grow in their abilities to "articulate their impressions and critiques of dances they observe as active, informed audience members" (College Board, 2011, p. 21).

Processes

Ms. Greves and her students use authentic dance processes such as imagining and experimenting, organizing and planning, and revising and refining as they create (NCCAS, 2014, DA: Cr1.1, 2.1, 3.1). Utilizing these processes, Ms. Greves encourages her students' social and emotional development "through opportunities to initiate, plan, and produce independently, but in coordination with others" (College Board, Dance, 2011, p. 21). This goal is evident through her actions in the vignette. First she invites students to think of themselves as choreographers. By assigning them the creative role of choreographer rather than setting movement on her students, she provides them with the opportunity to develop their own cognitive and aesthetic abilities as they experiment with creative ideas and expressive communication in addition to considering movement skills.

The creative project she introduces also helps her students to move beyond thinking solely of training the body into a mind-set in which they act as the creators. In the vignette students imagine and experiment as they engage with the photographs of Heloise Crista's work. In this early stage of creating they *talk* about what they imagine and how they might experiment using those imagined ideas in preparation to *do* what they imagine in future movement. In this way they are able to make plans verbally before they explore their ideas physically. Ms. Greves supports the students in this period of verbal exploration by asking them to focus on the "movement potential" of the sculptures and also modeling questions that students might consider as they amplify their budding ideas. Additionally she provides time in which they are invited to develop their own questions about the sculptures and their subsequent movement phrases. While she provides ample time for them to explore their ideas verbally, she also recognizes that these ideas eventually must be used to inspire movement, so she pushes them to find qualitative words that will result in meaningful and dynamic movement.

Ms. Greves also asks students to participate in organizing and planning. Her assignment simulates a long-established dance practice in which a choreographer organizes, plans, and presents an early vision of his/her work to others in order to receive feedback from peers who are invested in collaborating with the intent of revising and refining the work of art. In the vignette Ms. Greves enhances this practice by introducing students to dance literacies that aid in accomplishing their goals. For example, Ms. Greves and the class help Sierra refine her work during the processes of revising and providing feedback. Ms. Greves supports Sierra's understanding of the process by encouraging her to ask questions about her intent, how her intent might be understood by others, and which revisions to her work might offer more clarity for herself and her audience. In this way she introduces Sierra to critical questions that must be asked during the revision process. Importantly, Ms. Greves doesn't supply a solution for Sierra and instead encourages her to revisit her original ideas as she works to articulate a vision of the dance that serves her attempts to make meaning. In this way Ms. Greves helps Sierra to negotiate successfully difficult aspects of the revision process while maintaining her creative autonomy.

Literacies

Ms. Greves encourages dance literacy by introducing her students to ideas such as movement potential and qualitative words, which suggest that dancers can find inspiration for movement and choreography through other texts that can be embodied. Her students also are becoming dance literate because they actively engage in choreographic principles, which are introduced alongside dance processes (College Board, 2011; Hong-Joe, 2002). This practice builds cognitive understanding about dance that helps her students to negotiate the language and skills necessary for the process of creating. Ms. Greves also acculturates her students into professional dance discourse by providing instruction and activities that require verbal analysis, evaluation, and perspective as they discuss their physical work and intellectual ideas throughout the development of their choreography presentation.

Finally, Ms. Greves summons her students to participate in the discourse of a larger arts community by engaging them with artifacts such as photographs and sculptures that they use as impetus for their own creative work. This assignment to transfer from one discipline into artistic work in another (in this case from the visual arts to dance) allows students to see themselves as artists within a larger community. It also allows students to engage in dance as a holistic learning experience that genuinely influences and is influenced by learning that they do in other areas both in and out of school settings (NYCDOE Blueprint, 2005).

CONCLUSION

Like Ms. Greves, dance educators can provide young people with opportunities to create authentically. Real knowing and doing requires engagement with a variety of texts that are specific to disciplinary goals. The practical and intellectual knowledge necessary to create dance also occurs through rigorous curricular choices in which students experiment with processes where they imagine, experiment, organize, plan, revise and refine. Finally, educators should encourage dance-specific literacies that aid students meaning making as they use texts appropriate to dance settings and participate in processes apposite to the discipline.

REFERENCES

College Board. (2011). *Child development and arts education: A review of current research and best practices*. Retrieved from http://nccas.wikispaces.com/file/view/NCCAS%20Child%20Development%20Report.pdf/382049246/NCCAS%20Child%20Development%20Report.pdf

Dils, A. (2009). Why dance literacy. In C. Stock (Ed.), *Dance Dialogues: Conversations across cultures, artforms and practices*, Proceedings of the 2008 World Dance Alliance Global Summit, Brisbane, 13–18 July. On-line publication, QUT Creative Industries and Ausdance. Retrieved from http://ausdance.org.au/articles/details/why-dance-literacy

Hagood, T. (2000). *A history of dance in American higher education: Dance and the American university*. New York: Edwin Mellen Press.

Hong, T. (2000). Developing dance literacy in the postmodern: An approach to curriculum. In *Arts online: Dance professional readings*. Retrieved from http://artsonline2.tki.org.nz/TeacherLearning/readings/danceliteracy.php

Hong-Joe, C. (2002). Developing dance literacy in the postmodern: An approach to curriculum. (Doctoral dissertation). Griffith University, Brisbane, Australia.

National Coalition for Core Arts Standards (2014). National Core Arts Standards, *Dance: Creating. Core Dance Standards*. DA:Cr 1.1, 1.2, 1.3. Online at http://www.nationalartsstandards.org/

New York City Department of Education (2005). Blueprint for teaching and learning in dance. Retrieved from http://schools.nyc.gov/offices/teachlearn/arts/Blueprints/dancebp2007.pdf

3 Media Arts
Creating

Benjamin Thevenin

Scholars of media education, Douglas Kellner and Jeff Share, describe media arts education as "where students are taught to value the aesthetic qualities of media and the arts while using their creativity for self-expression through creating art and media. These programs can be found most often inside schools as stand-alone classes or outside of the classroom in community-based or after-school programs" (2007, p. 7).

In media arts classrooms, students might participate in more mass communication-oriented models of media production—producing video broadcasts of a school's morning announcements. They may be engaged in film studies—examining the aesthetic elements of classic cinema and then learning to implement similar techniques in the production of their own fiction films. Or students may be engaged in the production of alternative media—examining representations of their cultures and neighborhoods and using documentary as a means of giving voice to people and problems that are otherwise unrepresented.

Despite the variety in approaches to media arts education, a potentially unifying explanation of media arts education might include its emphasis on *the analysis and creation of multiple media forms*. Whether the goal of a particular media arts program is the production of televised news broadcasts, block-umentary films, Web sites, or video games, the students are engaged in examining how words, images, sounds, performances, and so on are integrated into multimedia communications and artistic expressions. And this engagement necessarily includes both critical analysis and creative production.

The following is one example of a literacy event in which students might participate in a media arts setting, an activity called the *social media adaptation*. Throughout the vignette, the students practice what the National Core Arts Standards for Media Arts describe as "refin[ing] and modify[ing] media artworks, honing aesthetic quality and intentionally accentuating stylistic elements," in this case, to reflect an understanding of the source texts which they are adapting (NCCAS MA:Cr3.1.I., 2014).

Mr. Kaufman's high school media arts classroom is in the middle of a unit on adaptation in art and media. The instructor and students have examined a number of historical examples of literary, cinematic, and other adaptations of existing works and discussed how the study of adaptations provides an opportunity to examine the interrelation of different media forms.

On this particular morning, Mr. Kaufman introduces a new assignment—the social media adaptation. He explains to the class that the students will work in small groups to (1) choose a work of classic literature to adapt, (2) identify significant elements of this work, (3) select a social media platform for the adaptation, and (4) successfully adapt the literary work to their chosen platform, making a special effort to retain those significant elements in their translation.

First, the class is organized into groups, and the instructor encourages them to survey their experiences with classic literature and determine which works might be best suited for such an adaptation. During the discussion, Mr. Kaufman visits each group and engages in dialogue to help the students brainstorm ideas.

Daniel, the spokesperson for one group, suggests, "We read Bram Stoker's Dracula last year in our British literature class, and we think that a horror story like that or Frankenstein or something might be cool to do."

"Well, Daniel, let's think about Dracula," responds Mr. Kaufman. "Is there an aspect of the story, a stylistic choice, a theme, or something about the book that you found particularly interesting or unique?"

"Well, a lot of the book is just letters," Daniel answers. "Instead of, like, a narrator telling the story or something, you know what's happening and how the characters feel through the letters they send each other. That's different."

"Okay. That's called an epistolary structure," Mr. Kaufman explains. "The story is told through epistles or letters, through the characters' interactions, rather than descriptions of events. Now, let's say you chose to update Dracula to today's times and use social media to tell the story. What could you do to keep this epistolary structure?"

"Well, people don't talk like they do in the book anymore, so maybe we could change the dialogue so it sounds more modern," another student suggests.

"Or you could have them texting each other instead of writing letters," offers someone else. "LOL:)," she laughs.

"Okay," Mr. Kaufman replies. "So, since the original story is told through letters, you might change that to text messages in your adaptation. What are the strengths and weaknesses of that approach?"

"It'd be shorter!" jokes a student. Mr. Kaufman and the students all laugh.

Daniel follows up, saying, "Yeah, but it'd be hard to explain a lot of the stuff going on in just texts. Like, it would be kind of hard to describe some of the places, or the stuff going on with just short messages."

Mr. Kaufman reiterates Daniel's point, and suggests that if the students have agreed on Dracula, they make a list of the elements they should be sure to retain in their adaptation—like the epistolary structure—and then consider how different social media platforms might encourage or limit the translation of these elements.

With the help of Mr. Kaufman, the students spend the following days doing some research—revisiting their chosen literary works, researching the authors' lives and work, and the culture and context in which they were writing, as well as looking at potential social media platforms. Then, they begin experimenting with different online social networking sites to see how their chosen works might be best translated to social media.

One day, Mr. Kaufman invites each group to report on their progress. Daniel's group shares the research they conducted about Dracula and discusses their interest in retaining the epistolary structure in their adaptation. Daniel addresses the class.

"We first thought it might be cool to tell the story with texts from each of the characters, but when we went back to study the book, there was so much going on that couldn't be easily described in such short messages. So, we decided that Skype would be a better platform for the story. That way we can have characters dressed up in costumes against backdrops that look like the old castles and stuff, and so we can communicate more information through the visuals, and plus it'll be more fun for us and interesting for the people watching it."

Mr. Kaufman praises the group's efforts and then prompts a second group to share what they have been up to. "Melinda," he says, "why don't you go next and tell the class a little about what we've been working on with your group."

Melinda explains that after listening to Orson Welles's radio play earlier in the semester, her group was interested initially in doing their own adaption of H. G. Wells's War of the Worlds but explains that when searching online, their group came across a number of news articles discussing controversies surrounding the social media site Reddit. Given that the site allows its users complete anonymity, there have been a number of widely publicized incidents of both online harassment—trolling and flaming—and circulation of offensive material within certain bulletin boards on the site. They discussed some of their findings with Mr. Kaufman but soon realized that while they found the controversy surrounding Reddit interesting, it didn't have much to do with their idea to adapt Wells's novel. Mr. Kaufman had worked with the group to do some additional research, and together they came across another of Wells's works, The Invisible Man. After learning about the book's plot, the students determined that a cautionary tale about a character who misuses technology, becomes invisible, and embarks on a reign of terror would provide particularly fitting source material for an adaptation on Reddit.

After the students' reports, Mr. Kaufman follows up with each group about the next steps in their creative process. He applauds Melinda and her group for the potential significance of their proposal while cautioning them about the sensitive subject that they are attempting to address. Mr. Kaufman reviews the school's Internet use policies with the students. He also emphasizes that while their proposed project involves translating the antics of the novel's antihero into contemporary times to make a point about internet culture, they must be careful not to engage in any of these behaviors themselves in their attempt at artistic creation.

Mr. Kaufman then visits Daniel and the *Dracula* group and discusses their plans to adapt the novel to Skype. The students are already busy casting their fellow classmates as actors, creating costumes (and fake blood), and writing out modern dialogue that still retains the feel of Stoker's work.

"I'm glad to see you're so excited about the project," says Mr. Kaufman. "Though, before you dive into making sets and costumes, there are still some aspects of preproduction that you need to consider. For example, have you thought about how you are going to share these video chats in your project?" he asks. "Vlogs are posted publicly, but Skype conversations aren't typically recorded or distributed. So, how do you intend to show them to your audience?"

The students consider their teacher's question and discuss options of recording screen grabs of the video chats or switching to an entirely different social media platform—like Twitter's Vine or even YouTube—that would facilitate sharing these conversations publicly. Mr. Kaufman again commends the group on their work and enthusiasm and requests that they check in with him soon with an update on their decision about how to share their project.

During the following weeks, each group develops their adaptations, reporting to Mr. Kaufman and their classmates as they go along.

UNDERSTANDING THE PERFORMING LITERACY EVENT

Texts

The previous description demonstrates the centrality of students' engagement with *texts*—in this case, both classical literature and social media—to their development of media arts literacies. In their examination of both literature and online social networking sites, the students seek to identify salient themes, stylistic conventions, as well as the affordances and limitations of the media. And through his design of the assignment and his interactions with each group, Mr. Kaufman works to scaffold the students' engagement with the texts—in particular, helping them use media analysis to more thoughtfully and creatively adapt their chosen literary works to social media.

First, the students examine works of literature to select source material for their adaptations. It is important to note that the students' engagement with these texts is not the end in itself but rather the first step in a larger process of connecting older texts (classic novels) with new texts (social media platforms) in their projects. In their analysis of these works of literature, students determine how particular elements of the texts are more or less suited for an adaptation to a social media platform. For example, when Mr. Kaufman prompts Daniel's group to consider what they find particularly interesting or distinctive about *Dracula*, he is encouraging them not only to consider different elements of the novel critically but to do so with their adaptation of this text in mind. The students' identification of the novel's epistolary structure and their decision to translate the work to Skype plainly demonstrate this idea. Ultimately, their analyses of literary texts provide an opportunity for students not to simply practice identifying tone or theme, allegory, or allusion but rather do so to enrich their creative production.

Next, students examine social media platforms as texts—analyzing how design, interface, legal agreements, various multimedia elements, and so on all contribute to the user's experience of the text. And given that social media often include multiple media forms (Pinterest includes images, text, and hyperlinks; YouTube includes video accompanied by online discussion, etc.), their study involves multiple areas of analysis. For example, the second group's research reveals that Reddit has a particular reputation for allowing anonymous users to post controversial content on its bulletin boards. Though, students just as easily might have considered Facebook's time line interface—to see how design structures the users' participation with the site—or its user agreement—to determine how privacy policies establish power relationships between the institution and its users. In each case, the teacher functions as a facilitator, encouraging students to consider these textual (and contextual) elements of social media as a means of helping them develop an effective, creative work.

Processes

In addition to the students' engagement with texts, their participation in *processes* such as critical analysis, research, and reflection is integral to their creative production. The previous section discussed how the students' analyses of both the literary works and social media platforms allows them to identify significant elements in each media and draw correlations between them that might prove productive in their adaptation. Additionally, Mr. Kaufman structures the assignment and interacts with his class in ways that encourage students to engage in further research and reflection.

After the first group identifies *Dracula*'s epistolary structure, Mr. Kaufman encourages them to research different social media platforms and determine which might be best suited for their adaptation. In this process, students are required to venture beyond their initial impressions, further engage with both the novel and different social networking sites, and read secondary sources for further relevant information. Then, with this newly gathered information, they are able to begin developing a creative work that is informed by research rather than fancy. And this process of research is ongoing. Even after the initial conceptualization of the project, the students continue to rely on research in their creation—in devising characters, dialogue, costumes, and so on. These media arts students come to understand that research is not something that is limited to the preproduction stage but rather continually accompanies and informs creative practice.

An essential element of media arts literacies involves the students' critical reflections on their own creative practice. For students' critical analyses of texts and additional research to be implemented effectively in their work, they must determine how this newly gained knowledge maps onto their artistic choices. For example, the second group's choice to adapt *The Invisible Man*, rather than *War of the Worlds*, indicates the development of their ability to reflect critically and constructively on the contradictions between their creative conceptualizations and their research. And like the research process, this reflection process is continuous. Mr. Kaufman applauds the students' interest in addressing such an important theme as the ethics of online behavior but cautions them that they must be conscious of how their artistic choices will shape their treatment of this issue. In all media arts—and particularly with an issue as sensitive as this group's project—creators must continually reflect on how their artistic choices contribute to the creation of narrative or communication of ideology. And as an outside observer, the teacher can prompt students to consider the consequences of those artistic decisions throughout the creative process.

Literacies

Given this chapter's emphasis on the creation of "*new* artistic ideas and work," an adaptation assignment may seem somewhat at odds with this notion of arts literacies (Jensen & Draper, this volume, emphasis added). This chapter argues that the work that students do to adapt a classic novel to a social media platform can be incredibly *original*, despite the fact that they are working with well-established (and often very *old*) source material. Given the recent revival of vampire stories, especially in youth-oriented media, the students' decision to adapt *Dracula* might be perceived as unfortunately unimaginative. But especially given the role of digital media in contemporary *remix culture,* the idea of art as necessarily *new* or *original* is now, more than ever, grounds for debate. Artists always have been influenced by, and have often alluded to, drawn from, sampled, and remixed others' work. An activity like the social media adaptation (consistent with much art in our postmodern age) simply makes this transparent. The *Dracula* group's decision to adapt the book's epistolary structure via enacted video chats nicely demonstrates their media literacy—creative uses of digital media acknowledge their artistic predecessors while presenting something novel. "New artistic ideas and work" are always already part of an artistic heritage (that might include both British Romantic literature and the *Vampire Diaries* TV show), and encouraging students to be conscious of (and even embrace) this heritage will better prepare them to participate successfully as media artists in the contemporary world.

Additionally, this example of Mr. Kaufman's class demonstrates how teachers might use creative projects like the social media adaptation to help students understand *the integration of multiple media elements* in media arts, regardless of curricular particulars. For example, students who adapt *The Invisible Man* to Reddit are learning concepts and skills that are applicable in any collaborative, creative media arts setting. Wells's text is not unlike a screenplay that a director simultaneously respects and creatively interprets in the production of a film. Any work of art (and especially media art) necessarily involves multiple collaborators—writer, choreographer, designer, performer, editor, and so on. By structuring the assignment as a group project, relying on students' collaboration and requiring their creation of something new from existing source material, Mr. Kaufman is providing them with an experience applicable to any media arts setting—from working in a newsroom to shooting a music video. Perhaps the most valuable literacy a student can gain from literacy events such as this is an understanding of the thorough interpenetration and remarkable interdependence of multiple media elements in any mediated communication or artistic expression.

CONCLUSION

Given the ubiquity of social media in contemporary culture, it makes sense for educators to address these platforms as part of their media literacy education. Too often, young people's participation in social media is passive rather than critical and creative. By developing a project in which social media Web sites are analyzed alongside classic literary works, Mr. Kaufman emphasizes to the students the necessity of critically considering their engagement with *all* types of media. And by uniting theory with practice, critical analysis with creative production, media arts educators are preparing their students to become active audiences and thoughtful, informed media producers.

REFERENCES

Kellner, D., & Share, J. (2007). Critical media literacy, democracy, and the reconstruction of education. In D. Macedo & R. Shirley (Eds.), *Media literacy: A reader* (pp. 3–23). Steinberg: Peter Lang.

National Coalition for Core Arts Standards. (2014). National Core Media Arts Standards MA:Cr3.1.I. Online at http://www.nationalartsstandards.org/sites/default/files/Media%20Arts%20at%20a%20Glance%20-%20new%20copyright%20info.pdf

4 Theatre
Creating

Amy Petersen Jensen

This chapter invites theatre teachers and their students to engage in aspects of creating that build theatre literacies. The skills and knowledge associated with creating can be a natural product of theatre work that involves students in *authentic theatre participation*. Authentic theatre participation in this case specifically refers to students engaging with theatre texts, processes, and literacies as if they were theatre practitioners working in real-world theatre settings.

The authentic theatre participation described here requires that students have facility with a variety of theatre texts. When creating, theatre practitioners must be dually responsible for both print and nonprint texts (Jensen in Draper et al., 2009, p. 102). Theatre practitioners read and create print texts (including written plays, stage diagrams, lighting plots, etc.) as they envision theatre. They also utilize nonprint texts (bodies, properties, lighting instruments, visual and aural landscapes, etc.) as they develop performance possibilities for the stage. While theatre practitioners must understand how to use both print and nonprint texts, they also are uniquely engaged in transferring words and other schematics (i.e., lighting or scenic designs, etc.) from a given print text to the stage, where what was printed is made live for an audience. Teachers invested in enculturating students into authentic theatre practices will help their students gain the literacies associated with these print and nonprint texts necessary to move theatre texts from the page to the stage as they practice envisioning theatre worlds.

Teachers guiding students in authentic theatre participation also introduce them to theatre processes as they create together. The National Core Theatre Standards invite teachers to use "envisioning, developing and generating" (NCCAS, 2014, theatre process verbs) processes (among other theatre processes) when formulating new ideas and work within theatre contexts.

Using these theatre-specific texts and processes, teachers can expose students to multimodal literacies appropriate for the theatre learning space. For example in theatre, literacy is more than the acquisition of vocabulary or the capacity to read a given print or nonprint text. Instead, it is the ability to negotiate theatre texts and processes or to "combine and coordinate words, deeds, thoughts, values, bodies, objects, tools, technologies and other people" (Gee, 2001, p. 721) to create within the context of the discipline. In the vignette below, the theatre teacher Mr. Moss accomplishes this by providing opportunities for students to envision, develop, and generate ideas for a future performance using theatre tools. In this vignette Mr. Moss and his intermediate drama students are in the early stages of creating a contemporary theatrical adaptation of Sophocles' *Antigone* to perform for their peers and community in six weeks. In preparation for writing their own adapted script, the class is exploring how they might portray themes from the original play in their work.

Readers of this chapter will note that within the vignette Mr. Moss exposes the students to a variety of theatre texts, introduces them to several theatre processes (in this case envisioning, developing, and generating), and through participating in the use of these texts and processes helps them to practice and employ theatre-specific literacies.

"Okay people, today we are going to envision what Antigone's world might look like here and now," says Mr. Moss. "By envision I mean that I want you to begin to think about what is important in Antigone's world and what that might look or sound like on our stage and how it might resonate with our audience. Let's go back to the original play text and revisit some ideas or themes in this very famous ancient text that seem important to us now. Then let's settle on a theme we might be able to further develop on stage. Developing in this case will include identifying useful themes in the play and then exploring how we can use our bodies on stage to fully represent those themes." Mr. Moss concludes by saying, "So what themes are expressed?" Julie speaks up immediately, saying, "Antigone buries her brother; that's an act of civil disobedience." Mr. Moss responds, "Good point, Julie. What do the rest of you think about Antigone's disobedience?" He waits for responses and then adds, "When might it be appropriate to disobey authority and when might it be important to comply with established rules that govern our collective societal interactions?" Ben responds. "She doesn't plan to disobey. She loves her brother, and family is everything!" Mr. Moss says, "Ben makes a good point. It seems like she defies the law for what might be a good reason to her. What else?"

While other themes like jealousy and power are discussed, the class decides together that these two themes—civil disobedience and familial love—will guide their creation of the contemporary script.

To develop these themes theatrically, Mr. Moss invites students to identify a few scenes from the original script where these themes are present. Once the students have identified three key scenes, he asks them to use the large strips of white poster paper that he has taped on the north classroom wall to engage in a silent written discussion about the scenes. He calls the paper a graffiti board and asks them to explore connections between the characters' lives in the play and their own lives. He suggests that these written discussions should point out comparisons between Antigone's world and their own. Providing a framework for the students to work within, Mr. Moss has established three categories of discussion on the large poster papers: *verbal conversations between characters in the play*, *ideas that characters present in monologue or dialogue form*, and *possible physical interactions that seem to occur between characters that display civil disobedience or family love*. Finally he asks them to spend some time thinking and writing silently on the graffiti board, promising that there will be plenty of time for them to talk about their ideas with each other.

Students silently examine the play for evidence and ideas and then write thoughts on the board. Citing the interactions and dialogue that occur between Hameon (Antigone's fiancé) and his father Creon, Sandra writes that "Antigone is like some of the reality shows I watch. There is so much awesome crying and dying going on in the play." She also notes on the graffiti board, "I hope our adaptation will have the same drama as *16 and Pregnant* or something like that."

Another student, Julio writes, "The girl's extreme reaction to King Creon's decision not to bury her brother Polyneices was not necessary. Antigone's speeches have power, but she is not protecting herself or other members of her family!" Later as the class converses about their writing, Julio says, "I understand that the Greeks believed her brother would not be able to make it to an afterlife unless his body was buried in the right way, and that bugs me, but I am positive that Antigone should not be risking her own life to dig his grave—this is her only life!" His statement gets a heated response from some of the students who express the importance of family honor, but others are more aligned with his position. A group of boys begins to chant, "Her only life! Her only life!" They're referring to their wish that Antigone had remained quiet and saved her own life.

Mr. Moss praises the group for their energy around this idea. He says, "I think we have made some good progress by examining what Antigone says and how it affects her relationships with other characters in this discussion. I am hoping that we also can begin to explore what she and the other characters do in these scenes we selected today that might help an audience further understand our themes. Sandra says, "I am interested in her character objectives. It might be good if we explore why she was doing what she did and why her objectives might be in conflict with King Creon's objectives or even her fiancé Haemon's objectives." Mr. Moss, responds, "Sandra gets a star! Great use of a theatre term, young lady." He then reminds the students about the purpose of theatre objectives, saying, "Remember that in theatre, a character's objective is shown by action. It is often something that the character is attempting to accomplish physically. I love your thoughts about what this play means, but now I think this would be an ideal time to get up on our feet and explore some of those meanings physically—let's think AND move."

Mr. Moss gives the class one last chance to examine what others have written on the graffiti board, and then together they assess which characters' objectives they are ready to develop using their bodies. He then assigns *groups of four to work with different segments of the play that they have discussed and reminds the students of the drama game that they learned earlier in the term titled "Slide Show." He says, "Let's play Slide Show to further investigate our thematic choices. I want each group to create a slide show; remember this is three sequential still images in which you represent the characters by embodying one of the themes we have discussed. For example in the first still image, or slide, you should show us something that Antigone wants that is related to familial love. In the second still image, you might show how she attempts to get that thing she wants—this may be her sister's acceptance or her fiancé's understanding. And finally in the third slide, share the result—or what happens when Antigone gets what she wants or is denied what she wants." He adds, "Remember these should be still images that are silent and physical demonstrations of what the characters want. You are welcome to use props or other objects available in the room if you think they will help you to tell your story."*

Students scavenge about the room to locate props and costumes that might enhance their performances. Thinking about the themes they have selected, students explore how their bodies might represent disobedience or familial love. In one group students play with levels and space between bodies to explore how they might convey defiance. In another group students experiment with ways they might express sisterly love simply through facial expressions. Julio and his group are attempting to tell the portion of the story where Antigone leaves the palace grounds to bury her brother. When Mr. Moss checks in with them, Julio says, "We can't get Antigone's stubbornness right!" Mr. Moss reminds them to think about how the positioning and movement of their bodies might provide an audience with clues about how a character feels about other characters, themselves, or ideas expressed within a scene. They begin to explore what might happen if they use their bodies to form the gate that Antigone has to go through to bury her brother. They try out various shapes and configurations and finally determine that they want to convey as much height in the gate as possible to demonstrate how threatening it might be to step through. After 10 minutes or so Mr. Moss gathers the class to perform their slide shows for each other.

They sit on the floor in a circle surrounding the small stage in the classroom. Mr. Moss invites each group to perform their series of images for the class. Several groups share their slide shows, and the students are excited by the images that have been created by their peers, but the one that sparks the most interest is the scene between Antigone and her sister Ismene created by Julio and his group. The first slide depicts the two young women—Antigone and Ismene—facing forward, hand in hand, ready to exit through the palace gates. Three of the boys in the group have used their bodies to form the shape of the ominous palace gates. The fourth boy lies dead just past the gates. In the second image the gates are parted and Antigone is depicted in a running position turned toward her brother's body, while Ismene is reaching out to Antigone still within the palace grounds. The final image depicts the gate closed again. Ismene stands stoically facing forward. Antigone is outside the gate, huddling over her brother's body. The images make it clear that the young women, who are only feet apart, are alone and isolated from each other now. Sharon gasps, saying, "Antigone really does lose everything." Jasmin notes how powerful the staging of the (human) gate was in each of the slides. She says, "The gate helped us to see how their relationship changed. In the first slide Antigone and Ismene looked so strong, like they could do anything together! But in the last slide, they simply looked defeated."

Mr. Moss acknowledges the creative ideas that were first envisioned in their thinking and writing and then further developed physically. He asks them to continue this investigation as homework. He assigns each of them to generate more focused work in pairs. Their assignment is to develop a short script based on the three slides they just viewed. He lists the requirements for the assignment. The script should express the ideas and attitudes that they explored verbally and physically today. He reminds them that they have decided to present their versions of the story in a present-day context. He also adds that quality scripts will include dialogue between characters or monologues where a character speaks what he or she is thinking as well as stage directions, which indicate what the characters are doing. Sending them on their way, he shouts, "Keep creating people!"

UNDERSTANDING THE THEATRE LITERACY EVENT

In the vignette described above, Mr. Moss introduces his students to theatre texts, processes, and literacies as they create together. In the following paragraphs I will discuss the specific ways that Mr. Moss aids the students in becoming theatre practitioners as he introduces them to theatre texts, processes, and literacies.

Texts

Mr. Moss invites his students to explore and utilize a variety of theatre texts. He initially shares the original printed play text with the students. Importantly he provides a theatre context for the print text by setting a clear theatre purpose for the reading of that text—the creation of a contemporary adaptation of *Antigone*. Within this parameter the class uses written and verbal inquiry skills such as the graffiti board to investigate the original play script. In this exercise he invites students to envision connections between their own world and the world of the play.

Mr. Moss also engages the students in the use of multimodal texts in the development of their new play. Through the explorations that occur in the Slide Show theatre game Mr. Moss helps students to see the important ways texts such as bodies, props, and other visual cues can aid theatre artists in making meaning. For example, students are encouraged to use only their physical presence or props as they physically develop portions of the story they had thought deeply about in the graffiti board exercise.

Finally the students are asked to generate a new written text as a response to the original play text and the verbal and physical work they did to envision connections between their own world and the world of the original play.

Processes

Mr. Moss's class creates using three theatre processes—envisioning, developing, and generating. Initially he invites the students to engage in envisioning possible themes represented in the play that might resonate with an audience of their peers. To help them express what they envision about those themes, he provides a graffiti board for the students to document their thoughts and feelings about the themes and ideas present in Sophocles's original text. He also supports their efforts to envision how they will tell Antigone's story in a contemporary context by requesting that they use theatre skills and knowledge as they express the ideas that they present on the graffiti board. He guides their noticing of the dramatic conventions used in the original text such as verbal conversations between characters in the play, ideas that characters present in monologue or dialogue form, or possible physical interactions that seem to occur between characters that display the themes they have selected. Additionally, Mr. Moss encourages discussion and even occasional dissent as they make decisions about the themes and ideas they want to express in their presentation of the story.

Mr. Moss and his students also further new ideas about the play that move beyond the *Antigone* playscript. Through the Slide Show activity, students begin to express new dramatic ideas physically as they use their bodies, props, and other found objects from the classroom to visually explore what the story of *Antigone* might look like on the stage. Mr. Moss carefully provides chances for students to take on the perspective of both performer and audience as each group presents their physical work to the other class members. This allows students to notice multiple ways to further develop and express the themes of civil disobedience and familial love physically. Because of this, students learn that there are many ways to convey meaning in theatre settings.

Finally Mr. Moss invites the students to combine their knowledge from the written texts and the physical work they participated in to generate a short script. To prepare them for success in this process, he invites them to draw on prior knowledge and skills used during class, but he also provides them with specific guidelines for the homework that provide a framework for their practice.

Literacies

Throughout the class period Mr. Moss involves his students in experiences where they read, write, listen, present ideas, and take on charter's perspectives within a theatre context. His students are invited to draw on traditional literacy skills; in fact, reading and writing are essential to understanding in this particular theatre lesson. However, Mr. Moss also engages his students in understanding new and expansive modalities (Kress, 2003) as they are uniquely used in theatre settings. In addition to reading and writing, he summons theatre students to negotiate and create using gestures, objects, images, and so on.

Mr. Moss empowers students to take ownership over the available semiotic resources by encouraging them to select from and organize those resources in ways that make sense to them and make sense in their world. In this way Mr. Moss encourages an awareness in his students that they can choose an "equitable participation in shaping the social and semiotic world" (Kress, 2010, p. 6) of the new play they are creating.

CONCLUSION

While this chapter provides one example of how texts, processes, and literacies can enrich a theatre arts classroom, it is important to remember that there are many and varied ways to engage in creation in theatre settings. Educators invested in developing theatre literacies in their students should consider using both traditional texts and the various multimodal texts used in theatre settings and then provide activities where students are posed with questions and problems that are essential to understanding in theatre. Authentic practice that allows students to envision, develop, and generate new ideas will increase their understanding of theatre in its context and improve students' future contributions in theatre settings beyond the academic environment.

REFERENCES

Gee, J. (2001). Reading as situated language: A sociocognitive perspective. *Journal of Adolescent and Adult Literacy, 44*(8), 714–725.

Jensen, A. P. (2009). (Re)imagining literacies for theatre classrooms. In R.J. Draper, P. Broomhead, A. P. Jensen, J. D. Nokes, & D. Siebert (Eds.), *(Re) imaging content-area literacy instruction* (pp. 97–112). New York, NY: Teachers College Press.

Kress, G. (2003). *Literacy in the new media age.* London: Routledge.

Kress, G. (2010). *Multimodality: A social semiotic approach to contemporary communication.* London: Routledge.

National Coalition for Core Arts Standards. (2014). Core Arts Theatre: Creating. Online at http://www.nationalartsstandards.org/sites/default/files/Theater_resources/Theatre%20at%20a%20Glance.pdf

5 Visual Art
Creating

Daniel T. Barney

I remember when I first heard about literacy initiatives in the school district in which I worked as a secondary art teacher. It was easy to make a short list of the various print texts my students and I utilized in the classroom that supported content area learning. These print texts included textbooks about artistic production in various contexts, art magazines, exhibition reviews, artist biographies, and artist statements. With the exception of the textbook, visual artists indeed engage with these print texts to participate in the discourses of artistic practice. The artists I know keep up with their fields by reading magazines and exhibition reviews and interacting with the discipline as a community of practice as they contextualize their own work. Artist statements and artist biographies also help an artist add to disciplinary discourses. But to be truly literate as a creator within the visual arts requires the ability to read visual art creations and to write visual art creations.

Eager to foster the literacy of art students, K–12 teachers like me create lessons and activities to help students engage in literacy activities using these print texts. However, teachers may want to scrutinize the authenticity of these activities to see if these texts are really texts that support more essential literacy practices in the visual art fields and, more importantly, if these texts are utilized in ways that parallel methodological inquiry within the visual arts. For example, the print texts listed above might be thought of as "readerly texts" (see Barthes, 1975, 1990) that are about the visual art but are not necessarily "writer-y texts" (see Barthes, 1975, 1990) that engage in meaning making through active creation. The point is that reading print texts about artistic practice is not the same as engaging in authentic artistic practices.

The literacy focus in a visual arts course should not be solely about the ability to read or even interpret what is written about art but to begin to contextualize and engage with art as a complex disciplinary practice, along with its discourses, methodologies, and interpretive frames for meaning making (Castro, 2007; Sandell, 2006) within and outside of regulating structures (Thomas, 2012). These structures may include but are not limited to schooling, business, culture, and politics. This critical, participatory, and active type of creative engagement still involves learning to read and write in a traditional sense, but visual art literacy instruction emphasizes creating in myriad ways. Students must have the opportunity to read and write authentically in the visual arts, which must include literacy instruction in artistic creation as a critical literacy process.

Art educator Julia Marshall (2002) uses the phrase "artmaking as research" (p. 280) to describe this process. To create in the visual arts means to engage actively with visual arts research methodologies—the disciplinary methods and philosophies surrounding the selection and use of methods, materials, processes, and contexts—that are utilized by contemporary practitioners within a "community of discourse" (Gude, 2009), or disciplinary field of inquiry.

A snapshot of what it might mean to begin to learn to write, or *to create* in the visual arts classroom, is provided as a vignette below. Mr. Baker and his students are discussing concepts of authenticity in the work of the jewelry artist Jan Yager. This excerpt highlights how students "generate and conceptualize artistic ideas and work" (NCCAS, 2014, VA: Cr1) and "organize and develop artistic ideas and work" (NCCAS, 2014, VA: Cr2) within the visual arts. It is not meant to be a summary of an entire lesson or curriculum experience but does provide us with a glimpse into visual arts literacy instruction that attends to authentic disciplinary engagement and inquiry in relation to creating processes.

Mr. Baker, the secondary teacher of an Art I: Visual Art Foundations class initiates a discussion with the students in his classroom. He addresses his class of 35 students, saying, "I've written the word AUTHENTICITY on the board here. I'd like you to take a moment to think about what authenticity in art making means to you. As you are thinking about how this term relates to artistic creation, please document your thoughts in your sketchbook. Feel free to draw from any sources you feel necessary to help you connect art making with this word as an idea."

Cherrie, a student, asks, "So we can draw or write our thoughts? Do we have to write in complete sentences?"

"No, not for this Cherrie—thank you for clarifying," replies Mr. Baker. "Think of this as an idea and thought-gathering sketchbook activity. As an artist, I often jot down quick ideas, drawings, and thoughts as small sketches, lists, and short sentences."

Mr. Baker waits a few minutes as students reflect, adding written thoughts and perhaps drawings to their sketchbooks.

"Would you please turn to a classmate and share some of your ideas about authenticity in art making?"

In pairs, students now take another few minutes to discuss the topic, utilizing their written as well as their visual representations to convey their thoughts. Listening in on some of these small groups, we would hear students compare and contrast their individual thoughts and ideas with their peers. They also would be able to practice communicating their thoughts via sketches if they chose to do so.

Visual Art: Creating

"For our next art making challenge, we are going to explore what it means for an artwork to be of its place and of its time." Mr. Baker writes this phrase on the whiteboard. "Before responding to this in a formal discussion, we are going to first explore, collect, and then reflect. Bring a bag with you and a means for collecting visual data, like your sketchbook and a drawing tool, and/or a camera. We are going to go on an artistic investigation."

Students are then given some instruction concerning policies about expected behavior if leaving the building. The teacher and students further discuss the challenge to be of its place and of its time as they exit the building to explore the school grounds, searching individually for inspiration regarding authenticity.

While outside, Mr. Baker instructs students on safe handling of found objects.

"I don't want to pick up anything gross!" shouts Devonne.

"Don't worry, Devonne. I don't want anyone to touch anything that is gross or dangerous. However, if you want to document something that you encounter, what other ways besides collecting the object could you utilize as an artist?"

"Oh yeah," says Devonne. "I can take a picture of it with my camera phone or draw it where it is. I get it."

After perhaps 30 minutes or more of independent exploration, data collection, documentation, and reflection, the students and Mr. Baker return to the classroom.

Mr. Baker encourages the students to take a few moments to share their findings in small groups or as a whole. They find pinecones, cigarette butts, various leaves and plant samples, aluminum cans, sprinkler parts, old football tickets, crumpled homework handouts, interesting rocks and sticks, images of graffiti, a lost shoe, orange peels, and lots of wrappers from candy and gum.

Mr. Baker asks, "What do these things mean, how do they make you feel, and what are the possible stories attached to these objects? Do these questions have anything to do with authenticity or being of its place and of its time?"

"I found a ticket from the football game from last night. I went to that game... unfortunately," laughs Evie. "Ricky and Jenn were there too, and I also found a cool rock in the shape of a goldfish."

The sharing continues, with some students talking about the connections they have or don't have with the objects found.

The class is then set up to watch a video clip about the jewelry artist Jan Yager.

Mr. Baker says, "Every artist has an individual way to create his or her work, but the jewelry artist Jan Yager asked the very question we have been discussing today. She gathered information, objects, questions, and answers similar to those you collected just now. I'd like you to examine the following questions (written on the board or passed out as a handout) as you watch this video about her art making: How did she arrive at this question concerning authenticity? What methods did she use to explore the concept of authenticity as an artist? How did she delimit her investigation, or what was the 'assignment' she gave herself as an artist? What were the processes she used to create an artistic response to this 'assignment'?" Mr. Baker answers questions about the task as needed. The video is then started.

In the short video clip, which describes the process Jan Yager used in creating work for the City Flotsam series and a specific work from the City Flora series called "The Tiara of Useful Knowledge, 2006," Jan Yager describes how she investigates the concept of authenticity by being inspired by objects she encounters within one block of her studio in Philadelphia. Mr. Baker returns to the questions asked before the video began. Mr. Baker asks for relevant responses.

Francie raises her hand and states, "Before starting this series Jan didn't think her art was very authentic, even though it was being shown in magazines."

"Yeah," says Billy, "just making the same kinds of objects over and over again became boring to her. She was really famous and all, but the work didn't have much meaning anymore."

"I thought her necklaces were pretty," says Maya.

"I think her work was pretty too, Maya. Having her work shown in magazines didn't seem to satisfy this artist, nor did the formal qualities of the work fulfill her desire to quit. They were aesthetically pleasing, and yet she continued to search and inquire," adds Mr. Baker.

"They looked great," agrees Arielle. "They were well made and all, but she wanted her work to matter more I think. . . . And so she gave herself a challenge to make something authentic."

Jairus chimes in, "To be authentic, she said it needed to be of its place and of its time."

"That's right, Jairus. That's what she said. Do you think that is the only way something can be authentic?" asks Mr. Baker.

"Probably not, but she did a lot of research while she was thinking about authenticity," suggests Aliyah.

Mr. Baker says, "What kind of research?"

Devonne shouts out, "She just walked around her neighborhood like we walked around the school!"

"That's not all she did! She also looked at old artifacts," recalls Stephen, "like that ancient bone necklace to get ideas. We didn't really do that."

"When she walked around, she thought about what it means to be authentic. She also read historical documents about her city, and she must have done other things to find out stuff." Ramona tilts her head and asks, "You know what I mean?"

Mr. Baker asks, "What other stuff do you mean?"

"Well, you know she knew a lot about the weeds she found around her studio, what they could be used for, and how not everyone finds beauty in them. She knows a ton about weeds," adds Ramona confidently. "She must have found out about them somehow."

"Authenticity is a pretty big concept," says Mr. Baker. "You are all recognizing that an artistic investigation draws from many sources and engagements. She kept her research question regarding authenticity in mind as she worked in the studio, outside of the studio, and even while she visited other places, like the library. What did Jan Yager do to narrow down or give focus to her investigation?"

Claire raises her hand and then adds, "Oh, she challenged herself to be inspired by things than happen one block from her studio, sort of like how we stayed on school grounds today. But then she also was open to bring in ideas from other sites and other interactions."

Mr. Baker notices that Eunice might have something to add. He calls on her. "Eunice, how did Jan Yager's artistic process of delimiting her inquiry relate to what we did today?"

Eunice, in a quiet voice says, "We collected things like Jan did. She even drew the weeds and took photos of them, but I think she might have done all that when she got back to her studio."

"Does anyone remember what Jan Yager said about drawing and photographing those plants?" asks Mr. Baker.

"She was drawing them and photographing them to help her make her jewelry," answers Maya.

"Hey yeah! She didn't just make her sculpture right away; it was kind of a long process," says Luz.

The class discussion continues, and the methods and possible reasons behind these selected methods are also discussed. The students and Mr. Baker will then elaborate on a line of inquiry and time line so that each student can begin to engage artistically in questions of authenticity on a personal level, sharing their artistic research with each other in a timely manner. So while the class eventually will create a single exhibition or a series of exhibitions, we will use just this short vignette to unpack the literacy instruction of visual arts creation.

UNDERSTANDING THE VISUAL ART LITERACY EVENT

Text

Texts within the visual arts hold disciplinary meaning. As noted in this classroom activity, this can include traditional print texts, drawings, paintings, sculptures, and even objects like a used football ticket, plants, or a bone necklace. In the visual arts, the site or location of inquiry or a space in which the performance or presentation of the work is exhibited or shared also can be a meaningful text. Jan Yager's one-block radius from her studio and the school campus become significant texts in Mr. Baker's literacy event. Being able to interpret or create meaning with these texts are the literacies of the visual arts.

Processes

Mr. Baker makes it evident that creating one's own "assignment" is an important aspect in artistic creation, which is key to the artistic process. The subsequent classroom discussion after watching the video supports these tenets.

To create in the visual arts then is to "write" visual arts texts. To be able to do this requires more knowledge than simply reading or interpreting print texts *about* visual art, although this is often an important aspect of being able to participate in visual art as a community of practice. More importantly, to write a visual arts text, one must have experiential understanding about how visual arts texts are created in context. To create a meaningful visual art text, one must engage *in* visual art discourses. Literacy instruction can support such understanding and engagement but must be based on contemporary practices and discourses within the visual arts. This may include but is not limited to thematic or conceptual problems, methodological positions, delimiting lines of inquiry or bodies of work, materials and process selection, contextualizing one's work within the broad discourse of visual art, presentation and representation concerns, and aesthetic paradigms and stances.

In this vignette, no object actually was created as of yet. Because the products of artistic investigation often are studied without knowledge of how and why they were created, we might teach artistic production in terms of skill acquisition only. Or perhaps we might overdetermine art as an expressive endeavor that is not about investigation but emotive visual catharsis. Both of these misinterpretations overlook the visual arts as a serious discipline of inquiry, cultural production, and critique. Mr. Baker supports authentic creation in the visual arts as a process of investigation and engagement that is not about simply reading or writing *about* art. Even though there are many artists who refuse to make objects in their artistic lines of inquiry (see De Bellis, 2009; Goldstein & Rorimer, 1995), Mr. Baker in this case, will undoubtedly help students eventually to "refine and complete [their] artistic work" (NCCAS, 2014, VA: Cr3) within a community of artistic discourse.

Mr. Baker might be asking too much from his students if he was looking for the "right" answers; however, in artistic production, creation is often a complex exploration and an organic juggling of thoughts, questions, memories, and hunches. Mr. Baker does, however, key into this particular artist's creation process as a methodology by asking students (1) to identify how Jan Yager became interested in questions about authenticity, (2) how she explored authenticity as a concept relevant to art making, (3) how she created her own "assignment" to focus her creative endeavor, and finally, (4) what artistic processes she employed to respond to her own "assignment." So, Mr. Baker is helping students realize that while some people might think that creating within the visual arts is all about using specific tools (paint brushes, canvases, clay, cameras, etc.) and techniques (chiaroscuro, linear perspective, hand building, impasto, etc.) to create a visual representation, obtaining creative literacy within the visual arts entails much more.

Literacies

While vocabulary is important to learn in any discipline, it is important to learn vocabulary in meaningful contexts. Mr. Baker doesn't simply define the word *authenticity*, nor does he use it in a sentence or have the students draw a picture to help them recall the word's meaning. Instead, he highlights the importance of understanding how those working within a disciplinary practice might utilize a word as a concept within the visual arts creation process. He asks his students to think about the word in relation to art making. Students are able to use dictionaries, online searches, or any other sources to help them gain an understanding of the word, but they will then have to make their own connections to how this word relates meaningfully to artistic practices. Mr. Baker encourages students to share their current understandings with others. This provides an aspect of accountability and interchange that relates to artistic practice but also connects to contemporary pedagogical practices (see Davis, Sumara, & Luce-Kapler, 2008).

Mr. Baker does not make an explicit transition from *authenticity* as a concept to being *of its place and of its time*. This possible oversight as an instructional strategy actually parallels how many artists create. Artists move between concepts, play with possibilities (Castro & Barney, 2012), problem *find* as opposed to always problem *solve*, and bricole or tinker (Kalin & Barney, 2014) with available understandings, objects, relations, and representations. Instead of defining authenticity for students, Mr. Baker invites the students to create meaning for themselves through a conceptual investigation as part of a contextualized artistic practice. This is a key process of inquiry. Mr. Baker, however, does return to the notion that conceptual investigation is a literacy that artists deal with when he states "authenticity is a big concept," and then he lays out the artistic strategy of how artists engage with a specific concept by making possible connections and relationships through a living inquiry outside of the studio or, in this case, the classroom. Mr. Baker then highlights another strategy, delimiting one's inquiry by creating one's own assignment, challenge, or body of work. In Yager's case, being of its place and of its time meant that inspiration should be generated primarily within one block of her studio site. The visual art texts that students engaged with were the found objects they related to concepts of authenticity. The photographs and drawings of these objects in situ also may be considered texts, but they are perhaps more related to drafts and preliminary research than completed artworks. They are indeed part of the inquiry process, and further literacy instruction may be needed if these are to be presented to the public. As a visual art teacher, Mr. Baker most assuredly would provide workshops on drawing, painting, photography, sculpture, and other traditional image- and object-making approaches for students. But without literacy instruction about how and why artists engage in artistic inquiry, these traditional skills and techniques act as isolated vocabulary acquisition and grammar building.

Mr. Baker doesn't solidify meaning for the students but encourages students to share their ideas with each other. Art can be quite ambiguous and subjective but is also self-referential, interdisciplinary, and rooted in specific discourses. These have a history and a contemporary set of practices. Mr. Baker does provide textual support for such a seemingly messy field of study. The video, for example, presents Jan Yager's process of inquiry in a fairly straightforward manner. Mr. Baker helps his students access literacy skills within visual art thinking and making by relating what is shown in this video to their own activity of searching the school grounds for that which might begin an artistic exploration of *the authentic*.

REFERENCES

Barthes, R. (1975). *The pleasure of the text* (Richard Miller, Trans.). New York: Hill and Wang. (Original work published 1973)

Barthes, R. (1990). *S/Z* (Richard Miller, Trans.). London: Basil Blackwell. (Original work published 1973)

Castro, J. C. (2007). *Constraints that enable: Creating spaces for artistic inquiry.* Proceedings of the 2007 Complexity Science and Educational Research Conference, Vancouver, British Columbia. Retrieved from www.complexityandeducation.ualberta.ca/conferences/2007/Documents/CSER07_Castro.pdf

Castro, J. C., & Barney, D. T. (2012). Playing the Spiral Jetty. *The Journal for Artistic Research,* Issue 2, http://www.researchcatalogue.net/view/2387/2388/0/0

Davis, B., Sumara, D., & Luce-Kapler, R. (2008). *Engaging minds: Changing teaching in complex times* (2nd ed.). New York: Routledge.

De Bellis, V. (2009). Tino Sehgal (Review of the exhibition *Villa Reale, Milan*, curated by Massimiliano Gioni). *International Contemporary Art, 101,* 38.

Goldstein, A., & Rorimer, A. (1995). *Reconsidering the object of art.* Los Angeles: Museum of Contemporary Art & MIT Press.

Gude, O. (2009). Art education for democratic life. *Art Education, 62*(6), 7–11.

Kalin, N. M., & Barney, D. T. (2014). Hunting for monsters: Visual arts curriculum as agonistic inquiry. *The International Journal of Art & Design Education, 33*(1), 19–31.

Marshall, J. (2002). Exploring culture and identity through artifacts: Three art lessons derived from contemporary art practice. In Y. Gaudelius & P. Speirs (Eds.), *Contemporary issues in art education* (pp. 279–290). Upper Saddle River, NJ: Prentice Hall.

National Core Arts Standards. (2014). *Visual arts standards.* Retrieved from http://www.nationalartsstandards.org/sites/default/files/Visual%20Arts%20at%20a%20Glance%20rev.pdf

Sandell, R. (2006). Form + theme + context: Balancing considerations for meaningful art learning. *Art Education, 59*(1), 33–37.

Thomas, B. (2012). Psychologizing and the anti-psychologist: Dewey, Lacan, and contemporary art education. *Studies in Art Education, 53*(4), 330–346.

6 Theatre in the Elementary Classroom
Creating

Jennifer J. Wimmer and Julia Ashworth

An elementary classroom is a space created for learning. In addition to learning the three Rs, it is a space where students learn about citizenship, responsibility, and caring. It is a space where students learn to ask questions, seek out solutions, and ultimately learn to make meaning of the world around them (Davis, 2008; McCaslin, 2006). In this chapter we argue that theatre and specifically process drama afford students the opportunity to explore, question, and experiment.

Process drama provides students with a tool to explore the human experience (Spolin, 1999). As students engage in creating process drama, they have opportunities to reflect and make meaning of their lives. As students share in the experience of a guided drama, they build community, empathy, and compassion (Davis, 2008). These types of complex ideas, though highly valued, are often difficult to teach, especially to young children. However, as students engage in process drama, they have opportunities to learn about and explore perspectives and others' points of view. For example, it states in the National Art Standards for Core Theatre Standards for Grade 1 that students should "propose potential choices characters could make" (NCAS, 2014, TH: Cr1.1.1 a). This type of learning activity provides students with the opportunity to try on characters' identities in a safe space. As a result, the complex ideas become understandable and meaningful because students are engaged in creating ideas using their bodies, voices, and minds (Heathcote & Bolton, 1995).

Those who have witnessed a drama performance are aware that it does not occur haphazardly or magically. Rather, creating drama in the classroom happens through thoughtful and skillful guidance by the teacher. The teacher must provide structure, pretext, and content (O'Neill & Lambert, 1982/1990). The teacher also must understand that in addition to foundational literacies (i.e., comprehension, phonics, vocabulary, etc.), there are particular literacies necessary to participate in process drama.

This chapter will first present a vignette from a first-grade classroom that demonstrates an integrated drama and literacy lesson; next, drawing on the vignette, we will discuss the processes, literacies, and texts used to meet both literacy and drama goals; and finally, we will discuss how the integration of the theatre with literacy impacts learning.

Ms. Barton's first-grade class is in the middle of a unit on personal responsibility. The unit explores ways personal responsibility is connected to choices and reactions to those choices. The desks in her classroom are pushed to the sides to prepare the students for drama work this afternoon. Ms. Barton and her students sit in a circle in the story corner to read Don't Let the Pigeon Drive the Bus by Mo Willems. After finishing the book, she asks students for observations, "What were some of the emotions the pigeon felt in the book?"

"He was excited," says one boy.

"It seemed like he was sad too," says the girl to his left.

"How did he feel when he didn't get to drive the bus?" asks Ms. Barton. "How did he react?" Almost all hands in the room shot up in the air: "He yelled." "He screamed." "He was funny." "I think he cried!"

Ms. Barton asks the students to stand up from their story circle and find their own spaces in the cleared room. "Make sure you have enough space around you to stand on both feet, stretch your arms, and not bump into your neighbors," she explains. "You will each work on your own; focus on yourself and your own choices. Can everyone please face forward in my direction?"

Ms. Barton tells the students they're about to begin a pantomime activity, but she would like them to do a practice round first, so everyone understands the directions. She explains that she will read lines from the book and the students will react to those lines. Ms. Barton reminds the students that one of the first times the pigeon asks to drive the bus, he says, "Please, I'll be careful." Ms. Barton's instructions include rules and guidelines for doing this type of drama work together. "Make sure you don't move outside of your own space. Keep your feet planted to the floor, and react with both your body and your face. When I say one, two, three, freeze, you'll each freeze in a frozen picture of 'Please, I'll be careful.' Okay? One, two, three, freeze!" Students create individual pantomimes by silently freezing in reaction to the line. "I see some really great images around me—make sure you stay frozen. Keep your mouths frozen too!" says Ms. Barton.

Students display various reactions and interpretations of the pigeon's plea. Some have exaggerated friendly or excited facial expressions; others are pretending to hug someone else; and several are down on their knees pleading. "I see some of you are making shapes with your bodies up high, some are down low, and others at a middle level. Let's all try something at a low level—you don't need to do the exact same things your classmates are doing, but it's okay if it's similar. Go with the first idea that comes into your mind. On the count of three, make a shape down low of what you might do if you were the pigeon on the line, 'Please, I'll be careful.' One, two, three, freeze!"

As students create various shapes, begging on their knees or laid out on the floor, Ms. Barton explores what emotions the pigeon might be feeling in this position. "What an excellent bunch of pigeons we have—as you pretend to be the pigeon, I want you to imagine what he's thinking right now. When I walk by and tap you on the shoulder, please share one word that might describe what the pigeon is thinking or feeling at this moment." Students' answers include: "scared," "happy," "nervous," "worried," "excited," "mad," and so on. Ms. Barton asks the students to relax from their frozen images, to stand up and stay in their own space, and ten, "Why do you think the pigeon might be nervous, excited, or worried right now?"

Jennifer raises her hand to answer, "He really wants to drive the bus but is scared to." A boy next to her exclaims, "He's worried he might get in trouble!" Ms. Barton wants to know if anyone in the class has ever felt the same way. "Have any of you ever been excited and worried at the same time?" Many students say yes. "When have you felt that way?" Students are quick to answer: "When I get candy out of the drawer without asking." "When I want to play outside before I do my homework." "When my friend comes over and I don't let my little sister play with us." Ms. Barton nods her head. "Those are great examples. All of those examples involve you making a choice—just like you have to choose if you're going to ask for candy, if you're going to play before you've done your homework, or if you'll let your little sister play with your friend, the pigeon has to choose if he's going to keep asking to drive the bus when he's already been told no." Ms. Barton asks the students to silently think of times when they've been told no, but they keep asking and pleading anyhow. After students have had a minute to think, Ms. Barton asks them to choose a neighbor nearby to be a partner, grab his or her hand, and raise it high in the air. The students share their ideas with their partners, and then Ms. Barton calls on several pairs to share their responses with the entire class.

Ms. Barton continued with the pantomime activity using another line from book.

"Let's do one more line from the book—on the count of three, I want you to freeze to the line, 'No fair!'" The students begin a similar process as before. Ms. Barton thanks bold and varied choices. She encourages them to use their intuitions and go with their first ideas.

After this line from the book, Ms. Barton asks half the class to remain frozen, while the other half relax but stay in their own spaces.

"Why do you think your classmates are frozen the way you see them?" Ms. Barton asks.

The students remark on how upset the pigeon is, how his face shows how he might be feeling. Jauna says, "His face looks like he's yelling." Ms. Barton says, "Why do you think he's yelling, Jauna?"

"His mouth is open, and his eyes are big—he looks mad." After both sides have had the opportunity to observe, she asks students to sit down on the floor in a circle.

Ms. Barton asks the students how it felt to freeze after each line and which line they liked to freeze for the most. The processes of creating multiple frozen images helps the students have empathy for the pigeon. As the students begin to describe what it was like to pretend to be the pigeon, she asks, "What did you learn about how the pigeon feels?"

"I think the pigeon is just really mad he can't drive the bus," says one quiet girl.

"Does anyone else agree?" ask Ms. Barton. Many hands go up. "Why?" she wants to know.

"He tries so many times to drive the bus, even though he knows he shouldn't," says another student in the class.

At this point the class begins to make connections to their own lives as Ms. Barton asks, "When have any of you said or heard someone else say, 'No fair!'?" Several students raise their hands to respond. Ms. Barton calls on several students: "My older sister says 'no fair' when my mom won't let her use her makeup!" "I don't think it's fair that I can only play videogames for one hour." "It's not fair that my brother gets his own iPad."

Ms. Barton asks the students to think about how people responded in those situations, "Did they respond like the pigeon and yell and scream? Or did they make a different choice?"

Ms. Barton reminds the students of the role choice played in how the pigeon responded to being told he could not drive the bus. She asks why the pigeon made the choices he made and if he showed personal responsibility for his choices.

A student remarks, "The pigeon might need someone to tell him not to yell so much."

Ms. Barton asks the students to give some advice to the pigeon; she asks them what they might say to him if they were to meet him to help him make better choices. "The pigeon needs our help. Now that you've played the role of the pigeon, you are better prepared to give him advice on how to behave more responsibly when upset. Will each of you create a piece of advice you would give the pigeon if he were to visit us today?" Ms. Barton gives them a few seconds as students whisper a line of dialogue to themselves. She then directs the students in the room to get on their feet and stand in two rows facing each other, leaving enough room for "the pigeon" to walk down the aisle they've created.

Ms. Barton, playing the role of the pigeon, proceeds to walk down the aisle, walking slowly and carefully listening as her students share advice with the pigeon. Although students' advice overlaps each other, she distinctly hears a few key phrases to share with the entire class when she's done. "I heard a lot of great advice, including 'speak nicely,' 'have good manners,' 'listen to others,' 'use your words,' 'count to 10 before you get mad,' and 'don't whine.'"

Ms. Barton concludes the lesson by asking the students to show her what the pigeon looks like now that he's listened to all this advice. "I'm going to walk down the aisle one more time—this time I'll be myself, and you all will imagine you are the pigeon. On the count of three, freeze as if the pigeon is being told no again. One, two, three, freeze!"

UNDERSTANDING THE THEATRE LITERACY EVENT

At first glance, the above vignette may appear to be a simple response activity to a read aloud. In fact, many elementary educators may read the vignette and say to themselves, "I already do this." However, a closer examination of this vignette begins to reveal a complex set of processes, texts, and literacies that the teacher and students are negotiating and creating. In the sections that follow, each of these components, which make up the literacy event, will be further discussed.

Texts

The vignette opens with Ms. Barton reading aloud a picture book to her class. This type of text is a key element of the lesson and a key component of the literacy event. In fact, literacy events are visible activities where a "written text, or texts, [are] central to the activity and there may be talk around the text" (Barton & Hamilton, 2000, p. 8). Therefore, it may seem commonsensical to view the picture book as the only text used in this lesson. Indeed, it is difficult for students to create unless they know something about the topic of study. While the text *Don't Let the Pigeon Drive the Bus* (Willems, 2003) is a key source of information, other essential texts in this lesson include the teacher's voice and body, the students' voices and bodies, and the classroom space. Each of these texts must be attended to and negotiated or "read."

While texts traditionally are viewed as print based with a set "reading path" (Kress, 2003, p. 3), an expanded definition of text is necessary to include the increasingly multimodal texts, which include image, sound, and gesture (Kress, 2003). Because students are required to negotiate or read a variety of multimodal texts both in and out of school, it is essential that teachers provide instruction in a variety of texts. In the vignette, Ms. Barton asked half of the students to examine the messages the rest of the class was presenting. Thus, the students were engaged with reading bodies, faces, and space. These texts became opportunities for students to move from consumers of knowledge to producers of knowledge; in other words, they became active participants in their learning rather than passive consumers.

Processes

In the vignette Ms. Barton engaged the students in the processes of imagining and exploring as they used their bodies to create messages based on the pigeon's actions, thoughts, and feelings. One of the great benefits of drama is that students are given opportunities to "imaginatively use [their] voice, body, and space to make others believe in a mood, idea, or message" (Cornett, 2011, p. 209). Instead of this learning activity being a simple response to a text, students are given opportunities to take up the social practices of actors as they learn how to use their bodies, voices, faces, and space to create and communicate a message. This does not happen by accident, rather "drama integration [must] include explicitly teaching students to concentrate, focus, and control their bodies, minds and voices" (Cornett, 2011, p. 204).

The students also had opportunities to explore their feelings and the pigeon's feelings through this drama experience. As Ms. Barton asked the students to think of advice to give the pigeon, they were asked to ponder and reflect on difficult concepts such as empathy, problem solving, and identity. Through the teacher's careful scaffolding, the students were given opportunities to negotiate these complex ideas as they created, demonstrated, and reflected upon differing viewpoints. Again, students were engaging in similar artistic practices and processes as theatre artists. For example, as theatre artists engage in exploration, they may ponder, "How does my artistic process change when experimenting with a variety of tools and skills, roles, contexts, and conflicts?" Similarly, Ms. Barton asked the students to experiment with roles as she encouraged the students to switch from the role of the pigeon to a parent or peer. Ultimately, the students were given opportunities to imagine and explore in a variety of ways.

Literacies

An arts educator may read this vignette and see no literacy. Similarly, a literacy specialist may read the vignette and see only literacy in the reading of the picture book. However, literacy knowledge and skills are present throughout the lesson as Ms. Barton guides the students through thinking, problem solving, exploring, and reflecting. Literacy is a complex and expansive term. While many definitions are available, it is important to expand definitions of literacy that extend beyond the printed word. This does not mean that foundational literacies are unimportant. Rather, they are used to create and negotiate particular texts at particular times for particular purposes. For example, "Vocabulary and conceptual knowledge is increased as students figure out how to take roles and convince, convert, coax, sell, feud, or bargain" (Cornett, 2011, p. 209). Therefore, another careful look at the vignette shows students engaged in drama that requires them to "concentrate, sense, perceive, imagine, and think" (Cornett, 2011, p. 209). These literacies are essential to their understanding of the texts, themselves, and their surroundings.

CONCLUSIONS

The Common Core State Standards document states, "To build a foundation for college and career readiness, students must read widely and deeply from among a broad range of high-quality, increasingly challenging literary and informational texts" (National Governors Association Center for Best Practices [NGA Center] & Council of Chief State School Officers [CCSSO],

2010, p. 10). We highly agree with this statement if the definition of text is broadened to include drama texts such as bodies, faces, and space. As students learn to negotiate (read) and create (produce) drama texts, they engage in learning that approximates theatre artists, which provides them with access to imagination, exploration, creativity, and problem solving—skills that are necessary for participation.

We strongly contend that as students engage with drama, they are provided with opportunities not only to learn to consume knowledge but also to take knowledge and transform it (The New London Group, 2000). We know this is not an easy task. However, we believe that as elementary educators, art educators, and literacy specialists come together and begin to dialogue that students will benefit.

REFERENCES

Barton, D., & Hamilton, M. (2000). Literacy practices. In D. Barton, M. Hamilton & R. Ivanic (Eds.), *Situated literacies: Reading and writing in context* (pp. 7–15). New York: Routledge.

Cornett, C.E. (2011). *Creating meaning through literature and the arts: Arts integration for classroom teachers* (4th ed.). Boston, MA: Pearson.

Davis, J.H. (2008). *Why our schools need the arts.* New York, NY: Teachers College Press.

Heathcote, D., & Bolton, G. (1995). *Drama for learning.* Portsmouth, NH: Heinemann.

Kress, G. (2003). *Literacy in the new media age.* London: Routledge.

McCaslin, N. (2006). *Creative drama in the classroom and beyond.* Boston, MA: Pearson.

National Core Arts Standards. (2014). *Core theatre standards.* Retrieved from http://www.nationalartsstandards.org/sites/default/files/Theater_resources/Theatre%20at%20a%20Glance.pdf

National Governors Association Center for Best Practices & Council of Chief State School Officers. (2010). *Common core state standards for English language arts and literacy in history/social studies, science, and technical subjects.* Washington, DC: Author. Retrieved from www.corestandards.org/assets/CCSSI_ELA%20Standards.pdf

New London Group. (2000). A pedagogy of multiliteracies: Designing social futures. In B. Cope & M. Kalantzis (Eds.), *Multiliteracies: Literacy learning and the design of social futures* (pp. 9–37). New York: Routledge.

O'Neill, C., & Lambert, A. (1990). *Drama structures.* Portsmouth, NH: Heinemann.

Spolin, V. (1999). *Improvisation for the theatre* (3rd ed.). Evanston, IL: Northwestern University Press.

Willems, M. (2003). *Don't let the pigeon drive the bus.* New York: Hyperion Books for Children.

Section II
Performing

7 Music
Performing

Paul Broomhead

Even though listening may be the predominant day-to-day music activity in young student's lives (Lamont, Hargreaves, Marshall, & Tarrant, 2003), performing may be considered the most prevalent process in music education as it dominates at least two of the most common music education settings for secondary-age students: the ensemble and the private lesson. The task of honing the skills involved in performance to the point of becoming an expert can require literally thousands of hours of practice (Ericsson, Krampe, & Tesch-Romer, 1993).

Performing literacies involve negotiating and creating texts in ways that are appropriate in musical performance. More specifically, performing literacies are characterized by the ability to interact effectively with texts that are commonly encountered while learning to perform, such as musical instruments, musical notation (scores), conductors, musical models, and surrounding ensemble performance (Broomhead, 2010). Sophisticated interactions with each of these texts require instruction, practice, and abundant repetitive experiences to develop the finely honed awareness and skills crucial to success.

Educators who aspire to escort students down the path toward becoming expert performers easily could use up every school hour on these skills as well as require regular home practice and would still have to acknowledge that this was little more than a good start. Accompanied by this sense of unlimited potential for performing expertise, it would seem that musical meaning deepens along with increased skill. Logic suggests that the deeper one can attend to nuances in performance of the music, the more he or she is able to access nuances of potential meanings.

Because musicians and music teachers desire for their students to experience the deep meaning potential of advanced performing, they might be tempted to focus their instruction only on performing processes—pushing students as quickly as possible through beginning stages to get them to higher levels of literacy and more deeply meaningful experiences. However, in an almost desperate approach to get beyond beginning stages, teachers may neglect the meaning making that is possible for students in even the earliest stages of musical experience. One of the ways to enhance meaning making from the beginning is to blend performance with creating, responding, and connecting experiences.

These processes—discussed in other chapters—contextualize and add variety and motivation to performing. For example, a student will play or sing differently with a higher level of expressive creativity, or with a deeper experiential familiarity with its genre, or with a deeper understanding of the background, structure, and purpose of a piece. These aspects of performance are rich with creating, responding, and connecting processes. This blend of processes is reflected in the National Music Core Standards (NCCAS, 2014, MU: Pr4,5,6-E), which state that a performing education in music should involve *selecting* musical works; *analyzing* their structure and context; *interpreting* creators' intent (and other factors); *rehearsing, evaluating and refining* personal and ensemble performances; and *presenting* a quality performance. Far from being a discrete process, performing always should be accompanied by some if not all of the other processes mentioned.

The performing literacy event that follows is based on the notions (1) that performing processes are important for meaning making in music and (2) that such meaning is enhanced by the presence of the creating, responding, and connecting processes interwoven with performing. As students engage in all of the processes, the teacher, Ms. Yarn, keeps the performing processes in the foreground, using recorded performances, feedback about the students' performing, and modeling of performing skills. This event, which takes place in the context of a middle school general music class, shows students negotiating recordings, musical instruments, and other's musical actions while preparing a small ensemble performance.

The air is brimming with nervous excitement as students meet with their small groups and engage in final rehearsals and discussions to prepare for the big performance. They will be performing a piece for the class today that they created based on their study of a genre, aided by performance instruction from Ms. Yarn. Class members recall her teaching and coaching session by session.

They recall the introduction two weeks earlier. She shows a video of a bluegrass band and asks, "Do you notice that 'boomp-chucka, boomp-chucka' feel in the accompaniment? See how the bass does the 'boomp,' alternating between [singing] one, five, one, five, and the folk guitar does the 'chucka' with his strumming? We'll call this a performing characteristic of the bluegrass genre. What other performance characteristics do you notice?"

The class engages in a discussion yielding several characteristics: the country twang in the vocals, the fingerpicking of the banjo, the drumsticks striking a wood box, and the melody alternating between singer and fiddler. Ms. Yarn calls special attention to the rhythmic unity of the group, warning, "One of the biggest challenges you will face in the project you are about to start is achieving unity with other members of your ensemble."

Ms. Yarn helps each student select a musical genre to study and forms five groups of peers with matching interests: two drum circles, a group of rappers, an a cappella vocal group, and a scream-o group (a student suggestion). Ms. Yarn goes from group to group helping them access recordings of their genres, identify performing characteristics of the genre, and focus on a characteristic compatible with some of their previous experiences and access to resources.

In a visit to the rapper group, Ms. Yarn says, "Okay. What resources do you have?"

Eric replies, "I brought some sick recordings WITH NO SWEARING, Ms. Yarn. I promise."

"How many songs have you listened to?" Ms. Yarn asks.

Norsa says, "Three. We're thinking the first one is our favorite."

"Let me hear it," says Ms. Yarn. They play it, and Ms. Yarn allows her body to respond to the rhythmic groove. "Nice! There's some real musical stuff going on there. Have you made your list of characteristics?"

"No, not yet."

"I'll be back to look at that in a few minutes. And don't forget to write down all of the performing skills you already have here in the group. Anyone play guitar?"

"Eric!" respond the group members.

"You've also got beatboxing here, right?" asks Ms. Yarn. John and Norsa both identify themselves as beatboxers. Ms. Yarn nods, "This is a start. What else have you got?" Before anyone can answer, she interrupts their thinking and says, "Okay. Think hard. Be thorough, and make a list. I'll look at that too in a few minutes when I get back."

In similar conversations with the other groups, Ms. Yarn helps students make sense of the recordings they are listening to; one group has no characteristics written down at all.

"Play it for me. Let's work on this together," she offers. She helps them identify several characteristics of the genre.

Students in another group are struggling to identify performing resources. "Anyone have an instrument at home that is not getting used?" Ms. Yarn asks. Jenna has a flute. Ms. Yarn pursues, "Have you ever played it?"

"Well, I took lessons for one year in fifth grade," Jenna admits.

"There you go. I'll get you a book that shows fingerings. It is gonna be SO fun finding a cool way to work flute into a drum circle."

Similar resources are found throughout the class. Several students have access to instruments on which they have received some instruction: a few play guitar, a bunch can beatbox, and all can drum. One student even has incredible facility with music apps on an iPad, and, of course, everyone can sing.

Ms. Yarn goes around to the groups again, making sure each student has a role to perform, and instructs students to decide on genre characteristics that their group plans to incorporate into their performances. After these initial observations and decisions, Ms. Yarn gives parameters for the pieces they will soon perform. "You may cover *(which means to reproduce or copy) a particular song, or you may make one of your own within the style of your genre.*

All songs must have an introduction, a conclusion, and at least two contrasting sections. You could think of these as verses and choruses if that helps."

Ms. Yarn continues her visits to the groups—two occupying opposite corners of the classroom, two in practice rooms, and one in her office—helping individuals develop skills in their selected performing characteristics. Visiting one of the drum circles, she stops beside Haylie and asks, "Could I borrow those bongos for just a sec?" She demonstrates how to get more ring from the drums by striking them harder and letting her fingers bounce off of the head more quickly.

Haylie tries the new technique and exclaims, "Ow! That's painful."

"Yup," says Ms. Yarn. "It's gonna hurt a bit. Your fingers kind of get used to it, though. Eventually you'll get good enough at the ring that you won't have to hit it so hard."

She then goes to the rapper group and listens for a few minutes. At a pause, she steps in and says, "Dudes! You know that all human beings without musical training speed up, right? That ain't you! Now try to really feel the groove, and just settle into it. Do NOT allow yourselves to speed up. Now everyone here do this with me." Ms. Yarn starts up and demonstrates a groove with her body and mouth.

After getting over the initial shock of Ms. Yarn's previously unknown ability to get down, the students join her, and they start to develop a feel for a more steady pulse. While there, she shows the bass guitar player how to slide down the fingerboard on an occasional anacrusis (the beat before a strong beat).

Ms. Yarn then goes to the vocal a cappella group and comes up with a harmony part for two singers; she gets students in the scream-o group moving their bodies to activate their visual sense of beat and improve their rhythmic tightness as an ensemble. She helps students in another drum circle discover the potential for making different sounds on several classroom objects that they can incorporate into their piece. Eventually, everyone receives help with some aspect of their performing.

After two weeks of practice accompanied by continual evaluation and feedback—by both Ms. Yarn and the students—performance day comes. Ms. Yarn has invited the band class and an English class to come and watch the performances. Before the other classes arrive, Ms. Yarn has time for a quick speech. "If you worked really hard these past two weeks to refine your performances, then your work is officially over as of this moment. Your performance today is simply a celebration of what you've achieved together. Mistakes will happen. Don't worry about them. Just focus on the music and on each other, and LOVE IT!"

The classes arrive; all five groups perform amid wild applause and screaming for each other. The energy is high, and the students are loving it. After the band and English classes have left, Ms. Yarn says to her class, "Well now! We've got us some real performers here, don't we? Some of you may have discovered things about yourselves as performers that you can continue to build on."

UNDERSTANDING THE PERFORMING LITERACY EVENT

This vignette is unusually free of direct instruction, focusing instead on feedback and coaching of individuals and small groups. Literacy instruction is highly individual in that each student is developing skill on a different instrument and groups are doing this within various genres. There are some families of literacies that all students must acquire, but there are also literacies that apply only to certain individuals. An example of a family of literacies is the ability to work together as ensembles. Varying individual literacies include getting the ring from the bongo drum, steadying the beatboxing pulse, learning the bass slide, and so on. The performing literacy instruction described in the vignette is both general and specific as well as both universal and individual.

Texts

In the introduction I briefly mentioned five types of texts that are common in music performance: musical instruments, musical notation, conducting, musical models, surrounding ensemble performance, and presentations. Of these, three are highlighted in the vignette: musical instruments, musical models, and surrounding ensemble sounds. I also included another type of text that is perhaps less common in performance instruction: music recordings.

Instruments are central to this activity: *instruments* meaning anything utilized to produce musical sound. In this vignette, these texts include actual instruments such as guitars and drums—these are the most prevalent in the vignette. But instruments also include students' voices (mostly singing), other types of sound produced by the mouth (e.g., beatboxing), and some nontraditional musical instruments (music stands, trash cans, and various other things that one drum circle found around the classroom). Even though some of the texts are nontraditional (along with the literacies involved in playing them), in almost all conceivable cases the students' interactions with these instruments have the potential to be musical and successful, and the literacies can be applied more generally to music performance beyond that particular interaction.

Providing musical model texts is really Ms. Yarn's primary instructional strategy. She provides a constant supply of musical models whenever she visits a group. For example, she demonstrates how to get more ring from the bongo, how to settle into a groove (avoid speeding up), and so forth. This type of text is significant because students are able to assimilate nonverbal information available through these demonstrations much more quickly than more lengthy or abstract verbal instructions, accommodating and achieving much higher levels of complexity as well.

Nonmusicians may be surprised at the inclusion of *surrounding ensemble* as a text, but all musicians who have spent substantial time in an ensemble acknowledge the extent to which its surrounding sounds and movements function as an important text to be negotiated. Music teachers talk about *vertical alignment, blend, locking chords, balance,* and so forth—all of which absolutely require students both to identify specific aspects of the surrounding ensemble performance and to make appropriate adjustments to their performance based on what they hear and see. For example, students in the scream-o group are challenged by Ms. Yarn to move their bodies in ways that enable them to achieve greater rhythmic unity. In the group with harmony, the singers must both sing in tune individually and listen carefully to the other singers and make whatever adjustments are necessarily to be in tune together. Surrounding ensemble performance is inevitable and central whenever performing music with other people.

Finally, two sets of recorded performance texts are involved in this instructional event. First, Ms. Yarn plays a recording of a bluegrass group and helps students learn to identify specific aspects that seem to characterize that style of performance. Second, the students listen to several recordings of performances in their specific genres and mine the performances for characteristic aspects just as they had done with Ms. Yarn's guidance with the bluegrass performance. These texts can provide rich, complex, and clear nonverbal information to guide student performance related to the text.

Processes

Performing is the process dominating the foreground in this vignette. Not only is performance the culmination of the project, but it is central to the preparation process as students select an instrument (including voice), practice individually, rehearse with groups, and present a formal performance for an audience. In Ms. Yarn's constant flow of questions, models, and verbal feedback, she refers frequently to the texts involved to help students focus on things that help them enhance their performing. It is important to note that the majority of student understandings from interactions with the texts are quickly, and sometimes immediately, applied to performance (such as when Ms. Yarn immediately gets the rapper group moving together).

This vignette demonstrates how conscious inclusion of creating, responding, and connecting can be addressed simultaneously and how these other processes can serve to strengthen literacy in performance. For example, creating is invoked by the requirement to create a piece of music, whether original or covered. Ms. Yarn provides general creative parameters to channel student creativity (introduction, conclusion, and two contrasting sections). This supports the performing process by providing something to perform that generates personal investment and motivation to excel.

The responding process is required as students are guided through responding-oriented interactions with the recordings and with Ms. Yarn's musical models. Ms. Yarn identifies and explains a performing characteristic of the bluegrass recording and then invites students to do the same, which nurtures responding literacies. She gives the students another task of identifying performing characteristics as they listen to their genre-specific recordings. This clearly supports the performing process by helping each student identify something specific to incorporate into his/her personal performance.

The connecting process does not appear to be involved actively in this vignette as the project does not include an aspect that is chiefly oriented to it. However, students must decide which genre to study, think through which genre characteristics their groups might be able to execute, decide how to use available resources to achieve their goals, and reflect on meanings that they have made from the experiences.

These aspects of the instruction support performing literacy indirectly by helping the students make choices regarding the context within which performing will be learned. Students easily could do some background work on their genres as well, but this project is already so intensive that Ms. Yarn leaves that for another time.

Literacies

Considering these interactions with music performing texts and engaging with the orientations that the different processes bring, it is not difficult to identify literacies that are nurtured and utilized in this instructional event. For the performance to succeed, students must develop the ability to create desired sounds using musical instruments—each aspect of which is a performing literacy. Because this experience varies for each person, Ms. Yarn supports the students by frequently visiting each group, giving feedback, and modeling performance techniques. Students receive frequent opportunities for exploration on the instruments aided by teacher feedback during multiple group practice sessions. Because the feedback given so frequently comes in the form of musical models provided by Ms. Yarn, students need to be able to make sense of what she is trying to get them to notice in her model. These abilities are literacies related to musical model texts.

Literacies related to surrounding ensemble sounds involve being able to hear and focus on specific aspects of these sounds such as pitch, timing, tone color, and for a choral setting, vowel shapes. In addition, these literacies involve the ability to make appropriate adjustments to one's performance based on those aspects in the surrounding sounds and movements. These literacies are nurtured in this instructional event when students make performing adjustments as they listen to and watch others in the group, which is constantly encouraged by Ms. Yarn as she goes from group to group.

Finally, students listening to the bluegrass performance with Ms. Yarn's prompts are developing the ability to identify performance characteristics of the recorded texts. She also requires them to practice this literacy by assigning them to try it on their own—extracting performance characteristics from genre-specific recordings that they are required to listen to and watch.

CONCLUSION

In this chapter I have focused the literacy event on the practice of enhancing performing interactions in the general music setting—a setting where performing can be an inadequately developed music literacy process if teachers see the class as an alternative to performing. But whether in general music or in ensemble classes where music performance instruction is well developed, seeing the processes, texts, and literacies clearly will enhance instruction as teachers conceive of learning in terms of literacy rather than merely in terms of skill. The beauty of the ideas in this book is found in the purposes and planning of the music teacher. This vignette shows performing, creating, responding, and connecting happening interactively, yet they need individual attention to ensure that literacy instruction regarding each will be included. Awareness of these processes will help to broaden and balance educators' conceptions of what comprises a comprehensive performing education.

REFERENCES

Broomhead, P. (2010). (Re)imagining literacies for music classrooms. In R.J. Draper, P. Broomhead, A.P. Jensen, J. Nokes, & D. Siebert (Eds.), *(Re)imagining content-area literacy instruction* (pp. 69–81). New York, NY: Teachers College Press.

Ericsson, K.A., Krampe, R.T., & Tesch-Romer, C. (1993). The role of deliberate practice in the acquisition of expert performance. *Psychological Review, 100*(3), 363–406.

Lamont, A., Hargreaves, D.J., Marshall, N.A., & Tarrant, M. (2003). Young people's music in and out of school. *British Journal of Music Education, 20*(3), 229–241.

NCCAS. (2014). *MU:Pr4,5,6-E*. Retrieved from http://musiced.nafme.org/files/2014/06/Core-Music-Standards-Ensemble-Strand1.pdf

8 Dance
Performing

Pamela S. Musil

Dance performance, like other performing arts, continues to evolve as notions of traditional concert performance are challenged and reframed. One such evolution that has explored not only the theatrical staging of dance but the idea of audience as well is that of site-specific, or site-based, dance performance, which offers alternative spaces for performing and experiencing works of art. Site-specific dance performance takes place in various environmental, architectural, or sociopolitical locations, which serve as the choreographer's response to and stimulus for performance. Performance sites and choreography vary widely, but commonalities of site-based work include using the site itself and its spatial parameters and qualities as inspiration. The interdependence between these two components is what makes site-based work unique (Hunter, 2009). In defying the boundaries of the traditional stage, site-based performance necessarily may require a shift or reframing of what we consider as performing literacy.

The National Core Dance Standards cite working and presenting in alternative performance venues as evidence of performance literacy—a standard that suggests the value the discipline places on site-based work. Additional evidence of performing literacies connected to this standard includes the ability to identify production elements that support the artistic intent of a work (NCCAS, 2014, DA:Pr6.1). Together, these pursuits offer opportunities for students to consider art making and performance in new environments as they contemplate production elements that may not normally be considered, such as the architectural and sociopolitical aspects of a space along with audience placement and juxtaposition.

Because the definition of performance can be elitist in terms of what performances and spaces are valued, Mr. Tanner, the teacher in the following vignette, explicitly chooses to challenge his students' preexisting views about performing spaces, settings, and purposes. He wants his students to understand that there are many viable and powerful ways and places to stage a dance performance and that one's choice of location, venue, and audience informs the art produced there. In so doing, he demonstrates teaching strategies that engage students on multiple levels within an authentic and relevant, learner-centered environment that ultimately leads students to analyze, interpret, and critique their own performances (Mainwaring & Krasnow, 2010).

A dance teacher who engages students in critical reflection encourages the development of higher-order thinking (Moffett, 2012), a process that rejects what critical pedagogy theorist Paulo Friere termed the *banking model of education*, where the minds of passive students receive deposits of knowledge from a narrating teacher (McLaren & Leonard, 1993).

To fully appreciate the scene, a synopsis of activities leading up to this moment proves useful in seeing its place within Mr. Tanner's full schematic.

Mr. Tanner, affectionately called Mr. T, is wrapping up a unit on site-based performance with his intermediate high school dance students. His goal was for students to consider how performance can go beyond the formal stage into community settings and how that shift would impact the performance outcome. He has primed students by sharing a brief introduction to site performances of the 1960s, and as a class they have viewed and discussed various YouTube clips of current artists' works, including examples of how sociopolitical aspects of a given space, or how architectural elements, evident in Stephan Kopplowitz's "Grand Staircase" project, might inspire site-based work. Additionally, students have researched online sources and selected and shared their own favorite site-based works within various settings and spaces, including ocean piers, beaches, phone booths, and train stations.

With permission from school administrators, students have investigated various sites on campus during their class time, exploring unconventional spaces and performance options including hallways, windows, elevators, and bleachers. Mr. Tanner has guided them through the creation of their own site-based works defined by the spaces and settings they have selected, and students have begun to transcend traditional boundaries of thinking about performance. For example, Yuki's group, having chosen the football stadium bleachers for their site performance, plans to place the audience under the bleachers, looking up from below at the performance above; and several groups have considered the possibility of spontaneously incorporating unwitting passers-by into their performances.

We enter the scene on performance day as students are about to present for their class peers the works they have created. Mr. Tanner greets students at the door, gives basic instructions about how they will proceed to each performance site, wishes them luck, and herds the class toward their first site—the elevators.

As the performance at the elevators begins, the audience, which stands only a few feet from the elevator doors, gets the impression that they are awaiting the elevator along with those performing. The elevator doors glide open, and the audience catches its first glimpse of the dancers inside—contorted in some unlikely conversational shape, as if frozen in time—as one lone dancer steps into the elevator with exaggerated, cautious, trepidation—and the doors close. Each time the doors open, a new, more absurd scene has evolved inside the elevator, creating a narrative of events happening behind closed doors. On the final opening door, an empty elevator punctuates all that has gone before.

Following the performance, Mr. T leads a quick discussion: "What production elements did you consider in how you chose to stage your elevator performance?"

Sam responds, "Well, we thought the effect of the doors opening and closing was sort of like a curtain opening and closing, and we wanted to use that to create a sort of story. We also talked about how being in an elevator with strangers is awkward—so we wanted the story inside to reflect that."

Yuki jumps in: "I totally got that! Those sick scenes inside the elevator— my cheeks hurt from laughing! And who hasn't thought about doing weird things inside an elevator?"

Xavier high-fives Yuki as Aubry says, "We were so close to the performance that I felt I was part of what was going on. And everybody gets the elevator culture of waiting and then getting in with total strangers."

Sally adds, "We thought there might be politics in the elevator—like you get on with your boss, and maybe feel like you have to stand behind him, or can't make eye contact or conversation unless he looks at you and speaks first."

Mr. T responds, "Yes, I could see those elements in your performance. The awkward situation of an elevator space was probably the most prominent message. When we have more time to unpack, I'd like to return to this idea and discuss how you might make your intent even more visible—but overall, really great work!"

Mr. T adeptly gathers students and points them to their next performance site, where they follow a similar process of questioning and discussion. As they rotate through each new location, Mr. Tanner notices that his methodical questioning about their performing decisions has led gradually to increased detail in students' responses as they revel in the singularity of each group's production choices and divulge the inspiration that informed those choices. By the last performance, which takes place at the football bleachers, students are thinking more specifically about the effect each performance has on them as audience.

At the bleachers, the audience is escorted below the bleachers and asked to look up. At first, all that is visible are the bleacher benches above, punctuated by blue sky between them; but suddenly, solemn faces peer down at them and disappear, and seemingly disembodied arms and legs, bent at odd angles, appear and disappear. At no time does the audience catch a glimpse of a full body. After the performance, Mr. Tanner asks, "What was it about this performance space that was unique?"

LeBron notes, "I thought it was cool how you put us under the bleachers. I mean, the space is so different from underneath. I don't think I've ever been under there before."

Susan blurts out, "It was freaky!"

Mr. Tanner prompts, "Can you explain what you thought was freaky about it?"

Susan responds, "It was dark and spooky under there, and looking up, all we could see was blue sky and stripes. And then from nowhere we see these faces peering down at us and these random body parts that were, like, disconnected from their bodies! Sometimes it made me laugh; sometimes it just freaked me out."

Mr. Tanner asks, "Yuki, is that the effect your group was after?"

"I think so," says Yuki. "We knew you wouldn't be able to see our bodies from below because we would be hidden by the bleachers—and we hoped the effect would be kinda bizarre."

Mr. Tanner asks, "Are there any social elements that you considered about the bleachers space that made you decide it should feel freaky and bizarre?" Students' eyes dart back and forth at one another as if they share a secret.

Senjay interjects, "Well yeah, but Mr. T—I'm not sure you want to hear it."

Mr. T challenges, "Try me."

Senjay continues, "OK—well, some sleazy activities sometimes take place under the bleachers during school and at football games, you know? So, we thought we should take that into account in our performance. We talked about how while all this dark stuff is going on below, people are jumping up and down on the bleachers above, cheering and all. We thought that in some twisted way, the cheering maybe supported what was going on below."

Mr. T is visibly impressed. "Okay, so how did that conversation inform your performance?"

Sally responds, "Well, the thought of people cheering for what was going on below really creeped us out. But we thought it was kinda funny too—in a dark kind of way. So we thought that the quirkiness of body parts and faces appearing would maybe be humorous while viewing from below, and seeing only body parts would also add sort of a dark element. So, yeah—I guess we were kinda successful, right?" The class acknowledges with nods of assent that the performance had met its mark.

This last group finishes as the bell is about to ring. With little time to unpack all that has taken place, Mr. Tanner summarizes, "Think about this, friends. The elevators, the bleachers—and all of your other awesome performing spaces—became a sort of sacred performing space with every bit as much import as a more traditional stage, perhaps more so because of the effects these performances had on you. I've seen you being transformed these past few days! And I think you've discovered that these performances would not be the same if you were to move them to a formal stage, right?"

Students nod in agreement as Yuki adds, "I suppose each type of performance serves its purpose—I won't deny that I like the thought of being in the spotlight on a big stage as well. But this was really fun. Can we do it again?"

Mr. T promises students they will revisit their performances for more unpacking and sends them from class with instructions to reflect on questions they are to write about in their journals for the next class period: (1) What makes a site performance engaging? (2) How has this experience influenced your previous definition of performance? As students pour into the halls in animated conversation, Mr. T hears someone shout, "Dude! That thing you were doing in the elevator today? That was SICK, man, SICK!" Mr. T smiles and ponders the vernacular's exact meaning in this particular context.

UNDERSTANDING THE LITERACY EVENT

In this vignette, Mr. Tanner and his class are exploring texts and processes that will lead to increased performing literacy in dance. Specifically, Mr. T's unit on site-specific performance gets students thinking about social, political, and architectural elements not always considered in traditional performing spaces. Though all performance spaces—including traditional stages—have social, political, and architectural elements that might be explored in performance, when students take their work into the environment, these elements become more apparent. Working and presenting in alternative performance venues and identifying production elements that support the artistic intent of a work present unique texts and processes that enrich students' prior understandings about performance.

Texts

While the body, its movement, and the written text and videos that Mr. T shares with students to introduce site-based work are obvious texts, the most relevant texts in this chapter comprise the defining elements of each performance space. Using space as text requires students to examine and interpret the possibilities for art making within a given location or site while making and establishing meaning that informs how they set up their performances. This includes reading and interpreting social, political, and architectural elements within a space and considering audience perspective and placement. For example, efforts to address sociopolitical aspects of each space leads the bleachers group to perform work informed by what happens simultaneously above and below the space. The audience's perspective of looking up at the performance scene from below creates a text that is simultaneously funny yet disquieting. Similarly, in the elevator scene, student choices to use the elevator doors as curtains and to create awkward body shaping and situations inside the elevator creates narrative (text) that suggests the awkwardness of the social environment within the elevator.

Processes

There are many processes imbedded within this schema that might be unpacked if this were a chapter about creating. What we witness in this vignette about performance are end-product processes: specifically, students performing for their peers, followed immediately by questioning and discussion about the performance event. Risner's assertion that "traditional dance pedagogy schools for obedience and emphasizes silent conformity in which dancers reproduce what they receive, rather than critique, question or create it" (Kerr-Berry et al., 2008) contrasts with the pedagogy in this vignette, where students are engaged in all three processes of creating, questioning, and critiquing as they make and identify artistic decisions relating to their work. Mr. T's use of critical dialogue, a key indicator of critical pedagogy wherein both student and teacher become active participants in creating and critiquing knowledge (Ottey, 1996), allows students to view their own performance and that of peers from a profounder perspective than what would have been available had they simply performed their work without discussion. For example, Mr. Tanner employs questioning and reflection strategies that help reveal students' decision-making processes. This post-performance unpacking discussion while the performance is still fresh in students' memories demonstrates several important processes: (1) It discloses the critical thinking that has taken place in the planning stages as performers reveal information that has informed specific production choices; (2) it engages performers in self-reflective assessment of the effectiveness of their choices; (3) it involves audience members in discussion and sharing that also informs performers about the effectiveness of their production choices; and finally (4) the discourse serves as a valuable means of assessment that allows Mr. T to determine the depth of students' thought processes and rationale in planning their performances. Students' informed and thoughtful dialogue indicates that this type of pedagogy and learning is common in Mr. T's classroom.

Literacies

Literacies within this vignette depart significantly from what might be considered in a more traditional performance environment. For example, the ability to recognize staging potential, architectural elements, and/or sociopolitical context within a chosen space and subsequently plan a successful movement event that is informed by the space and context often are not considered within traditionally staged performances.

The front matter leading to the performing moment cannot be overlooked as it is critical to the success of the final scene. Mr. T's activities scaffold sequentially from foundational to complex as he introduces students to significant site-based artists, has students conduct their own online research, then facilitates the creation of their own site-based works. This piece of the scaffolding is an important part of literacy building as it offers the opportunity to consider performance from a choreographer's viewpoint, positioning students as creators rather than mere performers or consumers of someone else's work.

One of the more important literacies that Mr. Tanner addresses is students' ability to identify production elements that would support the artistic intent of a work (NCCAS, 2014, DA:Pr6.1). Through Mr. T's skillful questioning, we are able to see how students' decisions about movement choices and audience perspective are influenced by their ability to collectively and socially read and interpret a space (text), infer how the product will be seen and interpreted by an audience (another text), and subsequently make decisions about the art performed there. As students identify architectural, social, and political considerations that have guided their decision making and draw conclusions about their own work and that of their peers, their emerging literacies become evident.

CONCLUSIONS

Dance performing literacies are multilayered and complex and can be influenced significantly by the performing context. Dance educators who, like Mr. Tanner, choose to approach dance performance in ways that challenge and expand students' assumptions about dance often open windows and doors of learning that reframe and redefine dance experience. Though this example is but one of many that could illustrate dance performing literacies in the classroom, it models pedagogical practice that can be successful in many settings and scenarios and, when applied, leads to engaged, relevant, and transformative learning.

REFERENCES

Hunter, V. (2009). *Experiencing space: The implications for site-specific choreography.* In J. Butterworth & L. Wildschut (Ed.), *Contemporary choreography: A critical reader* (pp. 399–415). London: Routledge.

Kerr-Berry, J., Clemente, K., & Risner, D. (2008). The politics of personal pedagogy: Examining teacher identities. *Journal of Dance Education, 8*(3), 94. doi: 10.1080/15290824.2008.10387363

Mainwaring, L., & Krasnow, D. (2010). Teaching the dance class: Strategies to enhance skill acquisition, mastery and positive self-image. *Journal of Dance Education, 10*(1), 14–21.

McLaren, P., & Leonard, P. (1993). *Paulo Freire: A critical encounter.* New York: Routledge.

Moffett, A.-T. (2012). Higher order thinking in the dance studio. *Journal of Dance Education, 12*(1), 1–6. doi: 10.1080/15290824.2011.574594

National Coalition for Core Arts Standards (2014). National Core Arts Standards Dance: Performing. DA:Pr6.1. Online at http://www.nationalartsstandards.org/

Ottey, S. (1996). Critical pedagogical theory and the dance educator. *Arts Education Policy Review, 98*(2), 31–39. doi: 10.1080/10632913.1996.9935096

9 Media Arts
Performing

Benjamin Thevenin

It may seem odd to discuss performance in relation to media arts, given the common understanding of performance—live, potentially improvised, immediately experienced by an audience who, typically, shares the same space with the performer(s). *Media* on the other hand, is associated with that which is *mediated*—pre-produced, produced, and post-produced, completely independent of its audience. While this perspective is understandable, it ignores the significant ways in which media arts and performance work together. For example, even though the National Core Standards discusses *producing* rather than *performing* in the context of media arts education, they are careful not to conflate production with creation, nor do they confuse production with mere presentation of media arts. Rather, much of the standards' discussion of producing emphasizes the moment when artist, work, and audience meet. For example, the first anchor standard explicitly discusses *expression* and *experience* and encourages students to "integrate various arts, media arts forms, and content into unified media arts productions, *considering the reaction and interaction of the audience*" (NCCAS, 2014, MA:Pr4.1.l, emphasis added). So, despite the absence of the word, the standards are interested in the production of media arts that exhibits the same sort of life as performance.

Perhaps the best demonstration of the interesting relationship between media and performance is hip-hop. Contrary to popular understandings of the term, hip-hop does not just include music (DJing and MCing) but also combines it with visual art (graffiti) and dance (break dancing) in a fantastic display of multimedia artistic performance. The personae adopted by DJs and MCs and their unique stylistic approaches to dropping beats and spitting rhymes are further demonstrations of the culture's interest in performing. For example, the Gorillaz—an alternative hip-hop band fronted by four animated characters—are as interested in visual storytelling (through music videos, animated shorts, online games, and live, animated performances) as they are in making music. Their project is the perfect marriage of media and performance—they make music, but simultaneously (and perhaps more significantly) they create unique characters, tell an engaging story, and build an entire fictional world.

Media arts educators who explore the relationship between media and performance help their students to create new ways of performing *and of understanding performance*. This is especially important when considering the daily, mediated performances in which especially young people are engaged through their use of online social networks—defining their identities and interacting with others and the world around them. The following vignette is an illustration of such an examination of performance through the lens of media arts.

Mr. Amerika's[1] *twelfth-grade media arts class has been exploring different intersections of media and art—interactive installations, performance art that incorporates projections, and crowd-sourced, Web-based collaborative projects—really wacky stuff. But these kids ain't seen nothin' yet. In the last few days, the class has discussed the ways in which artists remix media—appropriating images, audio, video, and so on and recontextualizing them in their work.*

Today, as the students enter the classroom, the lights are dimmed. Electronic music hums in the background. The chairs are stacked in the corner. And two glowing computer monitors are positioned on opposite sides of a high table at the head of the class.

Suddenly, Mr. Amerika enters the classroom wearing a red-sequined blazer and dark sunglasses with his hair styled into a neon-orange Mohawk. The students are amused but not entirely surprised, given their teacher's frequent, odd antics. But they break out in laughter and applause when they see their principal, Miss Bliss, enter the room wearing a full-tilt ice queen costume complete with white faux fur, icicle earrings, and a crystal scepter. Without saying a word, the two walk to the computers and face each other. A recitation of Robert Frost's poem "Fire and Ice" plays, and then suddenly Mr. Amerika clicks, and the classroom erupts in a series of sonic explosions. Sounds of engines revving and Metallica guitar riffs fill the room. Then Miss Bliss interrupts the barrage of sound with the intro to Vanilla Ice's "Ice Ice Baby," followed by sounds of waves crashing and avalanches thundering.

The performance continues for a few minutes, each performer furiously clicking and cueing their songs and sounds—machine-gunfire juxtaposed with the roar of a waterfall, Nelly's "Hot in Herre" followed by "Mr. Snowmeiser," sounds of hot and cold, fire and water, until finally Miss Bliss ends the sonic skirmish with a final, fatal blow—"Let it Go" sung by the ice princess herself. Mr. Amerika bows, as if to say, "I'm not worthy," and the students erupt into loud applause.

After the lights go up and the principal returns to her administrating, Mr. Amerika explains what just happened. The Webspinna Battle, the class's next assignment, will require pairs of students to develop personae that embody some concept—Fire versus Ice, Light versus Dark, Nintendo versus Sega, and so on. Then the pair will mine the Internet for songs and sounds related to these concepts. They will collect these links, creatively mix their collections of audio, and rehearse their remix battle before they, in full costume, perform a live battle by navigating, cueing, and clicking sounds from their arsenals. Mr. Amerika clarifies, "It's like Street Fighter 2 but with streaming sounds and songs as fireballs. Hadouken!"

"So, can we edit the songs and sounds together and then just play the remix on the day of the performance?" asks one student.

"Absolutely not," Mr. Amerika retorts, seeming almost offended at the suggestion. "As artists and media makers, we're like recluses in our studios or our editing bays. We're creative, but in private, self-conscious ways. Stage actors and dancers, musicians and stand-up comics—even TV weatherpersons—exhibit their skill and creativity in front of other people through live, enacted performances. They experience their art—bodily, corporeally! That's something I want you precious little hermits to experience. Adrenaline!"

After some additional instructions, the students pair up and spend the next week planning their performance. Mr. Amerika works with each pair, helping them craft characters, search the Web for clips, and rehearse their epic audio battles. And as per usual, Mr. Amerika constantly is peppering the students with questions about their artistic motivations and spurring them forward with off-the-wall advice.

"Angels versus Devils? Hmm," considers Mr. Amerika as he meets with a pair of students. "Pretty heavy stuff. You've got to ask yourselves what a couple of young punks can contribute to this age-old battle. Five-minutes of Mormon Tabernacle Choir versus Megadeath is going to get old. So, what do you have to bring to the table?"

The students hesitate.

"You, Beelzebub," Mr. Amerika addresses one of the pair. "Who is doing your bidding in the world these days? Wreaking havoc and raising mayhem at every turn?"

"Um . . . Justin Bieber?" the boy responds with a wry smile.

"HA!" Mr. Amerika laughs aloud. "Excellent! You're on to something. You don't have to abandon those medieval motifs of halos and pitchforks but just reimagine them within the context of American pop culture. The Biebs is a perfect place to start!" Mr. Amerika turns to the other student, "And you, Miss Celestia?"

The girl responds confidently, "Well, I think if JB is the devil, then Taylor Swift is definitely an angel." Mr. Amerika smiles with approval. Taylor Swift continues, "And so maybe it's a battle between pop culture we hate and pop culture we love."

Bieber chimes in, "I play 'Blurred Lines' and you play Pharrel's 'Happy.'"

Swift responds, "You play Chris Brown, and I come back with Beyonce's 'Single Ladies.'"

"Brilliant," Mr. Amerika jumps in. "And remember to consider not only your choices of songs and sounds but also your comportment. How does JB act? Miss Swift?"

Taylor responds, "I think he should be jittery and desperate, frantically clicking away, while I just calmly, confidently destroy him with pure awesomeness." Mr. Amerika applauds the pair's smart ideas and continues to help the class develop their performances.

The day of the battle arrives, and the students come to school in full costume—Waking versus Sleeping, Young versus Old, Zombies versus Aliens, Harry Potter versus Star Wars. It's better than Halloween. The students have carefully selected their audio clips, exploring soundboards and online games, and preparing live collages of movie quotes, sound effects, famous speeches, and pop songs.

As the first pair of students takes their places at the computer monitors, Mr. Amerika addresses the class. "Welcome gladiators! You have prepared well for this moment. But remember to ride the flow of the experience. If it makes sense to improvise, to rip into a face-melting solo, to pull a wicked killer combo, follow that impulse. Ready . . . fight!"

It's a riot. Pair by pair, students perform their battles, prompting applause, laughter, and dancing among the crowd. But perhaps even more fun is that between battles, the students take turns, impromptu, taking the open mic to freestyle rap, do impressions, cover popular songs, and tell funny stories. One kid even performed some tricks with his skateboard on the scuffed linoleum floor. Needless to say, by the end of the class, a crowd of other students and teachers has congregated in the back of the class and in the adjacent hallway to get a peek at the performances.

The following day, Mr. Amerika discusses the Webspinna Battle with the class. He starts by simply inviting their unfiltered responses, which include the word awesome quite a bit. Eventually, some more substantial reflections are made.

One student offers, "I really liked coming up with an idea for the battle—characters, costumes, sounds, finding things that fit together to make an interesting, tight performance. Ours was Waking versus Sleeping, which makes sense because that's a battle I fight every morning."

The students laugh. Mr. Amerika responds, "Costume design, sound design, scoring, acting, and choreography even. These are all elements we're familiar with in movies, and they're all here but in a jumble. But you did a great job at making this mess a unified mess—aesthetically, thematically. Talk to us about your creative process, you two."

Waking versus Sleeping discuss how their initial idea was to take something from everyday life and make it artful. "Who doesn't debate pushing that snooze button? It's something we all relate to, but it's not something we usually think of as material for an art project." They continue, discussing how they designed their characters—Sleeping came in rumpled pajamas with messy hair. "I didn't even brush my teeth or take a shower that morning—you know, for the sake of authenticity." Waking, on the other hand, wore a bright yellow warm-up suit and admitted to drinking no less than three energy drinks that morning.

The discussion continues. Later, a student adds, "I thought the coolest part was all the cool talents that people ended up sharing in between the battles. That was–"

"Awesome?!" interjects Mr. Amerika. "Yes, it was. What do you think, class? We've made a lot of cool art together in class, but no one has ever spontaneously done impressions in here. Why?"

A student responds, "Probably because you're getting us to feel comfortable around each other. We dress up and do this battle, and we're free to let loose a little. But that creativity and that energy doesn't end when the assignment ends. It just keeps going."

Mr. Amerika holds his hands to his face. "I think I may weep. Thank you. Thank you all." The bell rings, and the students continue to their next (and inevitably far more boring) classes.

UNDERSTANDING THE PERFORMING LITERACY EVENT

Texts

In this vignette, the performance of the Webspinna Battle relies on the selection, creation, and then integration of a few types of texts—the costumes, the sound bytes from the Web, as well as the final performance, involving additional elements like acting and dancing (or even freestyle rapping). Costume is an interesting text to consider first because it is something that, in varying degrees, is a component of all the arts. The costume is the visual design we choose to wear that, consciously or not, contributes to our identity as artists—whether it be a mask, cummerbund, or beret (all painters still wear berets, right?). So, while within the context of the Webspinna Battle, the role of costume is to indicate visually which concept each student has chosen to personify for the performance; a more general understanding of costume would include any attire that signals to either self or others the individual's relationship with or attitude toward the art.

Next, the role that the sounds and songs collected from the Internet play as texts in this literacy event is significant in that while they constitute an integral part of the final performance, they are not creations of the students themselves (at least not entirely). However, the conversation between Mr. Amerika and the students performing Devils versus Angels reveals an important point about the role of these texts in the final work. When he asks them to put a new spin on the age-old conflict between good and evil, he prompts them to look at the sounds and songs of contemporary culture with new eyes. The students then dig through the audio that populates our world to find those specific sound bytes that correspond with their themes and communicate their characters and then juxtapose those sounds—live—in a way that signifies this conflict between good and evil *to them*. The students make these texts their own through their performance of them.

But perhaps it is most helpful to consider these texts as interconnected rather than independent from each other. A sound effect from *Star Wars* or a line of dialogue from *My Little Pony* signifies very little alone, but when combined with other clips and even further with other elements like costume and the live setting, a performance emerges. And quite appropriately, Mr. Amerika demonstrates the necessary interdependence of each of these elements (or texts) in his own battle with Miss Bliss (a performance that also functions as a text). The curious and somewhat complicated nature of this assignment makes it difficult to describe. So, Mr. Amerika models the performance to show the students how to make a "unified mess" of such disparate texts as a sequined jacket, a Metallica guitar riff, and an engine roar.

Processes

As mentioned earlier, within the context of media arts education, some might prefer to discuss *production* rather than *performance*. My choice to focus on such a performative exercise is motivated by (1) the fact that this literacy event demonstrates how performance can be an integral and exciting part of media arts education and (2) because beneath the colored Mohawks and energy drinks, Mr. Amerika's students are engaging in the same basic creative processes as a kid producing, for example, a documentary film.

First, students develop ideas and make plans that will provide the foundation for the work that is to come. In the case of the Webspinna Battle, Mr. Amerika worked with the students to conceptualize their performance—choosing personae, searching for sounds, experimenting with different styles or approaches. In the case of Waking versus Sleeping, the students acknowledge that the idea came out of their everyday lives—them versus their alarm clocks. Then, students take the concepts they have developed and begin to realize them. Last, students assemble and polish these elements and fashion them into a final, unified artistic work. In the case of the Webspinna Battle, this included the final performance, but in other media arts classrooms, this may involve the final cutting and mixing of video and audio.

Interestingly, while this moment in the creative process is the most public for a performance like the Webspinna Battle, this post-production process takes place in much more private settings like the editing bay or sound studio. Despite this difference though, post-production allows for something that is also present in the public performance—the ability to take the pulse of the piece and determine what changes might be made. In this respect, the editor is not unlike the improv comedy troupe member who makes adjustments to the scene to make it work. Mr. Amerika's encouragement to his students to "ride the flow" and their subsequent, impromptu performances between each battle reflect this idea of intuition and improvisation injecting new life into the production of media art.

Literacies

The Webspinna Battle demonstrates how engaging with performance in the context of media arts education encourages new understandings of what constitutes performance. Throughout the activity, the teacher and his students comment on the interrelatedness of these different elements of the final performance. Whereas introductory film classes commonly identify the individual elements that contribute to cinematic storytelling—cinematography, editing, design, music, performance, and so on—Mr. Amerika's class engages with and employs these elements but without hard distinctions between them. If they see the work of art—in this case through the lens of performance—as inherently multimodal, as necessarily integrating each of these important elements, the relationships among these elements will be more productive, their work will be more unified, and they will open themselves up to more fruitful creative collaborations.

Some of other conversations about performance in this section address how exploring performance within the arts encourages students and teachers to recognize how we perform in other contexts in our lives. Waking versus Sleeping's discussion of their creative process nods to this notion of performance as an everyday occurrence. Everyone performs every day, and in an age of completely ubiquitous, Web-enabled, mobile technologies, we perform, perhaps most notably, using media. One might imagine Mr. Amerika using the creative exercise of the Webspinna Battle—of creating a character, selecting her attire, shaping her attitude, collecting media that best represent her—as a means of helping students explore how they shape their own identities, especially through social media. Here, maybe *performing literacies* lead to more traditional notions of *critical literacy*—prompting students not just to understand their art better or make art better but to understand themselves better and make themselves better.

NOTE

1. While my own media arts students perform a Webspinna Battle, I owe the idea for this activity largely to Mark Amerika, whose Remix Culture course at the University of Colorado, Boulder, has held Webspinna performances for years. For more information on these performances, check out "Net Sounds," a special issue of *The Centre International D'Art Contemporain de Montreal's Electronic Magazine* edited by Amerika.

REFERENCES

Amerika, M. (2010, April). Net sounds. *CIAC's Electronic Magazine*, Issue 36. Retrieved from http://magazine.ciac.ca/archives/no_36/en/summary.html

National Coalition for Core Arts Standards (2014). National Core Arts Standards Media: Presenting. Online at http://www.nationalartsstandards.org/

10 Theatre
Performing

*Amy Petersen Jensen
and Julia Ashworth*

Performance is central to theatre practice. Theatre teachers and their students spend much of their time inside and outside of class working toward fully mounted and completely realized theatrical productions. Countless hours are spent in preparation for these productions. This preparation often culminates in a fully produced performance. In this performance setting, students collaborate to showcase acting techniques, display technical acumen, and present an integrated work of art to the public—generally composed of parents, fellow students, and community members.

Performing a polished work of art in a public setting is often the hallmark of a student's drama experience. At their best these theatre productions allow young people to demonstrate individual and collective abilities to make convincing theatre choices that successfully convey meaning. When participating in this type of work, students often develop new and necessary learning and innovation skills, which are described by the Partnership for 21st Century Skills (2010). They practice making creative decisions, critical thinking, and problem solving as they develop the performance. Generally the culminating presentation demonstrates their abilities as communicators and collaborators.

While fully produced theatre work is often an integral part of secondary theatre practice, there are also affordances and limitations to that work. One potential limitation of fully produced work is the lack of equal opportunity for all students to practice performing. For example, the public nature of these performances may cause some students anxiety that prevents them from participating. Additionally some students may come from homes where time and resource factors prevent them from participating in these intensive performing experiences. These limitations can sometimes prevent interested and talented students from meeting the same theatre learning goals that their peers are able to meet.

In this chapter we argue that in addition to producing fully mounted theatre productions, theatre teachers can achieve parity among students through curricular opportunities that allow all students to practice performing. Drawing on the National Core Theatre Standards, we assert that pedagogical activities that lead to the theatre performing literacies should (1) engage all student participants in sharing and presenting stories, (2) invite students to use their bodies and consider others' bodies as they envision imaginary worlds, and (3) ask students to explore the human experience through shared creative work (NCCAS, Theatre Performing, 2014).

Process Drama is one model of theatre practice that can provide students with opportunities to practice the theatre performance literacies described above. Process Drama grows out of theories developed within the educational theatre movement (i.e. Bolton, 1984, 1992; Neelands & Goode, 2000; O'Neill, 1995; O'Toole & Taylor, 2006). It uses the same building blocks as traditional theatre production but uses those building blocks (story, context, action, and reflection) with different intentions. For example, while the intent of traditional theatre is generally to fully mount and produce a play for audiences, Process Drama uses the same theatre building blocks to structure drama solely for learning within low stakes environments. The performing processes inherent in theatre therefore become tools for making inquiry and learning together without the pressures associated with a fully mounted theatre production.

The following vignette provides an example of how students utilize Process Drama tools to explore performing and performance. We assert that this approach can be inviting to a variety of students because there is more room for error (and potentially learning opportunity) in these explorations than the fully produced experiences described above. The following vignette emphasizes how performing literacies might be experienced and practiced through these modes of expression. In the imagined world below, Mr. Martinez fully mounts two theatre productions each year, but he also engages his classes in performative work based in Process Drama.

Mr. Martinez' seventh-grade theatre class is currently studying Shakespeare's Twelfth Night. *Students are endeavoring to find physical ways to represent and stage the character of Malvolio. Today Mr. Martinez wants to work on Malvolio with everyone, not just those students who may end up portraying him in a scene or a play. His hope is that through this collective and collaborative work, more ideas and creativity will be fostered as well as students finding ways to apply today's concepts to other physical character studies. Students in the class have read* Twelfth Night *and are familiar with the story, so when Mr. Martinez asks them to stand in a circle to explore ways to embody Malvolio, they are ready to do so. He begins by asking students to stand by someone who will be a partner for today's activities.*

Mr. Martinez continues, "Today I want us to share ideas about Malvolio's story. I am wondering what you are feeling about Malvolio's state of being at the end of the play. You are all familiar with his last line in the play. Malvolio says, 'I'll be revenged on the whole pack of you.' What do you think of his statement?"

"He got what was coming to him," says one student.

"I don't actually think he deserved it. What Sir Toby and Maria and the others did to him was really worse than anything Malvolio had ever done to them," says another student.

"Okay, but how does he feel?" asks Mr. Martinez. "Let's think about blame later and try to explore how he might feel." Mr. Martinez continues, "In fact I think we might better understand his statement if we consider what his emotional or physical makeup is by the end of the story. I think we might understand his emotions better if we each use movement and actions to show how he felt."

Mr. Martinez further explains that he wants his students to do this by using their bodies to create two contrasting physical images with their partners. He says, "Partner A will create a frozen picture of Malvolio as he is at the end of the play, as a person who has been mocked and ridiculed. Partner B will create a frozen picture of Malvolio that represents an ideal image, what he might look like had he not been teased and bullied. Both partners are expected to create their frozen images simultaneously as well as collectively with the rest of the class."

The students move into partnerships and determine who will be Partner A and Partner B. Mr. Martinez reminds them not to share their creative ideas with their partners yet. Instead he encourages them to begin imagining what physical attributes they might take on as they demonstrate Malvolio's physical characteristics. After a minute he cues them to share their pictures by saying, "One, two, three, freeze!"

He responds to their work, "Wow, I see a lot of really interesting physical choices as well as a wide variety of choices—no one is doing the same thing as anyone else in this room," says Mr. Martinez. "I'm going to ask a few pairs to remain frozen, while the rest of us make observations on what we see. I will tap you on the shoulder if I want you to remain frozen."

Those students who are no longer frozen spend a few moments wandering around to the three different pairs of frozen images. They have been asked to observe their peers' choices, especially physical choices and facial expressions as well as the contrast between Partners A and B. Mr. Martinez wants to look at one partnership at a time and asks two of the partnerships to relax, while they observe one on their own. "Talk to me about what distinguishes the two images from each other and how these are both viable representations of the character Malvolio," proposes Mr. Martinez. "What words would you use to describe Partner A?"

"His body is crumpled, and his focus is so low on the floor it's hard to see his face," says one student.

"He almost looks like he has a disease—helpless, and abandoned," says another student.

"Does anyone else have another interpretation?" asks Mr. Martinez.

"I agree with what the others have said. He almost seems like he's given up; he even looks hopeless—as if he's beyond help, even if someone were to offer it," says a new student.

"Good observations—now let's look at how he compares to Partner B," says Mr. Martinez. "How is Partner B different?"

"I can clearly see his face, his body is standing up, and he almost seems proud of himself," says one student.

"Right, the contrast is stark—why is that the case?" asks Mr. Martinez. "How do their bodies connote what has and hasn't happened to both versions of Malvolio by what we see?"

"One of them has suffered," says one student, and several others agree.

"Let's look at another partnership to see if we can find out more about what's going on with these two different Malvolios," suggests Mr. Martinez.

The group situates itself around one of the other partnerships they spent time observing. After the pair freeze in their frozen picture again, Mr. Martinez asks them if they are interested in finding out what's going on inside the mind of Malvolio at this time. He tells the students that they can use a drama convention to see if they can find out any new information by inviting the characters speak. He demonstrates this by placing his hand on Partner B's shoulder, cueing him to answer the question he asks. After tapping the student's shoulder, he asks the boy playing Malvolio how he feels.

"I feel great, really happy—thanks for asking. I guess, I do wonder if I'm not a little uptight at times. But besides that, I am great!" exclaims Partner B in character. The students agree this answer was to be expected, although a few are surprised that he acknowledges that he has anything to work on, that he isn't perfect. They are eager to move on as they are more interested in knowing how Partner A feels and prompt Mr. Martinez to ask him what he's thinking but hasn't shared.

"It's hard for me to say this," begins Partner A, "but I feel so stupid. I can't understand why I was lied to and mocked. This didn't feel like a joke to me. I don't think I belong here. I might have to find a new place to live, a new town, a new job, a new life."

Mr. Martinez repeats this exercise with a second group. He then follows up with questions for the class, "So, what did we discover about Malvolio by observing the physical actions and thoughts of the actors in each of the partnerships?" asks Mr. Martinez.

"The way other people treat someone can make a huge difference in a person's life. How we treat people matters," says a student. "Even though Malvolio was irritating and he sort of mistreated Sir Toby and Maria, I'm not sure he deserved this. But he is the only one who gets punished. Why aren't they held responsible for their behavior too?"

"That's a good question and one for us to consider—although Shakespeare's language in this play doesn't include any dialogue that makes them responsible for these actions, what staging choices might we have? What could we do to portray this through physical actions?

Mr. Martinez then invites his students to further explore these questions on their own. He says, "Next class period we are going to build on the work we did today. In preparation for our next class, I want each of you to take some time this weekend to observe the physical choices of your friends and family. Think about how their physical choices make you more aware of how *they are feeling or what they are thinking. Really watch them in the same way that you really watched each other today. The things you observe in others might help us to consider more ways we might better understand and humanize Malvolio through our staging choices. See you all on Monday!"*

UNDERSTANDING THE LITERACY EVENT

In this vignette Mr. Martinez uses Process Drama techniques to explore texts, practice drama processes, and engage in using authentic theatre literacies with his students as they perform. Below we discuss the ways in which this type of small-scale performance experience can be equally as meaningful as participating in a fully produced theatre work. We do this by further examining how Mr. Martinez employed theatre texts, processes, and literacies to engage his students in theatre practice.

Texts

Mr. Martinez and his class engage with two texts in this vignette. First they explore a print text—the written play. The vignette explains that the class has been studying Shakespeare's *Twelfth Night* and that they have just completed the whole play with the intent of eventually performing segments of the work. However, during class Mr. Martinez chooses to focus solely on one short line that Malvolio speaks near the end of the play. The selection and use of this singular line—"I'll be revenged on the whole pack of you"— is important to note. While theatre classrooms are filled with print texts, the primary texts that we use to convey meaning are bodies. Because of this, significant arts learning opportunities can occur regardless of the print texts that are incorporated into our work. Therefore it is perfectly appropriate for Mr. Martinez to choose a key but very small portion of the print text to accomplish theatre work.

The primary texts used in this classroom vignette are the student actors' bodies. Mr. Martinez invites the students to find physical ways to represent and stage the character of Malvolio. While he prompts them to make decisions about how they will embody the character, it is clear that they must make clear and unique physical choices based on their understanding of the character Malvolio and his circumstances from their previous reading of the play. Mr. Martinez also asks the students to observe and comment on their peers' physical choices and facial expressions. His directions throughout aid the students in noticing that the staged body can be carefully read and interpreted and that expressions and gestures can be read as indicators of emotional well-being among other things. Additionally it is important to note that Mr. Martinez invites the students to act as creators and also participate as active consumers. For example, they create the physical text representing Malvolio using movements and actions, but Mr. Martinez also invites the students to take on the role of audience or observer. By doing this he engages students in the skills necessary to perform and to observe performance.

Processes

Mr. Martinez engages his students in three theatre processes during the class period described above. First he has them verbally share and present their ideas about the character Malvolio. Then he encourages them to use their bodies and consider others' bodies as they envision various versions of Malvolio's imaginary world. Finally he asks the students to use the shared creative expressions to make connections to their own lived experiences by inviting them to make further observations in their lives outside of school.

In this scenario Mr. Martinez initially invites the students to share their impressions about Malvolio based on their knowledge of the play and their own world experience. He calls on students to share verbal impressions about the character and his circumstance. He shapes the verbal conversation by reintroducing the students to Malvolio's final line in the play, but he immediately extends their ideas into the physical realm.

Mr. Martinez has carefully considered how the seventh-grade students might engage appropriately in physically envisioning Malvolio. He is conscious that they are aware of and nervous about the way their bodies might be seen by others. To create a safe performance space for everyone, he prompts the students to share their physical pictures all at once by saying, "One, two, three freeze!" This allows everyone in the class to perform without the observation of others. Eventually he singles several images out. He selects groups that he believes will be comfortable being seen and discussed by peers. However he continues to include the whole group in each of the creative expressions by specifically inviting everyone to observe and comment on the physical choices and facial expressions of those they observe. This cyclical interaction in which the students assume the role of performer and then observer potentially informs their future readings of Malvolio's physical actions and interactions with other characters. It also may further inform the ways that they are able to read and understand physical movement and actions in other drama work.

Students in Mr. Martinez's class seem comfortable drawing on their own experiences to form ideas and opinions about Malvolio and other characters in *Twelfth Night*. Mr. Martinez has established this atmosphere because theatre practitioners must draw on their knowledge of the human experience to develop characters that audiences will respond to. Mr. Martinez fosters their ability to make connections to their own lives throughout the lesson, but he formally encourages this type of work in his homework assignment by bridging the theatre activities in the classroom with the happenings of their real lives. Thinking in this way allows students to further consider the physical choices made by themselves and their partners and perhaps even become better and more thoughtful performers.

Literacies

Theatre-literate individuals can identify unique ways to discover and develop their own creative capacities through performance. Theatre artists often do this by exploring the mental, physical, and emotional makeups of the characters they play within imagined worlds. In this vignette Mr. Martinez supports his students in expanding their creative capacities through attainable performance goals that are accompanied by opportunities to observe others performing in low-stakes settings. These modes of inquiry engage students in beginning explorations of the mental, physical, and emotional makeup of the character Malvolio. Mr. Martinez uses traditional theatre building blocks (story, context, action, and reflection) but scaffolds performing opportunities to develop individual creative capacities without the risk associated with traditional theatrical performance. In this way Mr. Martinez successfully prepares those who may be interested in more formal performance opportunities with the performance, observation, and inquiry skills necessary for success in more formal theatre settings. Simultaneously he engages all of the students in exploring the universal ways in which the physical performance of self may impact how others understand the motives behind our actions.

CONCLUSIONS

As we state earlier in this chapter, fully produced theatre work is often an integral part of secondary theatre practice. However, there are affordances and limitations to that work. We argue that theatre classrooms also should work to provide alternative but equivalent learning opportunities for all students to practice performing literacies associated with theatre learning goals. A singular focus on high-stakes theatrical performance could prevent all students from participating in drama learning. Mr. Martinez's approach to theatre practice is more democratic. Like students in a fully mounted production, Mr. Martinez's students share and present stories, envision imaginary worlds, and explore the human experience through shared creative work. Additionally they develop theatre skills and knowledge, apply their own points of view to scenarios, and evaluate multiple perspectives on a given topic through playing different roles. Most importantly they do this in an educational space and within an educational paradigm that encourages the active participation of all students.

REFERENCES

Bolton, G. M. (1984). *Drama as education*. London: Longman.
Bolton, G. M. (1992). *New perspectives on classroom drama*. London: Nelson Thornes.
Neelands, J., & Goode, T. (2000). *Structuring drama work: A handbook of available forms in theatre and drama*. Cambridge University Press.

O'Neill, C. (1995). *Drama worlds: A framework for process drama (The dimensions of drama)*. Portsmouth, NH: Heinemann Drama.
Partnership for 21st Century Skills. (2010). *Mission statement*. Retrieved November 15, 2014, from http://www.p21.org/about-us/our-mission
Taylor, P., & Warner, C. (2006). *Structure and spontaneity: The process drama of Cecilly O'Neill*. Stoke on Trent, England: Trentham Books.

11 Visual Art
Performing/Presenting/Producing
Daniel T. Barney

Teaching students how to present their work to a public often is referred to as *presentation* in K–12 art education. There is certainly merit in gaining literacy in preparing a single piece or multiple works in a curated portfolio or exhibition that will be shared with a particular audience. Too often, however, the kind of presentation I see assessed in schools is a school-style exhibition or portfolio, emphasizing standardization, neatness, and low-quality matting or framing that superficially resembles authentic practices utilized by practicing artists. Assessing the neatness of a child's stipple drawing, drawn on sulfite paper and mounted with a glue stick onto mat board, which is then taped or stapled onto a carpeted wall, perhaps does not offer the presentation literacies potentially encouraged in (NCCAS, 2014, VA: Pr6.1.Ia): "Analyze and describe the impact that an exhibition or collection has on personal awareness of social, cultural, or political beliefs and understandings." Using student-grade media or materials is of course appropriate when learning skills and techniques within the visual arts, but substituting toilet paper rolls for deep sociocultural engagements with authentic totem pole discourses and practices would be considered literacy negligence (search *toilet paper roll totems* in an Internet search engine to view numerous problematic lesson ideas).

Of course, contemporary artists, even if object makers rather than socially engaged, conceptual, or performance artists, still are engaged in performing processes as an artistic literacy. Artists realize the sociocultural entanglements of their production and realize their work is hardly finished after it leaves a studio. They are aware that their production, if relevant at all, will have an aesthetic, experiential, discursive, and cultural impact. Presenting processes are certainly important in the visual arts, but focusing literacy attention on presentation of an artifact over an ongoing dialogue that includes the artist as performer tends to highlight a type of artistic production that, once again, emphasizes learning about art in lieu of learning with or through art. This subtle distinction in this chapter helps visual arts educators question how knowledge is constructed, positioning the audience or viewers of the work as part of a meaning-making performative activity. Presenting processes within K–12 education can become all but a preparatory process, complete and finished once presented as an exhibition, portfolio, and so on with the only remaining activity being to analyze the work as if the "reader" were a critic, historian, or curator. But these roles, along with cultural theorist and activist, should not be thought of solely as secondary discourses. They are part and parcel within the entire visual arts as a community of practice and (it is argued here) performing processes if they include the viewers as participants in the artistic form and gain key literacy understandings through the artwork.

Compartmentalized conceptualizations emphasize art as a form of linear communication rather than a discourse or conversation. For example, some art may communicate predetermined instrumental messages, but not all of it does, and we as teachers should not teach that all art must be about predetermined, clear communications within presentation or performance venues or sites.

Performance literacies, on the other hand, may draw out attention to processes concerning the interactive engagement with an audience, the contexts of the art event, and the iterative process of art making. Scrutinizing presenting and performing processes in relation to each other offers art education some key understandings into literacy within the visual arts, and this chapter challenges readers to consider performance and presentation standards in the visual arts, even though presentation is currently emphasized. It is the argument here that performing highlights the iterative, the improvisational, the pedagogical, and the continued investment with the artifact, artist, and audience, while presenting provokes issues of relevance, quality, mastery, and completion.

Artists present their work *to* and perform *for* and *with* a variety of audiences for myriad reasons. While the visual arts have selected to focus on the verb *presenting*, it is important not to underemphasize performing processes within contemporary practice. The following vignette illustrates an example of how Ms. Keyes and her students attempt to engage with current visual arts processes of presenting as a type of performing within a classroom experience. You will notice that questioning who one's audience might be during creation, as well as attending to processes of responding and connecting, deepens the meaning-making potential of the presenting or performing process illustrated here.

The high school Foundations 1 class is in the second term of the semester. Students have enjoyed learning about different image-making strategies in the visual arts in this primarily hands-on, process-driven course. They also have engaged in many interesting conversations about making art in contemporary practice but have not yet experienced some of the new genres or more social practices that have been a part of the discipline of art for the past 50 years.

The students begin to enter the classroom as usual but immediately notice Ms. Keyes is not dressed in her usual black pants, sensible shoes, and flow-y art teacher wrap shawl. Instead, she is wearing a long, red, knit dress, which appears to be a sort of costume; her hair is down, and her makeup is stark.

Ms. Keyes welcomes the students but uses a more dramatic, serious tone than usual, "Class, we are going to start a new project, but before we start making anything, I would like to visit the work of several artists today. The particular projects I'm going to share are diverse but have some things in common. I will introduce our first artist in the commons area, but this will require a degree of reverence and some seriousness. Please, quietly follow me."

The class follows Ms. Keyes as she walks slowly down the hall to the commons area. Ms. Keyes has already asked a few of the students before class began to help model a quiet yet purposeful gait.

A table with two chairs, facing each other, is located in the middle of the commons area. There is tape on the floor in a large circle that tacitly indicates where the students should stand. Ms. Keyes slowly sits down on one of the chairs, arms on her lap, lowering her head. One of the students, Kyle, reads from a script he had been given by Ms. Keyes before class began.

"The teacher is present for the next 10 minutes," boldly reads Kyle. "Any who desire to take part in this work are invited to sit in the chair across from the teacher's presence."

A very long 40 seconds pass, while students look at each other in shock and amusement. Ms. Keyes's head stays bowed the entire time, her body restful but statuesque.

Rudy, a gregarious art student takes his backpack off, leaves it on the tapeline, and sits in the wooden chair facing a bowed-headed Ms. Keyes. As he sits, Ms. Keyes's head raises slowly, as if a quarter has been inserted into the Zoltar Fortune Telling machine, animating his teacher. The expression on Ms. Keyes's face is pensive, soft, and at ease. Rudy stares into the teacher's eyes then shifts his gaze from left to right, noticing that every student is watching him intently. He returns his focus to Ms. Keyes, noticing the subtle color variants in her irises, a small scar on her left cheek, and one gray hair in her right eyebrow. He is lost in this unfamiliar gazing for a moment, disengages when he realizes he has lost track of time, and returns to stand over his backpack, smiling at his classmates, nodding and prodding others to test out Ms. Keyes strange object lesson. Meanwhile, Ms. Keyes has once again lowered her head until the next student is seated across from her.

Several others take part in this event. Two students even walk up together; one remains seated, while the other stands directly behind the chair. A few students giggle, while some are more serious. The 10 minutes pass, and during a break when a student rises from the chair, Ms. Keyes follows suit and leads the students back to class in a deferential processional. Upon reaching the classroom, Ms. Keyes comes out of her dramatized character and into her standard teacher self.

"So, what just happened, class?" asks Ms. Keyes. "Were you expecting this today?"

"That was so weird, Ms. K," shares Annabelle. "I can't believe you didn't bust out laughing. You stayed so calm the whole time!"

Blake adds, "I totally had to hold in my giggles at the end. That's why I didn't sit for very long. But for a moment, I think I understood what we were doing there. I can't put it into words, though."

"Uh, now you're being weird, Blake!" Nikki playfully chimes in. "No, I think Blake's right. We get it. It was this aesthetic event that we've talked about before—you know, how artists set up experiences so that audiences can feel differently, experience differently. I don't know. Now I'm being weird!"

Ms. Keyes says, "We are all weird. We are in art class!"

"That's true," three students state in unison, ending with some chuckles from all.

"But you know," teaches Ms. Keyes, "we also have shared experiences as well as unique perspectives. How did this thing we took part in relate to a shared and also an independent, unique experience?"

A few more minutes pass as questions and discussions arise. Ms. Keyes shares information about the artist, Marina Abramovic, and shows clips of her performances at the MoMA in New York City in 2010 during the exhibit "The Artist Is Present." Ms. Keyes asks the students about some of the decisions she and Marina made as she thought about the site of the performance, the styling of the artist's body, the lighting, the props as sculptural forms and objects that encouraged potential social engagement, and the invitation for the audience members to not only view the whole performance as a static work to be interpreted, but more significantly, actually to activate and transform the performance as an emergent work of art.

The students are eager to further investigate how these performance texts are constructed and what meanings are generated within the art community. Ms. Keyes invites students to research several artists and their work to further contextualize their newfound understandings. The students work in small groups using online sources (an abbreviated description of three of the possible artists' work is noted below to get a sense of the type of work Ms. Keyes selected).

Jana Sterbak's "Remote Control II" (1989) is a work in which the artist wore a very large aluminum, crinoline-like form on three casters that suspended the artist above the ground. The artist's feet were not able to reach the ground, but audience members watching the performance could control a remote that would move the sculpture around, the artist included.

James Turrell's "Heavy Water" (1991) acted as a minimalist-looking sculpture but invited viewers to further participate by wearing 1920s-style bathing suits, entering into the water surrounding the monolithic-looking sculpture, and diving under the monolith only to reach a platform inside that allowed them to look up to see the open sky, framed only by the edges of the monolith high above.

Tino Sehgal "This Progress" (2010) is a work performed in the Guggenheim Museum in New York City. All of the paintings and art objects were removed from the museum for Sehgal's piece. Viewers would begin to walk up the museum's famous spiraling ramp, where one of the more than 300 trained "interpreters" would ask to walk with them for a bit to discuss the topic of progress. First, a participant would talk and walk with a child, who would then introduce the participant to a teenage "interpreter" who would continue the discussion and ascent, ultimately passing the participant off to an adult at the top of the ramp (see Desantis, 2010).

"Those works are so powerful!" says Archer, after the students come back together for a full-class discussion.

"Weird, but cool!" expresses Lillian. "I can't believe Sterbak trusted her audience to control her movements like that! What an amazing example of feminist critique."

"Oh, and Sehgal's piece where the audience actually became the artwork," Jefra continues with an incredibly insightful comment relating to literacy. "Some people seemed to understand they were the significant form within the participatory installation, and others didn't get it at all."

"Yes," agrees Ms. Keyes. "Isn't it interesting as we engage with the various discourses of art, broadly defined, we increase our ability to make meaning?"

"Turrell's piece was really fascinating," shares Tiff, "but I'm not sure I would get the entire picture if I visited the museum. There is no way I'd change into a bathing suit at a museum, dive into pitch-black water, guessing there might be something to look at inside a seemingly solid structure."

"I agree, Tiff!" Ms. Keyes nods as she continues, "Many of the artists we engaged with today—well, actually, all of them—really presented a new system that challenged audiences to engage differently. All of the works, while beautiful, are not simply understood if read formally or technically. They are meaningful as the audience performs with the work." Aware that time is flying by, Ms. Keyes moves on. "Okay, now that we've talked about these works" says Ms. Keyes, "what we are going to do now is try to find what each of these has in common with our Abramovic experience today and how they fit into society as a whole. Will you get into groups of three or four and make a list together of traits each of these works shares? We will take a few minutes to do this."

Ms. Keyes walks around the room as students create their lists, helping students as needed by provoking, encouraging, and further questioning, especially in generating a "socially contextualized analysis of personal experience and events" (Ganesh, 2011, p. 26) as each artwork is deconstructed.

"Wow, I heard some amazing discussions and some great connections!" raves Ms. Keyes. "Who would like to share a trait that each of these artworks shares?"

Brad suggests, "These works were all displayed in a museum space."

"Yes, that's right Brad, good observation," encourages Ms. Keyes. "Other connections?"

Several more answers are offered, which are all insightful.

"Let's revisit your responses about the audiences' or viewers' roles in these works. Also, don't forget about your own feelings as we adapted Marina Abramovic's work," reminds Ms. Keyes.

Ms. Keyes leads the students into a discussion about how the artists all set up an artistic gallery space as an environment with specific staged objects, lighting, and some possible rules of engagement. One key point brought up by students is that the viewers still could choose to act autonomously in any of these situations; the actions were not scripted even though all of these sites were stark and the unwritten rules simple.

UNDERSTANDING THE VISUAL ART LITERACY EVENT

Texts

As radical as it seems, Ms. Keyes's body (Vergine, 2000); the entire school, including the ideologies embedded in that environment (Stables, 1996); the repositioning of the format of the commons area with table, chairs, and tape as markers also became significant texts. The student bodies and new social interactions that disrupted the school space were also texts that held significant meaning in the arts. The dialogue and script of Ms. Keyes's performance and the invitation to the students to engage as co-performers also became texts (Stevens, 2010) once the students began to gain understanding and disciplinary context of each of these texts within the visual arts.

Additionally, students collaboratively used online print texts (Kiili, Laurinen, Marttunen, & Leu, 2012) to review the work of several contemporary artists who think about not only the presentation of work to an audience but also about how the artwork is both transformative and transformed with and through an audience. Such a conceptualization of presentation relating to performing processes in the visual arts expands definitions of texts within the visual art classroom.

Processes

Ms. Keyes had to think about how teenagers, her audience, might act in the processional as a performance event. She helped students engage in the literacy event as co-performers even though they did not directly design the performance. The location of the performance started immediately once the students noticed their active roles within the performance. The processional was also a part of the presentation or performance. Ms. Keyes also invited a few students to model the form in which one could potentially participate, even though any number of anomalies could have resulted after such modeling. The process of how to engage with movement and interactive artwork was demonstrated, even if tacitly. She also prepared a script to open up participation rather than closing or dictating the form in which subsequent participation would take place. Ms. Keyes did not perform in the classroom but chose the commons area to show that some artwork requires even a small commitment or preparation to experience, as further discussed in Turrell's "Heavy Water" (1991). Space became sculptural and participatory as the audience activated the artwork as experienced in Ms. Keyes's object lesson and the works researched. A significant process within this example also emphasizes tension and the ordinary made unusual or aesthetically extraordinary. Finally, Ms. Keyes helped students connect the artistic forms presented with sociocultural discourses that generate significance and meaning. This is a key literacy process, for unlike the audience members in the examples presented in the vignette, Ms. Keyes was able to help her students increase their literacy of contemporary performative artworks by unpacking and contextualizing the event with them by discussing other works in relation to the event she set up. They did not simply get it or didn't get it but were supported through questioning, contextualizing, and sharing their experiential understandings.

Literacies

The texts in this chapter move beyond standard print texts and even beyond notions of neatly presented artwork within K–12 art classes. Ms. Keyes's presentation invited students to embody a literacy event (Kress, 2000) that was then unpacked together as students discussed other participatory works created by practicing artists. Hence, the participatory event in Ms. Keyes's classroom described above created a potential site of multiliteracies that encouraged creative discursive practice (Duncum, 2004; Fairclough, 2000; Kerry-Moran & Meyer, 2009). The literacy event was also multimodal (Albers & Harste, 2007; Graham & Benson, 2010; Kress & Jewitt, 2003) and challenged the normal order of the educational space of the classroom itself, upsetting existing social values of pedagogical players involved in a literacy event (Helguera, 2011). The artists described in this vignette thought deeply about not only how their work would be presented to an audience but how that audience would engage with their work to activate it as an art form. Framed in this way, the students may not have set up the conditions for the presentation of their own artistic production as Ms. Keyes did in this example, but they have initiated a literacy concerning the reader as a coauthor, which is no small endeavor.

This particular literacy event reiterates how texts become significant within contexts, including experiential and discursive communities of practice. The students in Ms. Keyes's classroom are beginning to learn new literacy skills as they understand presenting processes within the visual arts through active discussion and participation with art forms. Students will increase their literacy with presenting processes as they create their own works, either objects or social engagements, with and for audiences and as they search for opportunities to participate in contemporary art events like the ones described in this chapter.

REFERENCES

Albers, P., & Harste, J. C. (2007). The arts, new literacies, and multimodality. *English Education, 40*(1), 6–20.

Desantis, A. (2010, March 13). At the Guggenheim, the art walked beside you, asking questions. *New York Times.* Retrieved from http://search.proquest.com/docview/434331096?accountid=4488

Duncum, P. (2004). Visual culture isn't just visual: Multiliteracy, multimodality and meaning. *Studies in Art Education, 45*(3), 252–264.

Fairclough, N. (2000). Multiliteracies and language: Orders of discourse and intertextuality. In B. Cope & M. Kalantzis (Eds.), *Multiliteracies: Literacy learning and the design of social futures* (pp. 162–181): London: Routledge.

Ganesh, C. (2011). Futures for the American classroom: Where do we go from here? In E. Joo & J. Keehn II (Eds.), *Rethinking contemporary art and multicultural education* (pp. 17–26). New York, NY: Routledge.

Graham, M. S., & Benson, S. (2010). A springboard rather than a bridge: Diving into multimodal literacy. *English Journal, 100*(2), 93–97.

Helguera, P. (2011). *Education for socially engaged art: A materials and techniques handbook.* New York, NY: Jorge Pinto Books.

Kerry-Moran, K. J., & Meyer, M. J. (2009). Lighting the fires within: Pre-service teachers learning in and through drama. In N. Narey (Ed.), *Making meaning: Constructing multimodal perspectives of language, literacy, and learning through arts-based early childhood education* (pp. 207–228). New York, NY: Springer.

Kiili, C., Laurinen, L., Marttunen, M., & Leu, D. J. (2012). Working on understanding during collaborative online reading. *Journal of Literacy Research, 44*(4), 448–483.

Kress, G. (2000). Multimodality. In B. Cope & M. Kalantzis (Eds.), *Multiliteracies: Literacy learning and the design of social futures* (pp. 182–202). London: Routledge.

Kress, G., & Jewitt, C. (Eds.). (2003). *Multimodal literacy.* New York, NY: Peter Lang.

National Coalition for Core Arts Standards (2014). National Core Arts Standards Dance: Responding. Online at http://www.nationalartsstandards.org/

Stables, A. (1996). Reading the environment as text: Literary theory and environmental education. *Environmental Education Research, 2*(2), 189–195.

Stevens, A. (2010). Drama as text and performance. In M. Hattaway (Ed.), *A new companion to English renaissance literature and culture, volume one and two* (pp. 502–512). Oxford: Wiley-Blackwell. doi: 10.1002/9781444319019.ch77

Vergine, L. (2000). *Body art and performance: The body as language.* Milano, Italy: Skira.

12 Media Arts in the Elementary Classroom
Producing

Jennifer J. Wimmer and Benjamin Thevenin

Although students have an increasing awareness and involvement with media, there is often a preconceived notion that young children will learn intuitively how to interact with and make sense of media and technology as it is part of their everyday lives. The concern with this belief is that it positions children as passive consumers of media rather than active participants. Advancing technology and social network platforms have created a shift from Web 1.0 to Web 2.0. In other words, media and technology are no longer static, or something that we turn to in an effort to consume information (e.g., watching a movie, searching the Internet for facts), rather the user is able to interact with the media and technology to create, produce, and collaborate with others (De Abreu & Mihailidis, 2014).

The shift from consumer to producer requires elementary educators not only to acknowledge the media but also to take active roles in helping students learn the media literacies necessary to access, analyze, create, reflect, and take action (Hobbs & Moore, 2013) in the production of media arts. A focus on producing media arts also helps students to understand and develop the specialized literacies, skills, and techniques necessary to participate in the ever-increasing media world in which they live. Additionally, as teachers engage students in producing, they are invited to take up the discourse of media artists as they engage in developing and refining artistic techniques (NCAS, 2014, #MA: Pr5.1) such as tool selection, cinematography, sound, and editing.

In the vignette below, a third-grade teacher provides students with instruction and learning opportunities to produce a media arts project. The teacher has turned to the National Core Art Standards for Media Arts to guide her series of lessons; she is focused particularly on the Enduring Understanding, which states, "Media artists require a range of skills and abilities to creatively solve problems within and through media arts productions" (NCAS, 2014, MA: Pr5.1). With this understanding in mind, the teacher will guide students in the development of their skills and thinking processes as media artists. The specific standard that the teacher used to prepare the learning activities for the students reads, "Exhibit developing ability in a variety of artistic, design, technical, and organizational roles, such as making compositional decisions, manipulating tools, and group planning in media arts productions" (NCAS, 2014, MA: Pr5.1.3.a). As a result, while the students will be tasked with producing a media arts project, the teacher will focus instruction toward the students' development of artistic knowledge, skills, and decision making as producers rather than on the final project.

Miss Lasseter's third-grade classroom has been doing a unit on film language. In the previous weeks, the class has learned about different aesthetic elements—such as cinematography, editing, music, and performance—and how they contribute to the telling of a story and the communication of ideas in movies. They even have had a chance to try their own hand at some filmmaking—experimenting putting different soundtracks behind familiar movie clips, practicing different camera compositions and movements, and learning some basic editing skills in iMovie.

During the unit, Miss Lasseter has started class each day with a class discussion analyzing a short scene from a familiar movie. One afternoon, Miss Lasseter greets the class and introduces the clip of the day. "This is from a movie you all know pretty well, so I'm going to make it a little bit of a challenge. I want us to figure out how the scene uses different elements of film to create humor. What makes this funny?"

Together, the class watches a scene from Toy Story 3 *in which Ken invites Barbie to his dream house and gives an impromptu fashion show of various outfits. While Barbie feigns interest in Ken's clothing, she actually is perpetrating a ruse—she surprises Ken, tying him to a paddleball and forcing him to reveal the evil teddy bear Lotso's plan. She tears up Ken's favorite articles of clothing one by one until he's willing to talk.*

"So, I noticed a number of you laughing while we were watching. What is it that makes this clip so funny?" asks Miss Lasseter. "Were you able to figure out how the different aspects of film work together to make this a comedy?"

"Well, Ken kind of acts like a girl," giggles Chloë.

"No, Barbie, not the Tehru jacket!" says Jax *in a falsetto voice, quoting Ken from the scene.*

"And there are slow-motion shots of him trying on the clothes to that disco song. He's like a runway model or something," offers Jessie.

"And it's pretty awesome that Barbie takes him down," adds Chelcie.

"Great," responds Miss Lasseter, *"so you see how things like dialogue, vocal performance, body language, and even things like music and slow motion can create humor—can make the movie comedic."*

Miss Lasseter uses the rest of class time to introduce the idea of film genre to her students. In each genre, there are different types of stories told, different moods, and different uses of film language. She shows clips from familiar movies to demonstrate a number of genres. For example, she talks about the song and dance sequences in musicals like High School Musical *and* Frozen, *discusses Morgan Freeman's narration of* March of the Penguins *in relation to documentary film, and even shows a clip from* Bride of Frankenstein *to demonstrate the use of light and shadow in horror films. By the* end of class, the students are chatting with each other about how their favorite movies use these different techniques and fit into different genres.

The following day in class, Miss Lasseter starts with a film clip as always. She cues up the DVD for Toy Story 3, and there is an outcry from the students—"We watched this yesterday!" they exclaim almost in unison.

"I know we watched this yesterday," responds the teacher with a grin. "But we're watching it again. This time I want you to watch it with a different purpose. Think of a genre that we discussed yesterday that you like—Westerns, musicals, sci-fi, documentary, horror, whatever—and as you watch the scene, try and imagine how it might be filmed or edited or performed differently to fit into your chosen genre. The reason we're doing this is because your next assignment will be to work in groups to reconstruct this scene from Toy Story 3 but in a different genre."

The students express some enthusiasm and a little confusion. Miss Lasseter clarifies the assignment and answers some students' questions, and then together they watch the scene with Barbie and Ken. Afterward, the teacher organizes the students according to what genres they picked.

"Alright," Miss Lasseter says. "The first step is to brainstorm with your group. What are some of the changes to the film language that you thought of while watching that would make the clip fit into your genre? By the end of class time today, we'll want to have some idea of how you will stage and shoot and edit your own version of the Ken and Barbie scene."

As the students brainstorm, Miss Lasseter visits with each group, listening to their ideas and helping develop their approaches to the scene. The group that chose horror discusses how they might use the same footage from the clip but do some color correction and sound editing to make it seem scarier.

"There's some cool shadows and stuff, but you almost don't notice them because there are so many bright colors," offers Joye. "I bet we could make it black and white like the Frankenstein movie so that it gives it an eerie feel."

Bill suggests they replace the disco song Ken dances to with some heavy metal music. Jeff then asks the teacher if he can retrieve his iPhone from his backpack and play some techno music that might fit better. These ideas spark a debate among the students about what types of music best fit the horror genre. Miss Lasseter reminds the students of the clips from classic monster movies that they had watched previously in class, and the students eventually agree that some of the scarier scenes were those that used silence to create suspense. Miss Lasseter praises their good ideas, and they continue conceptualizing their scene.

The following day, students are finalizing their plans for production, and some groups are beginning to work on their scenes. Miss Lasseter is thrilled to see so many students participating in this project. She is particularly excited to watch some of the struggling readers in the class have an opportunity to showcase their funds of knowledge. As she approaches the sci-fi group, she notices that Kyle is leading the discussion and showing his group how to add special effects. Kyle often is unmotivated in class during the reading block and has been identified as a struggling reader. However, Miss Lassiter notices he has become a leader in his group during this project.

Shea asks, "Hey Kyle, how do you know how to do all of this cool stuff?"

He responds, "My brother has his own YouTube channel, and I watch him at home. Sometimes he even lets me work on his videos. It's really easy."

Kyle shows the students how to add cheesy special effects—adding light sabers, sound effects, and even the infamous Star Wars *wipe to transition from shot to shot*. His group continues to be impressed with his abilities. Miss Lasseter smiles and then walks toward the Western group. They have brought in costumes, and they begin staging their scene in which a Native American Barbie captures and interrogates a ranch hand Ken. The students are discussing excitedly how to best frame their scene; some students are sketching pictures, and others are setting up props.

Miss Lasseter meets with the musical group, who has brought Ken and Barbie dolls and is choreographing a song-and-dance number in which the characters lip-synch to popular songs. For example, while Barbie rips up Ken's treasured clothes, he sings The Supremes's "Stop in the Name of Love." The students perform the scene for their teacher, puppeteering the dolls and making Miss Lasseter laugh. Following their rehearsal, Miss Lasseter asks the group how they intend to shoot and cut the sequence to fit their musical genre. The students are unsure—they have been focusing so much on the song and dance that they haven't considered their use of cinematography or editing. Miss Lasseter reminds them of a previous lesson in which they looked at different storyboards and suggests that they try sketching out their sequence shot by shot. The students get out paper and pencils and begin plotting out the scene—debating about what to shoot, from what angle, and when to cut.

Over the next several days, the students continue to work on producing their scenes, and Miss Lasseter is there every step of the way, asking questions, demonstrating skills, and giving feedback.

UNDERSTANDING THE MEDIA ARTS LITERACY EVENT

The above vignette illustrates how an elementary teacher created a space for students to engage in their worlds as meaning makers, designers, and producers. As the students participated in the media arts project, they had opportunities to develop media literacies, production knowledge and skills, and collaboration experience. In the sections that follow, the texts, processes, and literacies that were utilized will be discussed.

Texts

Miss Lasseter provided students with opportunities to engage with several texts during the literacy event, including video, props, and discussions. The texts the students interacted with were multimodal, meaning that they attended to modes beyond print including visual, spatial, audio, and gestural. These types of dynamic texts require the students to attend to a variety of modes to make sense of the text. These types of texts often allow more students to participate because the students are not limited to their knowledge of the printed word. As you recall from the vignette, even though Kyle was labeled as a "struggling reader," he was able to share his knowledge and teach his group about adding special effects on the computer. As he interacted with multimodal text, he was able to demonstrate his understanding of content, including genre, and participate in the production process.

It is also important to note that the texts the students engaged with were quite complex. The students were not negotiating the multiple and multimodal texts to merely consume information; rather, they were reading across texts in an effort to create and produce a new text. Students' interaction with complex texts is promoted in the Common Core State Standards. For example, it reads, "Rather than focusing solely on the skills of reading and writing, the ELA/literacy standards highlight the growing complexity of the texts students must read to be ready for the demands of college, career, and life" (CCSS, 2015, para. 1). In the vignette, the short video clip became a complex text as students were challenged to analyze the clip for aesthetic elements such as cinematography, editing, music, and performance. The level of complexity further increased as the students were tasked with selecting a genre and producing a new scene that required them to work as a group to plan, make compositional decisions, and manipulate tools (NCAS, 2014, MA: Pr5.1.3.a). It is important to note that the video, as a text, never changed; rather, the text increased in complexity given the task the teacher assigned. In other words, the students were required to think about the text in more complex ways as they analyzed the aesthetic elements, made production decisions, and engaged in producing a new scene.

Processes

The time allotted for the students to engage in creation, collaboration, and production afforded them opportunities to refine their ideas, make educated choices about their scenes, and develop as media artists. It is important to note that the emphasis of this learning activity was on the students' development of artistic processes and not the final product. Miss Lasseter moved from group to group, applauding and directing the students' understanding and use of media arts tools and techniques necessary to create their productions. Miss Lasseter informally assessed each group and provided instructional support based on their needs. For example, the group working within the musical genre was focused only on creating dance moves. But through thoughtful questioning and guidance, Miss Lasseter moved their ideas toward production as she suggested sketching storyboards to sequence shooting. The emphasis of process over product also is evidenced in the Essential Questions identified in the National Core Arts Standards for Media Arts (2014) where it states: "What skills are required for creating effective media artworks and how are they improved? How are creativity and innovation developed within and through media arts productions? How do media artists use various tools and techniques?" (MA: Pr5.1).

As beginning media artists, it is crucial that students learn processes that contribute to the art rather than sacrificing substance over style. For example, Hobbs and Moore (2013) caution, "When it's too easy for students to create, they may take shortcuts that substitute snazzy visual effects for meaningful content" (p. 98). Indeed, as students collaborate and generate ideas, it is easy for them to lose sight of the purpose of the project. As was demonstrated with the horror genre group, the students wanted to add various genres of music to their scene to make it scarier. The students in this group were more interested in selecting a genre of music than making a production decision about creating a particular mood for their scene. Miss Lasseter used this discussion as an opportunity to assist the students in evaluating music selection. Through questioning and directing their thoughts to prior movies viewed, Miss Lasseter helped the students evaluate their decisions based on other productions, helping the students to realize that specific tools and techniques are consistent across horror genres.

Literacies

The students' participation in the media arts project provided them with opportunities to develop and use media literacies. Media literacies typically are defined as "the ability to access, analyze, and create" (De Abreu & Mihailidis, 2014, p. xxiii). Media literacies were evident throughout the vignette as students were tasked with analyzing video for aesthetic elements (e.g., cinematography, sound, and editing), recalling differing genres and then synthesizing that knowledge to produce a new video. Many elementary teachers may shy away from this type of complex assignment. Yet, the assignment provided students with opportunities to develop and practice media literacies necessary that are necessary for reading a variety of texts.

It is important to note that foundational literacies were present throughout the vignette such as genre, sequencing, and comprehension strategies. For example, Miss Lasseter encouraged the students to use their knowledge of sequencing to create a storyboard as a means of organizing their ideas. Media literacies are not meant to overshadow or replace foundational literacies; rather, media literacies are meant to extend students' learning and ways of interacting with the world. Furthermore, media literacy helps "children learn how to apply concepts like audience, message, purpose, and point of view to both familiar media (like TV shows and music) and unfamiliar media (like nonfiction textbooks and news articles) (Hobbes & Moore, 2013, p. 15). These are important literacies that support students' development and growth as literate beings.

CONCLUSIONS

As evidenced in the vignette, the media arts provide students with access to advanced content and concepts and with opportunities to demonstrate "complex reasoning and sophisticated thinking skills" (Hobbs & Moore, 2013, p. 15). While some elementary educators may be less than enthusiastic about the influence of technology and media on today's youth, as Hobbs and Moore (2013) state, "whether we like it or not, media culture is our culture" (p. 20). Rather than viewing media as something that encroaches on school time, the media arts afford teachers and students with opportunities to share their funds of knowledge as teachers create spaces for students to bring their out-of-school literacies and experiences into the classroom (Hull & Schultz, 2002; Pahl & Rowsell, 2005).

REFERENCES

Common Core State Standards. (2015). *Key shifts in English language arts*. Retrieved from http://www.corestandards.org/other-resources/key-shifts-in-english-language-arts/

De Abreu, B. S., & Mihailidis, P. (2014). Introduction. In B. S. De Abreu & P. Mihailidis (Eds.), *Media literacy education in action: Theoretical and pedagogical perspectives* (pp. xxiii–xxx). New York, NY: Routledge.

Hobbs, R., & Moore, D. C. (2013). *Discovering media literacy: Teaching digital media and popular culture in elementary school*. Thousand Oaks, CA: Corwin.

Hull, G., & Schultz, K. (Eds.). (2002). *School's out! Bridging out-of-school literacies with classroom practices*. New York, NY: Teachers College Press.

National Core Arts Standards (2014). *Media arts*. Retrieved from http://www.nationalartsstandards.org/sites/default/files/Media%20Arts%20at%20a%20Glance.pdf

Pahl, K., & Rowsell, J. (2005). *Literacy and education: Understanding the new literacy studies in the classroom*. Thousand Oaks, CA: Sage Publications.

Section III
Responding

13 Music
Responding

Paul Broomhead

This chapter provides an example of literacy instruction that involves responding in the discipline of music. The National Core Music Standards describe responding by identifying subprocesses: selecting, analyzing, interpreting, and evaluating (NCCAS, 2014, MU: Re7,8,9-E). Interactions that most directly correspond to responding processes and bring them to the foreground are primarily the consumptive aspects of music interactions such as listening and watching. When one equates responding with these consumptive activities, the processes listed in the standards work very well. But responding is often a prominent feature of musical interactions involving performing, creating, and connecting, which are participative in nature.

While listening and watching are frequently the primary aspects of musical activities such as attending a concert or listening to a recording, they also are important aspects of other interactions. For example, performing in an ensemble requires that ensemble members listen carefully to each other and make adjustments to achieve unified precision in rhythm, balance of volume, and unity of pitch, timbre, vowels, and vibrato (Titze, 2008). These adjustments reveal an aspect of responding that goes beyond the selecting, analyzing, interpreting, and evaluating that takes place during consumption and includes actions taken *as a result of* the interaction—actions that occur either during the encounter with the text or after (or both).

The example of an ensemble member listening and making adjustments shows multiple processes occurring simultaneously with "one aspect in greater focus in the foreground but with the others still in the background" (Cope & Kalantzis, 2000, p. 242). Performing is the primary process, while ensemble students are rehearsing, but good performing requires that responding also be in play as a background process. And for brief or substantial moments, responding may take the foreground as careful listening and watching reveal adjustments that are needed in an individual's performance to achieve ensemble unity.

I suggest that responding be considered active. The common image of a driver turning on the radio and passively listening while focusing on traffic certainly fits within the category of responding. However, responding interactions certainly can be more meaningful when the response is less passive, whether the individual is attending to surrounding sounds during ensemble performance, attending a concert, listening to a recording in the privacy of his or her bedroom, or listening to music during an unrelated activity. Some active responses take the form of physical actions such as dancing, swinging a hammer, or relaxing during a massage. (Yes, relaxing is an active response.) Or responding may take the form of musical actions such as the adjustments to sound during ensemble participation. Responses to music may invite innumerable experiences with feelings such as joy, sadness, loyalty, devotion, love, lightheartedness, determination, relief, and so on. Closely related is the realm of nonverbal understanding, which may include renewing the impact of memories, understanding some personal inner stirrings, and so on. Like the formal artistic processes described in this book, these types of responses to music often occur at the same time.

Teachers may utilize a wide range of instructional approaches to nurture responding literacies in any music setting. These include (1) providing musical training that helps students recognize certain devices in music (e.g., harmonic texture), (2) helping students focus their awareness on responses of their minds and feelings to the music, (3) sharing stories of personal meanings that others have made from music, (4) directing listening to a particular aspect of the music, and (5) nurturing openness to unfamiliar music.

Music recordings and live performances are prevalent contexts in which the general population would benefit from literacy guidance. Music educators have the opportunity to provide responding literacy instruction that helps students effectively interact as responders not only in the music classroom but in meaningful interactions with music outside of school and later in life. General music courses are favorable for this type of literacy instruction as performance expectations are often low. However, music educators also are charged with educating those who have chosen to specialize in music—usually in ensemble settings. Responding literacy is important for these students as well, but the performing demands of the ensemble setting prompt approaches to responding literacy that are compatible with performing. The literacy event in the following vignette represents a time when responding is brought to the foreground during a performing activity.

To illustrate the possibilities of music literacy instruction with regard to music responding, this vignette portrays instruction that nurtures responding literacies in a choral ensemble. The teacher treats the surrounding sounds of the ensemble as texts and nurtures literacies that are involved as the musicians make appropriate adjustments based on those texts.

The high school concert choir is starting to produce some great sound. Individuals have responded well to Mr. Perry's instruction regarding posture, singer's breathing, connection to the breath, vowels, and resonance. The overall ensemble sound is big but also warm. Mr. Perry's belief that each member of the ensemble must achieve his/her most brilliant sound individually really is paying off. However, although the students are singing their best individually and the group is producing a huge, beautiful sound, Mr. Perry can hear how the artistic merit of the singing is just not coming through because the group lacks unity. Unity is becoming an increasingly serious issue with the choir.

Mr. Perry knows that unity is needed in terms of volume (balance), tone color and vowel shape (blend), timing (vertical alignment), and pitch (tuning chords). He also realizes that all of these issues involve specific kinds of listening and responding to the ensemble sounds surrounding each of the singers. He starts with balance.

"Folks, we've got to work on achieving balance of volume both within our sections and across sections. First, each of you make sure that you are no louder or softer than the other singers in your section. This signal indicates the need to balance the volume within your section." Mr. Perry demonstrates his signal: elbows in, two palms facing the floor, and vacillating up and down. Then he conducts a cue to each section separately to sing the vowels i, e, a, o, and u on a pitch that will combine with the other sections to create a major chord. He uses a conducting gesture to indicate a hold on each vowel, gives his balance-within-section signal, and allows time for students to make adjustments in volume as they listen to others in the section. He gives frequent feedback: "I can hear a couple of sopranos who are singing louder than those around them. Try again."

Mr. Perry walks near the soprano section to hear if voices are standing out. "That's much better," he says. "Now, I think there are a few sopranos who actually are singing softer than the group as a whole. It's your job to match the volume of your fellow singers. Let's try again." He walks among the sopranos now and listens carefully for balance. "It's amazing how effectively you can hear and respond to others when you really bring your attention to it."

After allowing each of the sections to make similar adjustments, Mr. Perry says, "We're going to sing this basic chord on the same pitches and vowels you just sang. Watch for me to stop you on any vowel and point, like this, at a certain section of the choir." He demonstrates a subtle finger point. "At that time you will listen for and prepare to sing the pitch that that section is singing. You may have to adjust your volume to hear the new pitch. Then I'll use both arms to point, like this." He demonstrates both fingers pointing at the same section of the choir. "This is to show you it's actually time to switch to that pitch. Then after a moment I'll return you to your original pitches by sweeping my open hands apart, like this. The point of this, folks, is to listen so hard that you have to achieve a good balance to sing the correct pitches. This is about listening and adjusting!"

Mr. Perry has the accompanist play pitches of the chord, conducts the choir through the first two vowels, and stops on the third. He points at the soprano section, which has the root (i.e., the home pitch) of the chord; pauses for a few moments while students listen for that pitch; motions for the altos, tenors, and basses to switch to the soprano pitch; and then signals them to return to their former pitches in the initial chord. They are not terribly responsive on this first attempt. Not all find the note quickly. After the singers return to the original chord, Mr. Perry proceeds to the next vowel and repeats the process, pointing to the altos, who are on the third of the chord; and on the last vowel, he points to the tenors, who are on the fifth. The singers get progressively better at finding and singing the target note, but the tone starts to lack energy and fullness.

"Not bad. Many of you were quite tentative on the first one. The second went better because you made quicker adjustments in your volume. But I gotta say we really started to lose our good sound because the altos were quieter than the sopranos and the sopranos resorted to a less resonant sound as they softened to hear the pitch. On the third one, everybody else did the same thing to hear the tenor note. We were singing as if beautiful sounds didn't matter anymore. Uh . . . they still matter! And I know the beautiful tone you usually make. So sing that first chord again with your usual robust sound, and let's spend a few moments adjusting to each other's volume in both directions: softer and louder."

Students are ready to try again. "Keep in mind that you now have to worry about adjusting both to the singers in your own section and to those in the other sections. If your section is softer than the others, you all have to sing louder."

Students are ready to go, but Mr. Perry wants a slam dunk this time. "Raise your hand if you anticipate that you personally will need to sing louder. Good! Tenors, that's right; every single one of you will need to adjust up. Yep, some of you altos, too. Listen carefully for that. Obviously, basses were already perfect.

Now raise your hand if you anticipate that you personally will need to sing softer. Oh sopranos, how humble you are. Yes. Many of you will need to reduce your volume. Please be careful to maintain the core to your sound as you do so." Mr. Perry addresses the whole choir again. "Did you notice that more people raised their hands about singing louder than singing softer? Okay. Let's try this again."

The choir repeats the exercise with immediate feedback from Mr. Perry on each chord as he conducts a holding gesture. "We're starting to lose our core. Subtle changes please. Subtle! Raise your hand if you are having a hard time hearing the tenors.

"Yes, right there. All four parts are balanced, and I'm not hearing any individual voices. Beautiful!"

UNDERSTANDING THE LITERACY EVENT

Making sense of this literacy event invites several questions. What are the actual sources of content here that students negotiate and create as they develop responding literacies? What are the processes in play during these interactions, and what is Mr. Perry's role in guiding the students through the processes of responding appropriately to these texts? Finally, what literacies are being nurtured by Mr. Perry in this vignette?

Texts

The most prominent texts presented to students in this instruction are the sounds of fellow ensemble members. These surrounding ensemble sounds are grouped in the vignette as "within sections," the sounds of students in the immediate vicinity who are singing the same notes, and "across sections," sounds coming from students in the other sections. Listening across sections is particularly challenging as the students are standing according to section and must thus distinguish sounds from other sections of the ensemble from those immediately around them.

Another prominent text in this vignette is Mr. Perry's conducting and other gestures. Mr. Perry's students have been responding to his conducting daily. They can tell when he intends for them to hold a note, for example. In this vignette, he adds three meaningful gestural signals to their repertoire to let them know when to listen carefully to another section of the choir, when to go to another pitch, and when to return to their original pitch.

Processes

As discussed in the introduction, this literacy event portrays how responding processes can be brought to the foreground even while students are immersed in an interaction that is defined fundamentally by creating, connecting, or as is this case, performing. Ensemble students constantly are hearing the surrounding sounds of fellow ensemble members. But in attending purposefully to responding processes, Mr. Perry asks students to attend to these texts in different ways: more purposefully focused on apprehending certain aspects.

Mr. Perry calls on students to engage in responding by creating an environment where they must listen in a particular way to match the volume of voices immediately surrounding them or to find the pitch of a designated section of the choir while singing a different pitch in their own section. Then they must make volume adjustments as individuals within sections.

To facilitate the responding activities, Mr. Perry also calls on students to attend to his gestural texts in a way that is oriented primarily toward performance. He demonstrates the gestural signals while explaining what these gestures indicate the students should do. From that point on, he uses the gestures to help students maneuver into situations that provide particular kinds of access to the surrounding sound texts.

As is often the case in music, appropriate responding during negotiation of texts involves new text creation. By performing with adjusted volume while continuing to attend to the quality of personal sound production, students are creating personal texts that combine to improve balance both within their sections and within the ensemble as a whole. While this is text creation, Mr. Perry makes no real effort to nurture musical creativity.

Literacies

The literacies nurtured in this literacy event are fairly straightforward. First, students are learning to apprehend and understand the sounds from fellow ensemble members, both those from the immediate vicinity and those from other sections, in terms of volume. They must do this while continuing to produce a healthy sound of their own. Second, students are learning to adjust their volume to equalize it within their sections and across the entire choir by either singing softer to hear the others or louder to help others hear them.

Although these literacies are simple in concept, they are quite complex in practice. The vignette simplifies the types of response that are in real life very difficult to achieve. Some students must struggle just to notice sounds produced by others at the same time that they are producing their own sound. Then to hear specific aspects of that sound like volume (or pitch or tone color) and make appropriate adjustments is a challenge that rarely is achieved effectively by young singers. This task is made more difficult by the fact that the text is unstable. It transforms as it is being negotiated because all of the students are making adjustments similarly. This type of literacy often distinguishes inexperienced from experienced ensemble members. Yet conceptually it seems so simple that it may be tempting to simply yell "Listen!" instead of purposefully offering students guided opportunities to develop the literacies.

CONCLUSIONS

As students learn to respond appropriately and purposefully with music texts, they become more capable of meaningful interactions as music responders. In describing Mr. Perry's instruction, I have focused on only a narrow set of responding literacies: the ability to hear and adjust volume in response to the surrounding sounds of an ensemble. But the skills addressed in this literacy instruction have value considerably beyond negotiating the volume aspect of the surrounding sound text. The increased awareness of and familiarity with this text develop increased facility for dealing with other aspects of that same text. For example, as Mr. Perry's students strengthen their ability to hear the volume of the surrounding ensemble sounds, they will find it easier to attend to pitch, tone color, and timing.

I have focused on the ensemble setting in this chapter, but I suggest that making meaning through responding in musical interactions is valuable for all humans and in all settings where music is learned. None is favored over others because the types of meaning available have a richness that often touches humans in ways that are influential to effective living—not just to effective music performance. All music students should have access to the almost unimaginable variety of texts to which they may respond, texts rich with meanings to be made. It is crucial that music educators in every educational setting address students as responders and provide rich texts and guidance in responding appropriately to maximize meaning.

REFERENCES

Kalantzis, M., & Cope, B. (2000). A multiliteracies pedagogy: A pedagogical supplement. In B. Cope & M. Kalantzis (Eds.), *Multiliteracies: Literacy learning and the design of social futures* (p. 242). New York, NY: Routledge.

NCCAS. (2014). *MU:Re7,8,9-E*. Retrieved from http://musiced.nafme.org/files/2014/06/Core-Music-Standards-Ensemble-Strand1.pdf

Titze, I. R. (2008). Getting the most from the vocal instrument in a choral setting. *Choral Journal, 49*(5), 34–41.

14 Dance
Responding

Pamela S. Musil

As with any symbol system that communicates meaning, movement requires coding and decoding. As human beings, we are constantly immersed in a social and physical world that requires what Meltzoff (2007) calls *movement decoding literacies*, which allow us to understand or interpret bodily languages. Because movement occurs within "a perceptual-motor-emotional world, different than the symbolic world of letters and numbers" (Henley, 2014), the interpretation of movement requires access to perceptual and emotional as well as physical aspects of the movement being decoded.

Dance education offers access to the decoding of movement through verbal and kinesthetic language. Verbal language often is comprised of specific dance vocabularies, while kinesthetic language might comprise one's own internal sensations, perceptions, and responses to dance, including bodily or somatic knowledge, which includes "the ways we make meaning of the world through our bodily experiences" (Green, 2002). Verbal and kinesthetic languages both contribute significantly to one's ability to respond to dance.

In the act of responding to dance performance, the dancer or consumer calls upon prior experiences and understandings to construct meaning, which in turn inform how he/she responds to a given dance work. A response might be as simple and unstandardized as like or dislike, as commonly practiced in popular social media, or it can involve knowledgeable processes and reasoning based on informed practice. While liking or disliking a work may convey a personal aesthetic, value, or emotional response, it doesn't often produce productive dialogue about a work of art.

To respond productively to dance, Lavender (1996) and Lerman and Borstel (1996, 2003) both assert the importance of suspending value judgments, thereby avoiding the tendency to identify what one likes in a performance. In Lerman and Borstel's words, such valuing places emphasis on feelings "rather than the art itself and how it is communicating. When we start by naming the fact that the work has meaning at all, and offer options for responding to that meaning, we broaden the lens by which responders can experience and comment" (2003, p. 18). Thus, a dance educator's goal in transporting students past liking or disliking works of choreography would be to engage them in seeing dance through various lenses and experiences that, as suggested within the National Core Arts Standards, facilitate their abilities to analyze and describe dance, and students are asked to consider meaning as communicated through various texts (NCCAS, 2014, DA:Re7.1, 8.1).

This chapter illustrates how one teacher, Ms. Layton, introduces choreographic text to a class of beginners with limited vocabularies for discussing dance. The ability to decode and analyze a work is just starting to emerge as students learn to apply known vocabularies to describe complex movement.

Ms. Layton's beginning-level high school dance class has been exploring various dance styles and genres during a period of several weeks. As a class they have learned dance sequences and viewed video clips within classical ballet, modern and contemporary, and jazz and world dance forms, but they also have viewed and experienced movement inspired by choreography in various popular media settings from TV commercials to music videos to dance reality shows. Through these varied and diverse encounters, they have experienced and witnessed dance within a variety of contexts.

We look in on this class as they view YouTube versions of Microsoft's Surface television ads portraying rhythmically complex dances that evolve spontaneously in business and public spaces. Students' appreciation for the movement design and entertainment value of these short nuggets of choreography becomes immediately apparent in their smiles, body language, and verbal expressions throughout each clip. Josh exclaims, "I love this one! It's my favorite!"

Ms. Layton replays the ad and reminds, "Students, let's remember to avoid talking about it in terms of loving, liking, disliking, or hating for now. Instead, let's identify specific characteristics within the work that we can discuss. For example, Josh, are there any spatial, dynamic, or rhythmic elements that make you enjoy this work?"

Josh grins and says, "Yeah, for sure." Ms. Layton presses: "Okay, can you identify what some of them are?"

Josh thinks for a moment and says, "What stands out the most is the rhythm. It's pretty crazy."

Ms. Layton keeps pressing: "What's crazy about it?"

Josh thinks again, and continues, "Uh, it's fast and wicked—like, I can't keep from twitching while I'm watching it—I mean, I literally can't sit still!"

Ms. Layton acknowledges, "I'm happy that you paid attention to your physical response, Josh. You may recall from some of our previous experiences that a kinesthetic or bodily response can be an important indicator of how we are engaging with a work. When we find ourselves responding kinesthetically, the work tends to have a deeper connection for us—as if we are dancing the work instead of just watching it. In this case, you responded kinesthetically to the fast, complex rhythms. Thanks for that insight. Can someone identify other content that you noticed?"

Anna, an Irish dancer and one of the few in class with prior dance experience, says, "I liked all the quick, tricky body isolations—sharp, percussive, and, like, clear and precise."

Ms. Layton replies, "Thanks, Anna, for using some of our dance language and vocabulary. Yes, the isolated, percussive nature of the movement is clear, and because you indicated that you liked it, I'm going to ask you to describe in dance language what it is about this kind of movement that you personally relate to." Instead of responding verbally, Anna grins, stands up, and performs a short, fast-paced footwork sequence from her Irish dance training. Her movement has strikingly similar dynamic qualities to what she has described. Ms. Layton says, "Wow—we're all about kinesthetic responses today; aren't we? It seems that this particular TV ad really brings that out in us! Anna, I can see that your movement is similar to what you described to us. Can you articulate that?"

Anna smiles sheepishly and answers, "Well, that one ad actually had Irish-like dance moves in it. Did you notice that? Only they were using their hands instead of their feet! I loved that!" She checks herself for letting a value statement slip by putting her hand over her mouth momentarily then continues, "I mean—I guess the quick, sharp moves feel kinesthetically a lot like Irish to me, 'cuz it's also fast, and rhythmic, and—yeah."

Ms. Layton responds enthusiastically, "Yes! You've identified some similarities between this work and your Irish dancing. Excellent analysis, Anna!" Transitioning, Ms. Layton says, "Okay students, as we have experienced these various dance genres and styles over the past few weeks, we've also learned vocabulary that has helped us describe the movement, right? Today, we've discovered that our kinesthetic responses are connected to how we might perceive a work. So let's see if we can combine our kinesthetic understanding of the movement with the dance language we have been building over the past several weeks to describe the movement in these ads."

Ms. Layton references the "Elements of Dance" wall display that she and the students have been adding to in class all semester as they have explored various components and subcomponents of movement under general categories of body, motion, energy, space, and time. "Students, we've created this wall display together to help us document the verbal language we have used to describe our movement. Let's remember to use these terms in our descriptions." She quickly points out some of the vocabulary and definitions they have explored, such as locomotor *(movement that travels through space from one point to another)* and axial *(movement around the central axis of the body that doesn't locomote)*, and dynamic qualities, such as percussive *(a sudden, sharp release or burst of energy held in check or rebounding)* and sustained *(a smooth, ongoing release of energy that can be fast or slow without accents or changes in speed)*, focus *(where one projects one's gaze and/or movement intent)*, and body coordination patterns *(body part and joint isolations, body parts initiating or leading movement, or body parts in combination with other parts, and so on)*. She also points out various rhythmic concepts under the heading of "Time," including metric rhythm, accents, and basic rhythmic structures.

Ms. Layton asks students to use their verbal and kinesthetic dance vocabularies to analyze the TV ad choreography as she pairs them with partners and instructs: "With your partner, experiment with movement that feels similar to what you're seeing in these dance ads. You don't need to copy what you see—just improvise, and try to embody the main dance elements that stand out to you. Once you have experienced it, describe to each other how you think the movement feels kinesthetically. Describe how you understand the energy, timing, and spatial elements in this movement and how it relates to body attitudes, postures, and such. For example, some of you have mentioned percussive qualities and body isolations in the movement. What other dance descriptors can you find? See if you can identify at least two descriptive words or phrases for each element of dance, so when you're finished, you should have a minimum of eight descriptive words or phrases from your dance vocabulary."

Ms. Layton hands out written instructions for the task as students spread out and begin improvising and scribbling out descriptive words and phrases that come to mind as they analyze the choreography, which replays several times as they are working. As she circulates throughout the room, Ms. Layton helps students stay focused on vocabulary within the elements of dance. As Sally and Ella write "happy, and playful," Ms. Layton clarifies, "The emotion it conveys is important, for sure—but for now, how could you describe the movement using just the elements of dance language?"

Sally sighs, "I knew you were going to ask that! This is hard!"

Ms. Layton prompts, "What about the timing, focus, or body attitudes? Is there anything there?" Both students watch the video again, experiment more with movement, and alternately suggest "quick, tricky rhythms, and stiff, straight spines." Ms. Layton nods, encourages them to keep at it, and moves to the next group.

She allows this exploration to continue for some time as she circulates among the class, offering feedback and encouragement. Once she sees that most have identified their descriptive words and phrases, she continues, "Now that you and your partner have described it, let's see how well our observations align with one another as a class." The class shares their impressions in an open forum as Ms. Layton writes their responses on the whiteboard. Descriptors include predominantly axial movement with quick focus changes; percussive hand gestures; swiping hand and foot motions; stiff, upright spines and postures; confined use of space; and quick body part isolations. Ms. Layton sincerely notes, "Wow, students! I'm impressed with your level of discernment. Your ability to observe and describe movement content accurately really has improved! Your observations have captured some of the most prominent qualities of these clips. Tell me how you feel we've arrived at such overwhelming agreement on what we saw to be the most noticeable aspects of the movement?"

Shane reflects back on the various activities Ms. Layton has introduced throughout the past several weeks. "I think having all those experiences has helped us see stuff that we really didn't know how to recognize before. Like, we know more now what to look for, right? So I guess that makes us see some of the same stuff?"

Sena nods and adds, "The "Elements of Dance" vocabulary also has helped us describe the movement better."

Natalie inserts, "We've learned to be less judgey and more chill about stuff."

Ms. Layton asks, "Can you tell me more about that?"

Natalie explains, "Well, even though we may not like something right off, we don't need to judge its value that way. We can evaluate a work based on our dance knowledge instead of our biases."

Ms. Layton nods at Natalie and summarizes, "We've made some important discoveries today as we have increased our ability to read and respond to dance: First, we've identified how our kinesthetic response informs our own personal connection to a work, and we've taken that a step further as we embodied the movement characteristics in the choreography. Then, we described in dance language what we were seeing and experiencing. These activities have helped us discover ways of responding beyond simply liking or disliking a work. What's really exciting about these skills is that often something we initially didn't think we liked becomes something that we are deeply moved by—because we understand or can appreciate it more. Through varied experiences during the past few weeks, we have become more informed, literate participants and consumers of dance. For next time, I'd like you to be thinking about how certain types of movement might convey different meanings."

UNDERSTANDING THE RESPONDING LITERACY EVENT

In this scenario, beginner students have responded to choreographic texts by focusing on the prominent movement elements and qualities rather than their aesthetic preferences. Through a guided process of recognizing, exploring, and describing their own kinesthetic responses to the choreography, Ms. Layton has helped her students avoid making value judgments. Instead, she has offered them a means of coding, decoding, and discussing movement based on their emerging dance vocabularies. These activities will later aid students in recognizing and analyzing their own aesthetic preferences but from a more informed perspective than what was initially available to them. This distinction will be important to them as they continue developing as artists.

Texts

The most prominent text in this vignette is the movement students are learning to analyze and decode. As students struggle to identify and articulate characteristics of the movement they have witnessed, Ms. Layton's guided activities, questioning, and discussion about movement text—both embodied and verbalized—help to bolster students' ability to read the text they are decoding. Her focus on a defined vocabulary (the elements of dance) elicits greater specificity in students' verbal responses as they revisit the vocabulary, which reminds them of what they already know about movement that can assist them in their analysis of the choreographic text.

Placing vocabulary within this new context where students are asked to perform simple (but informed) analysis of a complex choreographic sequence allows them to make meaning out of the vocabulary (and text) beyond what they have experienced previously. For example, when Ms. Layton asks Anna what movement qualities she thinks are inherent in the TV ad that makes her like it, Anna is impelled to analyze her own Irish dancing using specific dance vocabulary. Anna interprets the movement as quick, sharp, percussive body isolations. In so doing, her understanding of this vocabulary suddenly becomes personal—an important component of meaning making. This in turn, imparts meaning to the choreographic text she is decoding. Without meaning, the text would hold no intrinsic value and quickly be forgotten.

Processes

Ms. Layton's progression of learning objectives throughout the semester has offered students opportunities to experience dance through multiple and multimodal exposures to dance vocabularies and languages. She has organized these experiences by helping students interpret and decode various dance languages through an "Elements of Dance" lens, which has offered a specific vocabulary for describing dance.

Having students analyze the choreography's movement characteristics from first a kinesthetic then verbal standpoint assists Ms. Layton's efforts to have them initially avoid the use of valuing language such as *like* and *dislike*. Instead, the focus is placed on students' use of dance language to articulate their own physical and verbal observations pertaining to the movement text they are learning to read. These experiences ultimately arm students with kinesthetic as well as cognitive language that assists them with categorizing and analyzing the works they are being asked to evaluate.

Literacies

As students are asked to analyze the complex choreographies they have witnessed, their kinesthetic response is the first to emerge. For example, Josh acknowledges that he literally can't sit still as he watches the choreography. Ms. Layton validates these responses while asking students to revisit verbal vocabularies they already know and have used in other contexts as a means for describing them. When she pushes Josh to be more verbally articulate about why the choreography makes him twitch, he realizes that the choreography's complex rhythms are part of what he is drawn to. The ability to recognize and describe one's kinesthetic response to a work of art is an important literacy that begins to emerge in this vignette.

Ms. Layton reinforces students' abilities to respond through physical, written, and verbal language as they first physically improvise and embody their interpretations of the main characteristics of the choreography, then cognitively classify the movement by assigning descriptive words and phrases from each of the four dance elements they have been studying throughout the semester, and finally, discuss and share their discoveries in an open forum. The meaning-making opportunities within these moments of reflective and analytical discussion are rich as they encourage students to use previously learned vocabularies in a new setting. As students begin as a community to discuss their shared understanding of the work, they recognize that over time, they have become more knowledgeable about dance, which has informed their abilities to respond meaningfully and productively within a conversation about dance. As a result, as Ms. Layton acknowledges in her closing statement, students have become more literate as participants and consumers of dance.

CONCLUSION

Certainly, this event does not encompass the many inroads, activities, or dimensions of responding literacy that might be explored as it represents only a beginning level of dance response and critique that does not venture into choreographic context or meaning. Rather, this singular example demonstrates one way that dance responding literacies might be developed and nurtured, particularly in the beginning stages, when students' dance language is still being formed. Ms. Layton's methodologies have bolstered learners' understandings of specific ways one might code, decode, and respond to a work of art. By requiring students to suspend (at least for the moment) their knee-jerk like and dislike responses, Ms. Layton has helped facilitate their use of dance language—both kinesthetic and verbal—to describe the movement they have observed. Consequently, students' abilities to observe and respond have been enhanced through tools that help them convey their understanding of dance beyond their own aesthetic preferences. Such practice facilitates attitudes and postures that allow participants to engage in authentic disciplinary practice.

REFERENCES

Green, J. (2002). Somatic knowledge: The body as content and methodology in dance education. *Journal of Dance Education*, 2(4), 114–118. doi: 10.1080/15290824.2002.10387219

Henley, M. (2014). Sensation, perception, and choice in the dance classroom. *Journal of Dance Education*, 14, 95–100. doi: 10.1080/15290824.2014.907497

Lavender, L. (1996). *Dancers talking dance: Critical evaluation in the choreography class*. Champaign, IL: Human Kinetics.

Lerman, L., & Borstel, J. (2003). *Critical response process* (p. 18). Takoma Park, MD: The Dance Exchange.

Meltzoff, A. (2007). "Like me": A foundation for social cognition. *Developmental Science, 10*(1), 126–134.

National Coalition for Core Arts Standards (2014). *National Core Dance Standards*. DA:Re7.1, 8.1. *Responding*. Online at http://www.nationalartsstandards.org/

15 Media Arts
Responding

Benjamin Thevenin

Long before the term *art education* was coined, scholars and artists asked questions about what constitutes beauty in art; what is the nature of the relationship between culture and society; and what does a work of art say about the artist, the audience, time and place, culture and politics. The purpose of responding in the media arts classroom is significant, then, as it provides an opportunity for teachers and students to explore these issues. Because while our students—and, to be honest, most of us—are constantly consuming media and art in their various forms, we often lack the ability to critically analyze these works and then articulate our perceptions, interpretations, and evaluations of them. The National Core Arts Standards for Media Arts discuss responding in relation to assisting students to be able to "analyze the intent, meanings and reception of a variety of media artworks, focusing on personal and cultural contexts" (MA: Re8.1.l) Author, audience, text, and context—*responding* is the means of making sense of the relationship between these primary elements of art.

Hobbs (1998) asserts, "At the center of media literacy education must be the pedagogy of inquiry, which is the act of asking questions about media texts. The cultivation of an open, questioning, reflective and critical stance towards symbolic texts should be the center pole of the media literacy umbrella" (p. 27). So while—in the context of the media arts classroom— responding most likely begins with the thoughts prompted or emotions elicited during students' primary engagement with a work, that is just the beginning. Laughs and tears in the movie theatre are responses, but so are the conversations that occur as the credits roll. And an effective media arts education helps students go beyond thumbs-up or down responses and encourages them to engage in discussions about media texts to develop their thoughts (verbally or through written work) and to use these conversations and analyses to inform their own creative endeavors. In the following vignette, Ms. Cage provides a simple demonstration of how we might facilitate responding literacies in media arts education—through class discussion, creative production, and self-reflection.

Ms. Cage's high school media arts class has spent the year exploring the creative process. The teacher has organized the course to help her students find new sources of inspiration for their work, to experiment with different creative processes, to draw upon various artistic traditions, and to learn tools that will help them practically realize their ideas. On this particular afternoon, Ms. Cage is introducing a new unit. The students enter the classroom and chat. They grab the chairs from the computer monitors around the room and form a small circle, facing each other. The bell rings, and Ms. Cage begins.

"When artists choose to work within a given medium or mode—whether it be photography, sculpture, interpretive dance, or film—they choose these approaches for their unique characteristics." starts Ms. Cage. "But how do you, as budding artists, begin to recognize the affordances and limitations of these different approaches? What makes film film? How is drawing unique from painting or printmaking? What am I able to express through music that I can't by writing a poem?"

To demonstrate this idea, Ms. Cage shares Maya Deren's A Study in Choreography for the Camera (1945). Before they watch, Ms. Cage introduces the film and prompts the class to consider some things as they watch.

"Pay attention to what you see, how you feel, and how you make sense of the film," she says. "And see if you can figure out why Deren might have chosen to work with film to make her art."

The class watches the short, silent film in which Talley Bailey performs a contemporary dance across various locations—a forest, a small apartment, a museum, and so on. The film ends, and a number of the students look confused.

Ms. Cage responds quickly. "Okay," she says. "First off, what do you think? How do you feel? Can anyone make any sense of what we just watched?"

The class is quiet, the students gathering their thoughts and working up the courage to answer the teacher's question.

"That was . . . different," offers a boy, Jon.

"I thought it was cool," replies Alice.

"Okay, Jon, Alice," Ms. Cage says. "What made it feel different? How was it cool? Tell us more."

Jon answers first: "Well, it's a movie without any talking. There are no real characters, except the guy dancing. And nothing really happens, except he dances in these different places."

"And that's why I liked it," retorts Alice. "It doesn't have witty dialogue or this intricate plot or anything. It's just simple and beautiful."

"Alright," Ms. Cage says. "So, here we have two different responses to Deren's art. Chances are some of you appreciated some of the things she's doing in the film, and others found it to be a little too out there or maybe some of both. And that's okay. Whether you liked it or not, I think it serves as an excellent demonstration of some of the things that film affords artists to do. What do you think, class? How does Deren's film highlight some of the strengths of film as a medium for art making?"

One student offers, "Well, the title says Choreography for Camera, so maybe she's talking about how films uses cameras to record people moving and dancing?"

"Okay, great," responds Ms. Cage. "So, among the unique elements of film is movement. That's where we get the word movie. Film is able to capture the movement of its subjects—in this case, a dancer. Deren determined the content of the film—Bailey dancing—in order to demonstrate a unique affordance of the medium of film: movement. What else?"

By this time, the students have warmed up a little to the discussion and offer answers more readily.

"You can edit shots together in movies. So, here, you see the guy start a dance move in one place, and then it cuts, and he finishes the movement in another place that's completely different."

"Also, even though there are no real characters or dialogue, the guy is still performing in front of the camera, just like an actor would do in a normal movie."

Ms. Cage discusses the students' responses—movement, editing, performance, and so on are all elements that, to varying degrees, distinguish film from other media. She then introduces the students' next creative project, which she calls "Medium Specificity." Students will—not unlike Deren—choose a medium, identify some elements specific to this medium, and then create a small work of art that explores these characteristics. The content of their work should demonstrate the unique affordances of their chosen medium, just as Bailey's performance revealed film's use of movement, editing, and so on.

Ms. Cage first has the students meet in groups and brainstorm together what media they might choose, and which elements of these media might be most interesting to focus on in their work. During the following days, students select their chosen medium and begin developing their "Medium Specificity" projects. Ms. Cage visits with each of the students and provides them with feedback on their progress. The deadline for the project arrives, and students take turns volunteering to share their work.

A student named Libby begins, saying, "I chose to focus on illustration—specifically pencil drawing. I was talking to Ms. Cage about how the reason I like drawing is because there's something about the feel of the paper, the pull of the eraser, the smell of pencil shavings—I feel like I'm making the characters I draw. I feel like I know them. And she shared with me this quote from Maya Deren, whose movie we watched at the beginning of the project."

Libby reads Deren's words from where she scrawled them down in her sketchbook, "The task of cinema or any other art form is not to translate hidden messages of the unconscious soul into art but to experiment with the effects contemporary technical devices have on nerves, minds, or souls."

Libby glances up from her paper and continues, "And so I thought I'd focus on drawing, and talk about how these devices—not movie cameras or anything but just pencils and paper—help me connect to the souls of the characters I create. I drew myself in the illustration, and I drew my character reaching out to me. Like we are connected through the medium."

Media Arts: Responding 127

Figure 15.1

The students applaud Libby and then dive into a conversation about her work. The students share their different interpretations of the drawing. Libby discusses other strengths and limitations of pencil drawing.

After a few minutes of discussion, Jon's hand shoots up, and he asks, "Why did you choose to draw that particular character?"

Libby considers the question for a second and answers, smiling, "Well, I like drawing dresses?"

Some of the students giggle, and Ms. Cage steps in, "That's a good question. Libby. You're talking about the relationship between the character and the creator. How does your design of your character contribute to this idea?"

Libby hesitates, and Ms. Cage follows up with another question, "For example, would the relationship between illustrator and character appear differently if you'd drawn someone like Batman instead of this little pixie girl?"

Libby pauses and considers Ms. Cage's question. She responds, "I guess you're right. I mean, I like drawing female characters. But maybe that's because I can relate to them more as a girl. And if I had drawn Batman, I don't know if it would've made the same point about the artist and the character being a part of one another."

Libby pauses again and looks contemplative. "I don't know if Batman and I would get along super well," she concludes with a smile.

Ms. Cage thanks Libby for sharing her work, and the students applaud again.

UNDERSTANDING THE RESPONDING LITERACY EVENT

Texts

In the previous scenario, both Deren's film and Libby's illustration are texts that provide Ms. Cage and her students with the opportunity to respond. However, the nature of the text, the context in which the students engage with it, and the types of questions that students are asked prompt different types of responses. First, Deren's film is a classic work from a renowned artist. Introducing the concept of affordances and limitations of a given medium and asking, "What makes film film," Ms. Cage invites the students to consider how Deren's film makes use of certain elements specific to the medium. Students' responses vary—some find the work interesting; others are confused by it. And when asked to analyze it further, students identify how Deren emphasizes elements like movement, editing, and performance as means of exploring the medium of film.

Following the class's engagement with Deren's film, they produce their own creative work in an effort to identify and explore the unique characteristics of other media. Libby's illustration provides the students with another opportunity to practice responding to a text. However, because of the difference in the type of text, the context in which it is examined, and the questions the teacher asks about it, the students' responses are somewhat different. First of all, Libby's drawing is a more accessible text to the students—both in that it adheres to a more conventional approach to illustration (as opposed to Deren's avant-garde film without dialogue or narrative) and that a fellow classmate created it. And because of their relative familiarity with the text, the students' responses are less about making sense of their perceptions of the work and more focused on interpreting and evaluating the work. These responses are also the product of the context in which the students engage with Libby's drawing. As mentioned in the vignette, students are accustomed to sharing their work with the class and giving and receiving feedback. The National Standards discuss the value of responding as it allows students "to evaluate various media artworks and production process, considering context, and practicing constructive feedback" (MA: Re9.1.7). While they are practicing some of the same analytic skills they employed in their discussion of Deren's film, their responses to Libby's illustration are not limited to understanding or appreciating the work but to helping their classmate improve as an artist. Ms. Cage has created a class culture in which respect is shown and constructive criticism is given in response to students' shared work. And because the creator of the work is part of the discussion, it is possible for not only the audience to respond to the text but the artist to respond to the audience as well. While the students' responses to a canonic work and a student's creative project differ in obvious ways, each text provides an opportunity to practice analytical skills and develop responding literacies.

Processes

There are a few different processes involved in these students' development of responding literacies, as they have the opportunity to respond through *discussion, creative production,* and *critical self-reflection*. First, after Ms. Cage screens the film, she engages the students in a discussion regarding Deren's work. Now, it is worth noting that at the beginning of this conversation, the students are noticeably hesitant, probably given their lack of familiarity with experimental film. But Ms. Cage has created an atmosphere in the classroom in which students feel safe to share their perceptions and interpretations, and she jump-starts the class discussion by simply asking for the students' gut reactions to the film. Then, Ms. Cage validates these first students' efforts to engage, identifies the strengths of their responses, and then prompts the class to dig a little deeper in their analyses. However, the responses that students offer in their analyses of Deren's film are only the first step in a larger process of responding.

Next, Ms. Cage creates the "Medium Specificity" project to allow students to respond not just to Deren's film but more importantly to the concepts she is introducing to them. To determine whether her students understand the idea that different media have unique elements, Ms. Cage gives them an opportunity to practice these concepts. While another class might require a test as a demonstration of students' understanding of the concepts, Ms. Cage allows *them* to test out the concepts, to make sense of them, by attempting to implement them in their own creative work. As Libby's presentation suggests, the students are encouraged to produce something that is unique to their personal artistic sensibilities but is still grounded in an understanding of the concepts introduced in class.

Last, Libby is encouraged to respond to the class's feedback on her work and, in so doing, engage in some critical self-reflection. For decades, the principles of "access, analyze, evaluate and communicate" have functioned as guiding principles of media literacy education (Aufderheide, 1997). Focusing on these principles is an effective way of understanding how students can respond to texts. However, there is a growing acknowledgment among media educators and scholars that media literacy necessarily involves an engagement not only with media texts but also with one's own critiques and creations (see Hobbs, 2011). And as is demonstrated in the dialogue between Libby and her classmates, this is not always an easy process. She is asked difficult questions and struggles to provide adequate answers for her creative decisions. Notably though, Ms. Cage recognizes this, and reframes the student's question in a way that prompts Libby to consider more thoughtfully the motivations behind her art. In this way, Libby's practice of responding literacies is not limited to analysis of media art, or the implementation of concepts in her own creative work, but also to reflecting on her own development as an artist.

Literacies

This discussion of the role of responding in this example helps us identify how Ms. Cage is able to facilitate her students' development of media arts literacies. This scenario from Ms. Cage's classroom demonstrates the importance of students being able to identify the affordances and limitations of a given medium. Ms. Cage is helping the students not just understand why artists choose to work within a given medium but also determine what media or modes might allow them to best express themselves and communicate their ideas. In the words of Gunther Kress, students are encouraged to ask "What can a specific mode do? What are its limitations and potentials?" and "What are the affordances of a mode?" and to make artistic choices that utilize these "affordances in ways which arise and reflect their concerns, values and meanings" (2003, p. 45). And this is no arbitrary skill but one essential to each student's development as an artist and their practice of responding literacies. The National Standards state that responding literacies necessarily involve them to be able to "describe, compare and analyze *the qualities of and relationship between the components* in media artworks" (MA: Re7.1.7, emphasis added). Through responding to media texts, students begin to identify their different elements and how they function in relation to one another.

Last, by examining these texts—both Deren's film and Libby's drawing—and sharing their responses to them, the students are exploring firsthand the potential for *polysemy* in a work of media art. That is, there is no single authoritative meaning inherent in a work of art. Rather, there always exists the possibility of multiple meanings, determined by both the characteristics of that work and the diverse experiences, perspectives, and associations that the audience brings to it. By sharing their different readings of a single text, students are beginning to explore how meaning is made—that texts are *encoded* with certain meanings (e.g., through the use of particular aesthetic elements) and that individuals *decode* these texts differently (see Hall, 1980). And the articulation of these interpretations in class discussion is particularly interesting because it allows students to share and compare their individual processes of signification. The introspection involved in seeking to understand one's own meaning-making process also relates to the concept of critical self-reflection, or responding to *self*. Here, not only Libby is able engage in some self-reflection. Rather, when encountering their classmates' different responses to works of art, students are invited to consider their own meaning-making processes.

CONCLUSION

Ultimately, Ms. Cage provides her students with an opportunity to develop responding literacies by inviting them to critically engage with a variety of media texts, respond to these texts, to the concepts from classroom instruction, to classmates' creative work, and ultimately to each other. And given their development of these new skills, students become better prepared to engage critically with media arts outside of the classroom—moving past passive popcorn chomping to talk through the credits, having critical conversations about authors and audience, text and context.

REFERENCES

Aufderheide, P. (1997). *Media literacy: A report of the national leadership conference on media literacy*. Aspen, CO: Aspen Institute. Retrieved from http://www.medialit.org/reading-room/aspen-media-literacy-conference-report-part-ii

Hall, S. (1980). Encoding/decoding. In S. Hall, D. Hobson, A. Lowe, & P. Willis (Eds.), *Culture, media, language* (pp. 128–138). London: Hutchinson.

Hobbs, R. (1998). "The seven great debates of the media literacy movement." *Journal of Communication, 48*(1), pp. 16–32.

Hobbs, R. (2011). *Digital and media literacy: Connecting culture and classroom*. Thousand Oaks, CA: Corwin.

Kress, G. (2003). *Literacy in the new media age* (p. 27). New York: Routledge.

National Coalition for Core Arts Standards. (2014). National Core Media Arts Standards MA: Re9.1.7. Online at http://www.nationalartsstandards.org/sites/default/files/Media%20Arts%20at%20a%20Glance%20-%20new%20copyright%20info.pdf

16 Theatre
Responding

Amy Petersen Jensen

Theatre educators should provide students with opportunities to respond (Gonzalez, 2006; Lazarus, 2012) critically to theatre work. For the purposes of this chapter, *responding critically* means that theatre students actively interact with the ideas presented in the process of creating a theatre work when participating as artists. It also means that theatre students actively interact with the ideas presented on stage in a fully realized theatre production when participating as audience members. In both roles (artist and audience member), students can practice using the critical literacies associated with responding by building the contextual understanding necessary to make meaning.

The National Core Theatre Standards invite teachers and students to engage in critically responding by "reflecting, interpreting, and evaluating" (National Core Theatre Standards, 2014). Theatre teachers and students utilize these responding processes when participating in the creation of a theatre work. For example, actors respond as they reflect on what they see, hear, or feel when portraying a character; directors interpret a written script and then translate that into the verbal and physical realm of the stage; and scenic designers evaluate what utilizing a particular color or texture of a fabric to dress a set might convey about that setting.

Responding processes also occur when viewing a theatre work. For instance, audience members often critically reflect on an actor's successful portrayal of a character; viewers interpret meaning in the aesthetic choices made by the director when staging a play; they also evaluate the technical success of the designs used in a production.

Students can become critically literate creators and consumers as they practice responding (reflecting, interpreting, and evaluating) through inquiry within a play's various contexts. The Core Theatre Standards describe this type of inquiry as "formulate[ing] a deeper understanding and appreciation of a drama/ theatre work by considering its specific purpose or intended audience." (NCCAS, 2014, TH: Re9.1.I.c). In this vein, the Core Theatre Standards also encourage teachers and students to examine a theatre work by gathering supporting evidence about its interrelationship to other "art forms, history, [and] culture" (NCCAS, 2014, TH: Re9.1.I.a) as well as considering the aesthetic choices evidenced in the "production elements" presented in a theatre work (NCCAS, 2014, TH: Re9.1.I.b).

As already stated, it is important for students to practice responding literacies when they are creating and also when they are participating in viewing theatre. Students can become critical consumers as they make purposeful inquiries about a work of art and thereby increase their abilities to create works ripe with meaning and contextual relevance (Gallagher, 2014, p. 213).

In the following vignette, Mrs. Quint and her beginning drama students have been participating in an exceptional experience across the school year. Every other month students have been invited to attend a play performance at a professional children's theatre in the city. Before and after each play viewing experience, Jade Reyes—a teaching artist who is also a dramaturge for the children's theatre performing company—comes to their school to explore aspects of each staged performance. This month the students attended a staged version of *Esperanza Rising*. The play, which is based on Pam Munoz Ryan's award-winning novel, explores what happens to Esperanza, a privileged thirteen-year-old Mexican girl, when she is forced to leave behind her beautiful home and her beloved mother to form a new and challenging life in America. The play follows Esperanza and her former servants as they cross the Mexican border into the United States and attempt to find work to survive. The story centers on Esperanza's coming of age through her realization that she can actively contribute to her new community even though she is only thirteen.

Mrs. Quint and Jade recently prepared students to see the performance of Esperanza Rising *and for the responding activity that the students are now preparing to present. In class periods prior to viewing the play, Mrs. Quint invites the students to think about ways that audience members might actively respond to a performance. She instructs the students, saying,* "As we watch Esperanza Rising, *I want you to put your dramaturgy hats on, while you view this play. Remember that one role of the theatre-viewing audience is to interpret intent and meaning in a theatre work. As you know, Jade helps interpret intent and meaning in plays as a dramaturge. She does this by doing cultural and historical research about the play and then providing that information to the director, designers, performers, and even to the audience members.*

Jade adds, "Here is one example of how I work. I want to share some behind-the-scenes information about this particular production of Esperanza Rising." *When describing the creative processes of the company, she says,* "As they (the director, designers, and actors) began to create this play together, the director invited all of us to think about how this play might communicate different messages to different people. This was a really important question for the director because he holds dual citizenship in Mexico and in America, and he wanted to communicate to people from both places his love for each land. He even told us that he feels like a part of his heart belongs in both countries, and he wants to share that idea through this production because he thinks it strengthens him. After the director shared his story, I did some research into how Mexican and American cultures might express love for their homeland. My research findings eventually aided the company in strengthening the visual design of the production. Mrs. Quint and I are interested in each of you recognizing and then sharing how artistic choices like the director's or dramaturgical choices like those I described earlier might influence how we understand and feel about Esperanza and her journey."

Mrs. Quint jumps in, saying, "Responding to a play in this is way is not about giving it a thumbs-up or a thumbs-down. Instead Jade and I are looking for thoughtful, active responses to the production you view. Actively responding to artistic choices made in a play is an important part of participating in the theatre. To prepare to do this, we are going to form three study circles. Each circle will be responsible for observing the play with a critical eye, like a dramaturge. For this assignment, each group will watch the production and then identify one or more production elements—characters, setting, costumes, lighting, sounds, or others—that stand out to you and seem important to your understanding of the play. Then we want you to ask some questions about why those artistic choices might have been made. Finally we would like you to gather some supporting evidence for possible answers to your questions—perhaps some historical, cultural, or artistic information—this is the part where you find out more about something that you hear or see in the play that makes you curious about a potential meaning.

Jade adds, "Your job is then to assess the possible impact those elements might have had on you and your study circle as audience members viewing the play."

Following their viewing of the play, the students have several days to work with their study circles to form responses to the play. During the preparation days, the study circles have prepared responses to two prompts about the play performance of Esperanza Rising: "In the performance we noticed that . . ." and "We saw/heard _____ in Esperanza Rising, and it made us wonder why . . ."

Today is "Response Day." Each study circle has selected a unique way to respond to the prompts. One group is thinking about aesthetic choices made in the presentation of the play. Students in this study circle are focusing on the role of the mariachi in the play. They are listening to audio recordings of mariachi music on the Smithsonian Folkways Web site, which was listed as a resource in the Esperanza Rising program study guide and which Mrs. Quint had pointed out when they showed interest in the play's mariachi music. They also are carefully examining colorful facsimiles of Saltillo serapes, traditional Mexican scarfs, which were worn in the production and provided for the class by the company costume shop at Jade's request. When Jade brought the serapes, she also shared information with the group that she had gathered for the designers prior to them designing the costumes for the play.

A second group is concentrating on how the play represented homeland and culture. One group member, Lila, had read the book on which the play was based; she brought it from home, and the group compared descriptions of Esperanza's home and culture in the book and those in the play. With the help of Mrs. Quint, other members of the group also investigated the Library of Congress Archives, which Jade had shared with them in earlier lessons. They gathered news stories and photographs from Mexican and American newspapers from 1929 and 1930—the years that the play takes place—and then made comparisons to the action within the play. They also located a map of the Mexican/American boarder from that time period and are considering the perils Esperanza and her friends might have faced as they made their way from Mexico to California and ended up in labor camps just as the Great Depression was beginning.

Genevra, a member of the third group, noted that the play presentation was bilingual and that although the play was primarily spoken in English, most characters throughout the production used Spanish language at some point. Because most of the group has a limited background in Spanish, they could not read many of the Spanish words in the playscript from Esperanza Rising that Jade provided. Mrs. Quint suggested they use a digital translator to understand more fully the words chosen by the playwright to express meanings within the bilingual frame.

At the beginning of Response Day, the study circles get ready to present their responses to Esperanza Rising. Mrs. Quint and Jade then gather the class members together and invite one of the groups to present. Tyler stands, introducing the first group's response, saying, "In the play we noticed that a male band played throughout."

Alina chimes in, "The play program calls the band members mariachis. The band was with Esperanza in Mexico, and they were a part of her fancy birthday party. But we noticed that they were also in the work camp with her when she got to America. This seemed strange."

Jethro adds, "We also noticed that the band members were all dressed up as if they were ready to perform all of time, even in the work camp. We're talking big hats and tight, black pants with a sort of sparkly ruffled trim—pretty snazzy."

Alina counters, "The actors performing as mariachis sometimes took off their hats and covered their ruffled pants with a big, tentlike blanket called a serape so that they could play extra roles like bandits or field workers."

Mrs. Quint asks the group, "These are great observations, but tell me why you think the mariachis were used throughout the play?"

Keandra pipes up, "So obviously we needed to do some research about mariachis and their music to find out why they were always onstage and almost always singing in those extravagant costumes, even when it seemed out of place."

Tyler also contributes saying, "Jade helped us do some research on the Smithsonian Folkways Web site. We listened to a lot of music and also found out that mariachi bands play at important cultural and personal moments in Mexico, like baptisms, weddings, patriotic holidays, and even funerals.

Alina says, "Jade reminded us that some of the words they sang might be important, so she brought a copy of the script, and we looked at all of the words in the songs with her. I really liked the words in the last song. The song happens when Esperanza and her mother are planting the rosebush roots from their old home on the work campgrounds. One of the mariachis sings, 'If you look up at the sky,/What do you see?/The same slivered moon,/That always shined on me' (Alvarez, p. 55)."

Genevra, a member of the third study circle, raises her hand and says, "Hey, those words remind me of the story Jade told us about the director—how his heart belongs in both Mexico and America. That's the same with the mariachis—they belong in Mexico, but in this play, they also belong with Esperanza wherever she is."

Jade asks, "So how do you think the artistic choice to have the mariachi band present all the time, even in the work camp, might have had an impact on the way audience members viewed the play? That is your assignment, right?" Several hands from the class go up in response to her question.

Tyler says, "Well, none of us have any real connection to Mexico, so I am not sure, but it does seem like the mariachi band followed Esperanza through a lot of important moments, not just her birthday, but really growing up and then getting her mother back, so yeah."

Lila, a member of the second study circle says, "I have a thought about that. In our group, we looked at the book the play is based on, and there are no mariachis in the book. But the book does talk a lot about the heartbeat of the land. In the book, Esperanza discovers that she has brought the heartbeat of her Mexican land with her. Maybe the playwright used the mariachis as a way to represent physically what Esperanza thinks about and feels in the book."

Responding with enthusiasm, Mrs. Quint says, "This is a great conversation! I really appreciate your efforts to better understand the purpose of the mariachis. I am curious about what the second group might add to your good thinking about the play. I know your study circle has been thinking about Esperanza's journey from Mexico to the United States. Why don't you share what you have discovered? Lila, you started us thinking about the original book and its connection to the play. Do you want to begin your response there, or are you prepared to begin at another point?"

UNDERSTANDING THE THEATRE LITERACY EVENT

In the vignette, Mrs. Quint and Jade Reyes engage their students in critically responding by inviting them to view and respond to the production of *Esperanza Rising* by practicing some dramaturgical research skills. In the following paragraphs, I will outline how Mrs. Quint and Jade help students to reflect, interpret, and evaluate the play and its contexts using a dramaturgical lens.

Texts

The students in Mrs. Quint's class primarily respond to the live performance of *Esperanza Rising*. This performed text is ephemeral in nature—it is performed only once in one particular way for this specific audience. Because of this, Mrs. Quint and Jade prepare the students to actively participate in this singular viewing. First they assign the students to work in dramaturgical study circles. Then they specifically guide the students' noticing by asking them to reflect on and then interpret potential meanings (i.e., aesthetic, social, cultural, etc.) developed within the play. Jade models this type of reflection and interpretation when she shares contextual information about the company director's artistic intent and the impact her own active response to the information had on the visual design of the play. She then invites them to consider the possible ways this information might help them to *read* or interpret the play as they watch and then later reflect on what they have seen and heard. Finally they ask the students to identify key production elements (designs, staging, actor choices, etc.), ask questions about artistic choices relating to those production elements, and then search out plausible answers to those questions.

Mrs. Quint and Jade support their inquiries into the performed play by sharing associated texts, which further inform their understanding of the live production. Jade provides the *Esperanza Rising* playscripts and actual costumes from the theatre company for students to examine and then situate within their study of the performed play. Both educators expose students to databases that have historical images and printed texts that provide context about the work. Most importantly they provide students with prompts that guide their investigation of these texts.

Processes

Mrs. Quint and Jade engage students in dramaturgical processes to help them develop their responding skills and knowledge. They do this by placing the students in study circles in which they are invited to interpret potential meaning in aesthetic choices made by the *Esperanza Rising* director and his team. The study circles each identify key aesthetic choices made in the play. For example, group one identifies the use of the mariachis as a key aesthetic choice. Once they have identified these key aesthetic choices, Mrs. Quint and Jade engage the students in dramaturgical research processes. They do this specifically by inviting students to participate in contextual research related to the aesthetics they have identified. As the students investigate the use of mariachi and its value within the context of the play, the teachers encourage students to locate and use research materials that provide further information about the aesthetic or cultural aspects of the play. Some of these include the playscript, the book on which the play is based, and the costumes from the actual production. Students make assertions and then derive potential meanings from the performed play as they gather evidence from resources beyond the play to support those assertions.

Importantly Mrs. Quint also provides her students with additional access to theatre knowledge and theatre processes that she could not have provided on her own by inviting a teaching artist into her classroom. Jade Reyes has specific contextual knowledge about the play that aids students in understanding general theatre processes and especially dramaturgical processes. Jade also provides access to texts, artists, and inside information about the production that enhance the students' ability to respond to the various contexts that inform the play.

Literacies

Throughout the vignette, Mrs. Quint and Jade support students' emerging responding literacies. First they invite students to identify production elements within the play, and then they ask them to reflect on the aesthetic choices that make up the production. In this case, reflection occurs as students consider the possible contextual reasons for the choices the artists made (i.e., use of the mariachis, bilingual performance, etc.). The students further formulate a "deeper appreciation for the play as they interpret the performed text through the lens of dramaturgy. In their roles as dramaturges, they make inferences and observations about the production of *Esperanza Rising*. They do this by considering the play in the context of other art forms, especially the book from which the play originated. They also study historical information, such as the information they gathered about the Mexican/American border and the Great Depression. Additionally the students discover cultural information related to the play. For instance, they ponder the poetic language of the play's music and what it might reveal. They also question why the play is written and performed mostly in English but also in Spanish. Because they are invited to investigate the play from so many points of entry, they never respond to the play by evaluating whether it is a good performance or a bad one. Instead they evaluate and then value many possible interpretations of the work—and this ability is one hallmark of critical understanding.

CONCLUSION

Learning to respond to theatre work is an important part of theatre practice. Students learning to respond can be introduced to responding literacies as they create and perform themselves and also as they observe and investigate theatre work created by others. More importantly, as students practice responding by reflecting, interpreting, and evaluating their own work and/or the work of others, they should be empowered to actively engage in processes that value contextual understanding as a means of knowledge making.

Where this is possible, I believe that students will respond with a critical awareness and an expanded vision of the theatre and its meaning-making capacities.

REFERENCES

Alvarez, L. (2006). *Esperanza Rising*. Online at http://www.broadwayplaypubl.com/

Gallagher, K. (2013). *Why theatre matters: Urban youth, engagement and a pedagogy of the real*. Toronto: University of Toronto Press.

Gonzalez, J. (2006). *Temporary stages: Departing from tradition in high school theatre education*. Portsmouth, NH: Heinemann.

Lazarus, J. (2012). *Signs of change new directions in theatre education: Revised and amplified edition*. Bristol: Intellect.

National Coalition for Core Arts Standards (2014). *National Core Arts Standards Dance: Responding*. Online at http://www.nationalartsstandards.org/

17 Visual Art
Responding

Daniel T. Barney

Opportunities to teach traditional reading strategies in the visual arts do exist of course, but focusing on a general definition of literacy in the traditional sense, for example, to extract predetermined information from a print text, would compromise the learning within a disciplinary context within the visual arts (O'Brien, Stewart, & Moje, 1995). The event described in this chapter elucidates disciplinary literacy concerns that exceed the "generic recommendations" (Maniaci & Chandler-Olcott, 2010, p. 5) that permeate traditional literacy research.

Within the field of art education, responding to art as a visual text that holds significant sociocultural meaning is not a new concept (Duncum, 2002; Smith-Shank, 2004) and is at the core of what many call visual literacy (Chung, 2005) and an important concept of a visual culture art education (Duncum, 2003, 2004, 2009a, 2009b; Freedman, 2003). However, this type of semiotic responding (see NCCAS, 2014, VA: Re7 and Re8), although important, touches on only one type of responding. The approaches mentioned in these visual arts anchor standards focus on visual analysis and interpretation for meaning making, which often is lacking in print-based textual literacy strategies. But, more importantly, the vignette below also suggests contemporary artists, like Walton Ford, utilize additional responding literacy strategies as they generate their artworks. Hence, students can use responding as a literacy strategy to not only reflect on finished works as texts but also while in the process of creating art, as does Walton Ford.

Ford's artistic creations, by his own admission, respond to the "wildlife work of John James Audubon" (Buford, 2009, p. 8). Ford responds, however, not only to historical methodologies of process, style, and ideology but also to historical print texts that are humorous, dark, and ironic when brought into a contemporary context (Buford, 2009). Walton Ford's reading of these historical texts is not to find facts or information as knowledge but to rethink, to surprise, and to play within a contemporary art discourse. When Ford researches a topic at a library or archive, he is searching for stories and perspectives that were perhaps once common but seem ridiculous or darkly poignant in our current worldviews. And even though Ford's paintings are rendered much like Audubon's paintings to show detail and the subject's position in the world, they are not simple illustrations or diagrams to document natural history from an Audubonian (early nineteenth century) perspective; they respond to that time of making and documenting as it relates to now. Ford's works make historical facts and perspectives bizarre and reflects our own dark dilemmas and situations.

Walton Ford's process of creating his paintings, not simply the painting of these works but the inquiry and research as a literacy engagement, models a type of critical literacy for the teacher described in the following vignette, as well as for her students, "where the whole world becomes a text, i.e., the icons and symbols that represent dominant and subdominant ideologies are 'read' as texts" (Carter, 2011, p. 239).

Students in Ms. Rao's high school painting class have been learning watercolor techniques, including the manipulation of aqueous media with various brushes onto different supports and grounds, management and care of supplies, and some basic color theory exercises and image-making strategies. The students just finished a technical challenge in which Ms. Rao asked each student to create a small shoebox-size diorama-as-still-life-scene from found objects they brought in from home and around their town. These looked like miniature dioramas that one might find in a life science museum but with the inclusion of contemporary life. The students exhibited their watercolor paintings alongside their dioramas in the town's local library gallery. Ms. Rao has been focusing her teaching on technical workshops for this aqueous media unit but is now moving on to more historical and conceptual literacies, desiring to foster additional authentic literacies used by contemporary artists today.

"I'm really proud of the work you all did to make our exhibition a success," Ms. Rao exuberantly tells her students with a smile. "Your friends and loved ones who came to see your work seemed very interested and engaged with your ideas and efforts. So, congratulations to all of you!"

"I loved making those dioramas," shares Natalie.

"I am so glad, Natalie. I could tell most of you enjoyed setting up your own little worlds to paint. I think we learned a lot from that portion of the lesson. What are you all going to do with your dioramas, may I ask?"

"Those things took way longer than I thought they'd take," says Bronson. "I'm keeping mine forever unless I sell it for a million dollars."

"Well, I think we learned quite a bit in creating them in relation to our paintings," suggests Ms. Rao.

Keely nods her head in agreement, but adds, "I actually felt like the dioramas were more art than our paintings. Do you know what I mean?"

"Tell me more," probes Ms. Rao.

"Well, Tasha, Skylar, and I were just talking about how our paintings were mostly about making technical decisions—you know, choosing the color's intensity and value and making soft or hard edges, while the construction of our dioramas was more about . . . well, us. I guess what I am trying to say is I felt that the diorama was where I was putting things together

to make meaning for myself and anyone who cared to ask; the painting was a representation of that experience that already took place."

"Wow, thank you, Keely! Your comment really relates to the next lesson in our painting class. Thank you for sharing," says Ms. Rao appreciative for the unexpected transition into her next curricular idea for helping students gain conceptual and historical responding literacies during their artistic practice.

Ms. Rao prepares students to watch select video clips from an Art21 series, showing how the artist Walton Ford responds to the illustrations of naturalist John James Audubon and to a wide variety of historical accounts, photographs, and dioramas. She stops the video every so often to discuss issues the students either have discussed previously or even missed during their past aqueous media forays. She also passes around a book with Audubon's illustrations of birds in their natural habitats. However, Ms. Rao is interested particularly in challenging the students to scrutinize the methodological or creative processes Ford uses to create his watercolor paintings. We return to the conversation as this point.

"Wait, so Walton Ford paints these amazing watercolors because he thinks the stories they are based on are funny?" asks a perplexed student named Simone.

"I think that is awesome!" Atticus states enthusiastically. "He's like this ridiculously killer watercolor artist who has sick skills but who seems mostly driven by sarcasm, irony, and dark humor."

Trista disagrees, "He seems like a junior high school kid to me, seeking the naughty and dark puns in everything. I like his style, his abilities. The content is just . . . difficult sometimes."

Several hands are raised in response to these last few comments. It appears half the class has strong opinions either in agreement with Atticus or with Trista.

Ms. Rao mediates as a few opinions are expressed simultaneously. "Wow, I'm glad we found something that excites us today! Who would have thought watercolor could be controversial," she says wryly. "Remember that as we discuss contemporary art, we don't always care about whether we think it is good or bad but rather what it might limit or afford. How does it make us see, think, or act differently?"

Trista thanks Ms. Rao for the reminder, "Thank you Ms. Rao. That makes sense, but I guess I just don't appreciate potty humor as much as some people do."

"Point taken, Trista," reassures Ms. Rao. Thank you for your willingness to share your thoughts freely with us. That goes for all of you. You may not like how artists like Ford choose to use their skills or vision in art, or you might love it, but either way, I'm grateful you can respectfully engage in the discourse of art. These educated opinions matter, and you are not the only ones who have differing thoughts about artists and their work. Let's return to Ford's work and his process to see what we can learn. Let's skip the paintings' content for the time being and highlight his approach."

"I thought it was cool how he researched so much," says Gill.

"Oh," agrees Lauren," I know! He went to natural history museums and libraries. It was pretty cool that he would get so carried away with an idea. It seemed like one idea would lead him to another and so on and so on. Remember when he found an old photograph of a dove and those written accounts of those huge flocks of birds that are now extinct! Passenger pigeons, I think? His painting of that fallen branch with so many birds on it is pretty dark but so interesting! I can't believe his watercolors are so huge!"

"I know," recounts Darryn. "It seems impossible that those birds were once one of the most common birds with flocks in the hundreds of millions, and now they are extinct!"

Trista nods in agreement and adds, "I may not love the content of his paintings, but I do see how they mirror some of our current cultural beliefs and practices. Like Lauren, I find it interesting how he was inspired by so many accounts but kept each painting focused on a particular concept."

"Maybe that is why so many of his paintings have notes on them," suggests Allen, "you know, to keep reminding him what really inspired him in the first place."

Ms. Rao is excited about this insight, having read a curator's review of Ford's work, suggesting a very similar insight. "That's a terrific idea, Allen! When we made our dioramas, did any of you keep notes about what you were thinking about at the time?"

Louette, Tasha, Skylar, and Keely all indicate they took some notes in their sketchbooks as they were constructing their small dioramas, also collaging images from photographs, magazines, and books, but after asking the students, it appears that none of them responded to historical narratives like Ford did. They also did not write words on their watercolor paintings like Ford. Ms. Rao listens to all the different ways the students developed their dioramas in preparation to create their paintings and is excited to challenge them to focus on two new responding literacies used in contemporary artistic practice.

"I love hearing about how we prepared to paint our own watercolor paintings. As we learn about how other artists work, it helps us notice the cool things we do on our own, doesn't it? But I for one am inspired by Walton Ford's inquiry process as well as his technical abilities. Our next project will provoke us to try out a few of Walton Ford's strategies. First, we are going to do some historical research, not as historians but as artists. We are going to return to the library, where our current exhibition is taking place, to search for stories and images from the past that may be incredibly interesting and meaningful if brought into our current times. We can focus on irony if that would be a good place to start, but you need not look solely for dark narratives as did Ford. Does that make sense?"

As the students nod, smiles on most of their faces, Ms. Rao continues, "In addition, I want you to look at your finished paintings and find an artist from the past who you can learn from or respond to in a critical way, like

Ford did with Audubon. We will talk about this more in depth later, but the artist you choose undoubtedly will change the meaning of the narrative with which you decide to work."

The bell rings, students begin to gather their backpacks, and Ms. Rao, raising her voice as the students shuffle about, says, "I'll see you all in the library next time we meet!"

UNDERSTANDING THE VISUAL ART LITERACY EVENT

Texts

The texts students engage with in this vignette include traditional print texts such as Ford's writing on his paintings and the assignment to engage with historic narratives in books found within the library. Like the artist presented in this vignette, however, students began to scan historical print texts, not to seek factual information but to find stories that relate to contemporary life in surprising or interesting ways. Therefore, the perception of this traditional print text is different within the visual art disciplinary practice described above.

Likewise, the artworks themselves, the reproductions of both Audubon's illustrations and those shown in the Art21 video about Walton Ford, are texts that can be interpreted and analyzed through semiotics, but this vignette highlights responding through artistic practice as an art maker and critical cultural producer. So, while these images and the video are visual texts, once again, they are not used solely to find information that is complete or fixed but to provoke an artistic response from students.

Contemporary artists do not always create new objects and forms but respond to past and present conversations found in visual culture. These narratives, objects, and images act as complex texts with potential cultural significance. These texts are then recontextualized in our contemporary world perspective as artworks that function as new texts, often holding radically altered meanings and significance to their referents. Walton Ford recontextualizes texts in this way, as described in the vignette above, but artists' projects, like Fred Wilson's *Mining the Museum* (1992) further illustrate how objects and images as texts do not hold meaning in isolation but create dynamic intertexts (Barney, 2013) within cultural contexts. In *Mining the Museum,* Fred Wilson only utilized the objects already in the Maryland Historical Society's collection to create an installation that recontextualized how meaning is made by juxtaposing objects in close proximity to each other and adding title cards.

Students noticed the print texts written on the watercolors, but instead of reading them solely for information, students in Ms. Rao's class read them as part of the artist's methodology or process of responding in the creation of a visual text. Hence, they read them in context of the artistic practice itself.

Processes

Ms. Rao asked the students if they utilized some of the literacy strategies Ford uses as he responded to Audubon and to his own found narratives. She also asked if the students added written texts to their own watercolors, suggesting to them that they might consider doing so if they felt so inclined. The addition of written words in the paintings were analyzed informally in this classroom as a strategy for helping the artist to keep focused on the main concept and perhaps to help the viewer recognize this artistic perspective, but this was only inferred and is not a universal practice in artistic production.

Ms. Rao did not use traditional formal analysis in evaluating Walton Ford's work, as some might interpret the visual arts standard "Apply criteria to evaluate artistic work" (NCCAS, 2014, VA: Re9). She also did not use such a frame to evaluate student work. She did, however, offer an open set of criteria about the quality of an artistic text by stating, "Remember that as we discuss contemporary art, we don't always care about whether we think it is good or bad but rather what it might limit or afford. How does it make us see, think, or act differently?" Hence, a key process she introduced to students was to begin to scrutinize texts within artistic discourse for affordances and limitations rather than good or bad evaluations.

Students learned that Ford creates artworks as responses that carry forward meanings from primary-source texts, in this case from Audubon, along with the additional meanings generated from the historical narratives in the print texts Ford finds to focus his inquiry and artistic vision. Ford remixes key features of these texts to create a new text with new meanings (see Knobel & Lankshear, 2008). Even Audubon did this very thing as an illustrator during the early nineteenth century, but he focused on different features. For example, Audubon did not simply document birds in their natural habitats, but he also collected specimens and constructed his own dioramas as a naturalist, based of course off of his own ideologies and those available to him at the time. His artistic responses, the texts he generated, were imbued with the perspectives and discourses of his cultural and historical context. This is an important process the students are beginning to engage in with Ms. Rao.

Literacies

Researching like an artist is a significant literacy that Ms. Rao offers to her students. She states, "First, we are going to do some historical research, not as historians (see Nokes, 2013), but as artists." Ford relishes the irony and expanding the actual stories he discovers with possible narratives through visual metaphor, utilizing a wide range of image-making strategies. He draws on history and information but elaborates to create potential meaning. His informational search with historical writing is not for fact gathering for general understanding and recall but to elaborate an aesthetic sense of being in the world. Ford responds to Audubon by suggesting what a modern-day naturalist might look like if keeping with the style of Audubon. He responds artistically to narratives and images as potential visual textual fodder. He attempts to connect the viewer to past ideologies and perspectives while asking them to scrutinize their own in relation to his creations. He asks readers of these newly created visual texts to ponder the intellectual, humorous, and aesthetic repositioning of media, process, style, subject matter, and narrative. Such an experiential potentiality (O'Donoghue, 2015) is also a key process students are initiating in this literacy event.

Ms. Rao will of course have much to discuss as she continues her lesson with her students, but Walton Ford's example about what an artist reads as text, how an artist reads a text, and likewise, how and what an artist writes as text helps us as we engage with literacy in relation to responding. As the students begin their search, attempting to respond to print texts, she will need to recall the authentic literacies artists use to engage with such texts. This is a daunting task if curator and art scholar Linda Weintraub (2003) is correct in her assertion, claiming "the quantity of inspirational sources made available to contemporary artists is mind-boggling. In fact, it includes the entirety of recorded human experience" (p. 122). Students in Ms. Rao's class will not simply read the words found in texts. Nor will they be searching for facts or even seeking some predetermined understanding, but they will be looking for aesthetically moving passages and relevant imagery and image-making strategies. They are looking to be surprised. They are looking to expand the possible as responding is not a passive event that analyzes fixed meaning but active and generative in the creative processes of the visual arts.

REFERENCES

Barney, D. T. (2013). Interlude: What saved me. *Multi-Disciplinary Research in the Arts: Special Issue on A/r/tography and the Arts, 3*(1), 1–13.

Buford, B. (2009). *Walton Ford: Pancha tantra*. Cologne, Germany: Taschen.

Carter, Y. G. (2011). Sociopolitical consciousness and multiple perspectives: Empowering students to read the world. In R. Powell & E. C. Rightmyer (Eds.), *Literacy for all students: An instructional framework for closing the gap* (pp. 233–257). New York, NY: Routledge.

Chung, S. (2005). Media/visual literacy art education: Cigarette as deconstruction. *Art Education, 58*(3), 19–24.

Duncum, P. (2002). Visual culture art education: Why, what and how. *Journal of Art and Design Education, 21*(1), 14–23.

Duncum, P. (2003). The theories and practices of visual culture in art education. *Art Education Policy Review, 105*(2), 19–25.

Duncum, P. (2004). Visual culture isn't just visual: Multiliteracy, multimodality and meaning. *Studies in Art Education, 45*(3), 252–264.

Duncum, P. (2009a). Thinking critically about critical thinking: Toward a post-critical, dialogic pedagogy for popular visual culture. *International Journal of Education through Art, 4*(3), 247–257.

Duncum, P. (2009b). Visual culture in art education, circa 2009. *Visual Arts Research,* 35(1), 64–75.
Freedman, K. (2003). *Teaching visual culture: Curriculum, aesthetics and the social life of art.* Reston, VA: National Art Education Association.
Knobel, M., & Lankshear, C. (2008). Remix: The art and craft of endless hybridization. *The Journal of Adolescent & Adult Literacy,* 52(1), 22–33.
Maniaci, K., & Chandler-Olcott, K. (2010). "Still building that idea": Preservice art educators' perspectives on integrating literacy across the curriculum. *International Journal of Education & the Arts,* 11(4), 1–41.
National Core Arts Standards. (2014). *Visual arts standards.* Retrieved from http://www.nationalartsstandards.org/sites/default/files/Visual%20Arts%20at%20a%20Glance%20rev.pdf
National Coalition for Core Arts Standards (2014). *National Core Arts Standards Dance: Responding.* Online at http://www.nationalartsstandards.org/
Nokes, J.D. (2013). *Building students' historical literacies: Learning to read and reason with historical texts and evidence.* New York, NY: Routledge.
O'Brien, D.G., Stewart, R.A., & Moje, E. (1995). Why content literacy is difficult to infuse into the secondary school: Complexities of curriculum, pedagogy and school culture. *Reading Research Quarterly,* 30(3), 442–463.
O'Donoghue, D. (2015). The turn to experience in contemporary art: A potentiality for thinking art education differently. *Studies in Art Education,* 56(2), 103–113.
Smith-Shank, D.L. (2004). *Semiotics and visual culture: Sights, signs and significance.* Reston, VA: National Art Education Association.
Weintraub, L. (2003). *In the making: Creative options for contemporary art.* New York, NY: Distributed Art Publishers.

18 Visual Arts in the Elementary Classroom
Responding

Jennifer J. Wimmer and Daniel T. Barney

Young children are inquisitive beings, and they need opportunities to respond to significant issues such as poverty, social justice, and environmental concerns. The visual arts allow students access to complex ideas and issues because students are able to view and analyze images based on their ideas and experiences rather than their ability to read print-based texts. We argue in this chapter that students' engagement with the visual arts as creators, viewers, and responders provides opportunities for students to think about and engage in conversations about participation, including issues of access and voice.

Responding is not a passive activity; it involves more than simply liking or disliking a piece of art. Responding involves perceiving, analyzing, and interpreting artworks based on personal experiences (NCAS, 2014, VA: Re7.1). While responding may take the form of a written response, classroom discussion, creation of a new artwork, or a combination of forms, the form of response is not as important as the students' thoughts, questions, and connections to the artwork. The artwork plays a key role in the response activity; therefore, it is important that teachers carefully select works of art that invite thoughtful reflection and encourage meaningful discussion. In this chapter we are interested in helping students think about art as participation. As a result, we focus on socially engaged art. This form of visual arts transforms time and space, invites others to engage, requires thoughtful interaction, and promotes others to act.

As students create and respond to works of art, they develop and utilize literacies that encourage them to ask questions and seek answers to better participate in their lives. The visual arts, and particularly socially engaged art, provide a space for engaging in critical literacies and specifically in thinking about issues of privilege and injustice (Vasquez, 2004). Indeed, participation in socially engaged art necessitates critical literacies because one of the goals of socially engaged art is to help students become "more imaginative, open-minded, critically-thinking and responsible citizens" (Naidus, 2004, p. 207). When students have opportunities to participate in responding to artistic practices within this art form, they can develop literacies that will increase their cultural understanding and personal engagement with the world. Specifically, it provides opportunities for students to ask and ponder important questions about who is invited to participate and who is left out.

In the following vignette a fourth-grade teacher carefully guides her students through the process of creating an artistic response to a socially engaged piece of art. Miss Shaw creates a space for students to reflect about the purpose of art, to think about what it means to respond to a work of art, and to begin to create an artistic response. Throughout the learning activity the teacher and students engage in important discussions about issues of access and voice as they select a location for their artistic response.

Miss Shaw and her fourth-grade class just finished watching a TED Talk given by the artist, designer, and urban planner Candy Chang (2012). Chang believed she could improve the community in which she lived by encouraging introspection and providing a space to make collective wisdom visible. In this talk, she focuses on one particular work that was a response to having lost someone very close to her. She transformed an abandoned house in her New Orleans neighborhood by painting a side of the house with chalkboard paint, stenciling the question, "Before I Die . . . _____," and leaving chalk in baskets attached to the house. Within a day, the entire side of the house was filled with responses to her question. A few of the responses include, "Before I die, I want to sing for millions," and "Before I die, I want to hold her one more time," and "Before I die, I want to be completely myself." Candy states, "This neglected space became a constructive one, and people's hopes and dreams made me laugh out loud, tear up, and they consoled me during my own tough times. It's about knowing you're not alone. It's about understanding our neighbors in new and enlightening ways. It's about making space for reflection and contemplation, and remembering what really matters most to us as we grow and change."

Miss Shaw and her students discussed Candy Chang's talk in relation to her work as a socially engaged artist. They talked about her beliefs about what art can and should do as well as the particular approach to the work titled "Before I Die," including the medium, process, context, concept, and form. Miss Shaw and her students connected this work to other works they have seen in past classes. They also talked about what kinds of responses they might have added to such a wall in their own neighborhoods.

Following this discussion, Miss Shaw directed the students to think about the artwork as a whole. Then the students were tasked with responding to Candy Chang's work. Interpreting responding as writing, several of the students retrieved their field notebooks from their desks. However, Miss Shaw informed them that responding could take on many different forms, and while a written response was one way, the students would be creating an artistic response to Candy Chang's work. As a result, instead of simply recreating this work in their own community, like others have done, Miss Shaw encouraged her class to create a new response while keeping Chang's methods in mind. Following a great deal of discussion, Miss Shaw's students decided to create a similar wall, using a question to incite introspection from their own community, where they can aggregate the wisdom of those around them. After quite an engaging discussion, the class is excited to ask, "Even though I haven't entirely grown up, I can still . . . _____."

We enter the discussion at this point:

Miss Shaw proudly states, "I am so impressed with this question. It assumes that anyone who stops to respond in writing will consider themselves still in the process of growing."

"Some grown-ups might participate, but I want to tell everyone what I can do," says nine-year-old Bruno.

"That's an interesting point, Bruno," says Miss Shaw, "but did Candy Chang answer her own question?"

Cynthia quickly shouts, "No, she did NOT!"

Amber agrees, "No!" Then adds, "But does that matter? Maybe our project can be different? Maybe we can add our own answers to our question we made up."

"Where should we do this project?" questions Miss Shaw.

"We could do it on our classroom blackboard, Miss Shaw," offers Miranda.

"Nobody would see it! Well, except for the custodians after we all leave when school's out," replies Josefina. "That wouldn't be a very good project."

"Why wouldn't it be a very good project if nobody saw it, Josefina?" asks Miss Shaw.

"Candy Chang had, like, her whole community responding to her artwork. We would write our own responses, but we'd only find out what the custodian thought. I'd like to have more people involved. That's all," Josefina responds.

"Well, I think you are understanding that context, place, and time matters in this type of artistic practice," responds Miss Shaw. "If we are creating an artistic response similar to Candy Chang's, then it is important that we think about who has access to our artwork. Maybe we should give some thoughtful consideration as to how and where to best present our work. Should we go on a search for a meaningful location? Keep in mind that we need to find a place to create our response that allows as many people as possible to contribute to our work of art. You know what? Everyone grab your field notebooks. Let's go find a spot to do this thing!"

Miss Shaw and her students leave their classroom in search of a site for their art project carrying their field notebooks, which they use to take notes, create thumbnail sketches, and create reflective responses to daily prompts.

"Miss Shaw," Nnamdi says, "we could just do our project right here outside of our classroom on the wall. We sometimes hang our other projects in the hall for people to see."

"Yeah," agrees Sarah. "That would be super easy. We could use black butcher paper and white chalk."

"Those are good ideas," encourages Miss Shaw. "Who would likely answer our question if we put a sign up right here?"

Visual Art in the Elementary Classroom 151

"Some of my friends in other classes," replies Jenni.

"Maybe some teachers," suggests Frederick.

Miss Shaw nods, saying, "Alright, let's jot down some of those ideas in our field notebooks before we scout out other possible locations."

Miss Shaw notices students are drawing sketches of the possible location, while others are listing pros and cons. Miss Shaw encourages the students to think about providing as many people as possible with access to their artwork. Once students have had a few minutes to take notes, they move on to their next location.

Upon arriving at the cafeteria, several students are excited about the space.

Sara is first to state, "This would be perfect! We could paint the wall right here with blackboard paint, and people who finish their lunches can respond to our question."

Dillon agrees, "Yeah, and everyone would see it because we all have to eat!"

"Excellent ideas. Let's remember what this spot has to offer too," states Miss Shaw.

Miss Shaw encourages the students to think about materials, placement, and access. The students jot down some ideas in their field notebooks, and then everyone walks to the front entrance of the school.

"Here's another place that might be an option," suggests Miss Shaw.

"Well, some of our parents pick us up here, and we all walk in through these doors," adds Annabelle.

Frederick is hesitant, but offers, "I like how our parents can be involved, but I don't think as many students would add to our artwork as they would in the cafeteria."

Miss Shaw agrees, stating, "That's an interesting insight, Frederick. It is important for us to think about who we want to participate in our work. A lot of thought sure goes into selecting the right place for a socially engaged art project. This experience helps us better understand the process Candy Chang went through as she prepared to share her art."

Miss Shaw and her students continue around the schoolyard, discussing media selection, size of the work, and a variety of methods in which an audience participant might be encouraged to leave a response. They also talk about possible off-school sites in their own community along with the potentials and limits of each of these artistic choices.

UNDERSTANDING THE VISUAL ARTS LITERACY EVENT

The above vignette explored how socially engaged art provided the teacher and students with opportunities to respond to works of art while attending to issues of participation and artistic method. Additionally, the vignette highlighted the crucial role teachers play in planning and guiding students through a learning activity. Miss Shaw carefully crafted a lesson that wove together artistic texts, processes, and literacies that encouraged students' careful consideration of ideas. Each of these key components will be detailed below.

Text

As the students engaged in creating an artistic response, they interacted with a variety of texts made up of various semiotic systems such as film, language, and space (New London Group, 2000). The video served as a key text throughout the vignette. The video provided students with access to Candy Chang as an artist. Additionally, the video allowed students to see her, listen to her experiences, and finally view her artwork. While the entire video assisted students in understanding socially engaged art, Miss Shaw directed the students to think about the artwork in particular. The students and teacher reflected on this video throughout the learning activity to ensure that they were using appropriate methods and meeting the goals of socially engaged art. For example, early in the vignette, the students were discussing who would respond to their artwork, and Miss Shaw asked the students to recall if Candy Chang had responded to her own question. The artwork as a text was crucial to the students' understanding of art and to their development as socially engaged artists.

Other key texts included the school building and the class discussions. The space of the school building became an increasingly important text throughout the learning activity. It is important to note that the school building was not a new space for the students. By fourth grade, the students had walked the halls and were very familiar with the space. However, given the purpose of locating a place to share their artistic response, the school building became an unfamiliar text that they had to learn how to read. As the students moved from space to space, discussing ideas and taking notes, they quickly came to realize that the different spaces afforded different things. For example, the lunchroom provided access to all students but prevented adult participation. Miss Shaw was careful to ask thoughtful questions that prompted further thinking and questioning by the students. During the conversations, students had opportunities to jot down ideas, questions, and images. It is important to note that the notebook was not used as a response in and of itself; rather, the notebook served as a place to gather ideas. These texts were crucial for creating dialog and moving the creation of the artistic response forward.

Processes

As the students created their artistic response to Candy Chang's socially engaged artwork, they participated in two responding processes, which included sharing and analysis. Miss Shaw was aware that her students' thinking and sharing of ideas and questions were crucial to their understanding of socially engaged art. As a result, Miss Shaw did not dominate the students' conversations as they sought out a space for their artistic response; rather, she asked clarifying questions that encouraged and opened opportunities for students to grapple with the ideas put forth by Ms. Chang as well as those shared by classmates. This type of sharing is supported by the National Core Arts Standards for Visual Arts. For example, an Enduring Understanding listed under responding states, "Individual aesthetic and empathetic awareness developed through engagement with art can lead to understanding and appreciation of self, others, the natural world, and constructed environments" (NCAS, 2014, VA: Re7.1). Because Miss Shaw positioned the students as creators and active participants in the development of knowledge and ideas, they had opportunities to learn from one another while thinking about their school and community.

Students also had opportunities to analyze and discuss Ms. Chang's work as they viewed the video with an emphasis on her artistic methods, which included the medium, form, and concept. The students also had the difficult task of simultaneously responding to Ms. Chang's work while considering the potential responses of others to their artwork. For example, as they focused on Candy Chang's artwork, the students were able to analyze and discuss how her artistic methods helped convey her intended message (NCAS, 2014, VA: Re7.2.4). And then as the students began the process of creating their artistic response to this socially engaged artwork, Miss Shaw encouraged them to move beyond a simple reproduction of Candy Chang's work and to create a response that was relevant to their lives as students and community members. Through the video and class discussion, the students came to realize that socially engaged art is activated through audience participation. Therefore, as they analyzed the school space, their conversations centered on issues of participation. While they could not know for certain who would participate in their artistic response, they were aware that providing the potential to participate was crucial to their artwork.

Literacies

Creating an artistic response to Candy Chang's socially engaged artwork required the students to develop and use literacies that provided them with greater access to the world. For example, the students developed literacies that allowed them to read and analyze the various texts for issues related to access, prejudice, and privilege. Specifically, the students had opportunities to think about the importance of time and space as a means for providing voice to their community members. As students engage in learning literacies, it is important that they learn that literacy is powerful and should be viewed as "a means to broader human agency and individual and collective action" (Luke, 2012, p. 6). The students in this vignette came to realize that as creators of their artistic response, issues surrounding participation, including access and voice, had to be thoughtfully considered and addressed.

It is important to note the critical role of the teacher in creating opportunities to develop and utilize critical literacies. Miss Shaw created a space for the students to engage in critical literacies as they observed, questioned, and responded to Candy Chang's art. At first glance, it may seem that the statements made or questions asked by Miss Shaw were very simple. For example, she stated, "If we are creating an artistic response similar to Candy Chang's, then it is important that we think about who has access to our artwork." In another instance, Miss Shaw questioned, "Who would likely answer our question if we put a sign up right here?" These types of statements and questions invited the students to think about complex issues of access and specifically about who would and would not have opportunities to participate in their artistic response.

CONCLUSIONS

Traditionally, elementary students' participation in the visual arts has focused on creating an interesting-looking product that can be hung in the hall and taken home to be attached to a refrigerator. This notion of the arts eclipses students' abilities "to see the arts as a significant contribution to their lives" (Gude, 2007, p. 6). As evidenced in this chapter, young children are capable of participating in the arts in meaningful ways. With guidance from the teacher, students are able to gain access to complex ideas through responding to art. Furthermore, as young children develop as artists, they need to understand that the visual arts impact the personal and public lives of themselves and others.

REFERENCES

Chang, C. (2012). *Before I die I want to . . .* [Video file]. Retrieved from https://www.ted.com/talks/candy_chang_before_i_die_i_want_to

Gude, O. (2007). Principles of possibility: Considerations for a 21st-century art & culture curriculum. *Art Education, 60*(1), 6–17.

Luke, A. (2012). Critical literacy: Foundational notes. *Theory into Practice, 51*, 4–11.

Naidus, B. (2004). Outside the frame: Teaching a socially engaged art practice. In M. Miles (Ed.), *New practices new pedagogies: A reader* (pp. 191–208). New York, NY: Taylor & Francis.

National Core Arts Standards. (2014). *Visual arts.* Retrieved from http://www.nationalartsstandards.org/sites/default/files/Visual%20Arts%20at%20a%20Glance%20rev.pdf

New London Group. (2000). A pedagogy of multiliteracies: Designing social futures. In B. Cope & M. Kalantzis (Eds.), *Multiliteracies: Literacy learning and the design of social futures* (pp. 9–37). New York: Routledge.

Vasquez, V. M. (2004). *Negotiating critical literacies with young children.* Mahwah, NJ: Lawrence Erlbaum Associates.

Section IV
Connecting

19 Music
Connecting

Paul Broomhead

A common characteristic of many chapters in this book is the focus on interactions with texts as *participating in* the disciplines in contrast with the notion of *learning about* the disciplines. In music, the creating, performing, and responding processes clearly are rooted in participation in music. On its face, the connecting process in music may seem to point to the act of thinking *about* and forming conceptual meanings *about* music. Indeed, countless traditional language texts present information about music, including books and articles about music history, harmonic theory, music philosophy, world music genres, music psychology and philosophy, and so on. One could spend a lifetime accumulating information only about music from these traditional texts. And meanings made in this way can be deep and significant as insights regarding motivations of composers, beauty of formal craftsmanship, influences of music on historical events, and so forth bring fascination and enlightenment in themselves.

But connecting during participation is the focus of the National Core Music Standards, which include two connecting standards for music. The first relates the concepts clearly: "Synthesize and relate knowledge and personal experiences to *make music*" (NCCAS, 2014, MU: Cn10-E, emphasis added). The second standard, "Relate musical ideas and works to varied contexts and daily life to deepen understanding," does not appear to insist upon participation until the accompanying "enduring understanding" is joined with it: "understanding connections to varied contexts and daily life *enhances musicians' creating, performing, and responding*" (NCCAS, 2014, MU: Cn11-E, emphasis added). Music students need to connect music to their daily contexts outside the music classroom so that they can then apply these understandings to improved music making.

I experience some discomfort with the notion that all goals of music literacy should be realizable through music making—as if meaning cannot be musical if music is not directly present or as if meaning made through music is not significant if it is not strictly musical. This is clearly not the case as potential meanings from music include feelings, attitudes, insights, actions, and so on that may be applied outside of music. Music may be significant, for example, in its power to buoy a person up at a time of discouragement, strengthen one's resolve to endure an affliction, help an individual to understand and develop self-identity, stabilize one's sense of well-being, contribute to experiencing and expressing spirituality, and so on (Minichiello, 2005). Whether or not these meanings make a person a better musician seems somehow superfluous compared to the immediate influence they have in one's life. They are fully realized before any return to music participation, and their significance is not diminished because the meaning was not strictly musical in nature.

Having expressed this concern, however, I feel that music educators are obligated to focus on interaction with music itself and the literacies needed to make meaning. Because music teachers are trained in music but not in psychology, therapy, or some other extramusical field, I feel responsibility requires us to keep our focus primarily on effective participation in music. After all, higher levels of literacy result in enhanced meaning, whether that meaning is fundamentally musical or not. We recognize and honor extramusical meanings and do our best to prepare students to interact with music in ways that maximize *all* kinds of meaning, but I suggest that music teachers focus primarily on goals that can be manifest through musical participation rather than on how effectively students may manage their emotions and other extramusical goals. Thus without denying or turning away from such meanings, we leave psychology to psychologists and so forth.

I propose that connecting in musical interactions be understood as the process of negotiating and creating music texts for meaning using reason, comparison, association, inquiry, analysis, and other mental and emotional activities. Musical interactions where connecting is the foreground process indeed often will be *about* music and not necessarily musical in themselves. But connecting can be musical as it is nurtured in moments of participation. The processes clearly have been shown to be interwoven in music with one or more processes in the foreground and others in the background. Position in the foreground need not necessarily be stable. Thus a student may be performing and focusing on intonation one moment, a performing literacy, and then switch to unifying his/her timing with others just a moment later, a listening literacy. Similarly the performer could reflect on the relationship between the sounds he/she is making and the occasion of the performance, perhaps a funeral, and suddenly the connecting process takes the foreground. When this occurs, we may expect not only that the performer makes meaning as a thinker and feeler but also that the performance itself is impacted—hopefully improved.

While I continue to celebrate all musical connecting, including connections that involve the study of music history, theory, cultural studies, psychology research, philosophy, and so forth, in this chapter I wish to call special attention to connecting focused on participation in music. In the literacy event described, the music educator's goal is to trigger moments frequently where the connecting process takes the foreground during performance participation—even if only for a few moments—and the performance improves as a result of the meaning made through the connecting process.

Mr. Besenkopf's orchestra is playing the second movement of the Surprise Symphony by Franz Joseph Haydn. Participants have pretty much learned the notes and rhythms and have a few weeks to refine it and make it special for their festival. Of course, what Mr. Besenkopf is really after is more than a great rating at competitions; he wants students to have meaningful experiences with music. He has found that the more connections students make to and within the music, the more meaningful it is to them. As a bonus, it also sounds better.

Mr. Besenkopf says, "We've got the notes and rhythms basically learned; now it's time for this piece to come alive inside and out. By inside, I mean inside of you. By outside, I mean what it sounds like out here in the external world." He's talking a bit above some of their heads, so he rephrases. "Basically, you are now going to figure out how to connect this music to your personal lives and learn to love it. Then it's going to sound better; mainly it will be more expressive." Instruments propped on their laps, students wait for the assignment they can tell Mr. Besenkopf is about to give them.

"This is what you're going to do. Look up Franz Joseph Haydn on Wikipedia and read the following three sections: "Early Life," "Struggles as a Freelancer," and "The Years as Kapellmeister." I have here three things for you to complete by Friday." Mr. Besenkopf displays the assignment prompts to accompany the reading.

1. Assemble a list of three of Haydn's personal characteristics.
2. Identify at least one similarity between Haydn's childhood and your childhood.
3. Identify one connection you see between Haydn's personal characteristics and the musical characteristics in the Surprise Symphony.

After reading through and clarifying each prompt, Mr. Besenkopf says, "Remember that the goal is for you to connect to this music. If you find an aspect of Haydn's life that interests you, dig deeper in your reading, and focus on that element."

On Friday, students turn in their assignments, and with a big smile, Mr. Besenkopf says, "Prepare to tell me a personal characteristic of Haydn that you found most interesting. I'm going to choose students randomly to tell me that one thing. Jake, you're first."

Jake responds, "Uh . . . He, like, had a sense of humor?"

Mr. Besenkopf asks, "What makes you say that?"

Jake gives a knowing grin and says—not without sarcasm—"Well, he wrote the Surprise Symphony designed to make people jump out of their seats."

Mr. Besenkopf smiles and says, "Oh, I bet you think you just took care of all our business, huh?" (Polite laughter trickles from the students.) To the class, he says, "Yeah, can anyone remember the name of his first opera?" Several call out, "The Limping Devil."

"Yep. Sounds like a funny show to me, but maybe it was a little extreme in those days; it actually got shut down by censors! Okay. Raise your hand if sense of humor *was one of the three characteristics you wrote down.*" A bunch of hands go up. "Okay," says Mr. Besenkopf, "we're gonna keep going. Andrea?"

Andrea responds, "I thought it was cool how he took care of his wife her whole life even though they were separated and they never loved each other. He seemed kindhearted."

"Okay. Good. How many of you wrote something like kindness *as one of your three?*" asks Mr. Besenkopf. Again several hands are raised.

The discussion continues similarly for a few minutes, and students comment on the absence of parental love during Haydn's childhood and the independence he had to assume from an early age. Mr. Besenkopf goes to the next prompt. "Mark, if it's not too personal, will you tell the class a similarity between your childhood and Haydn's childhood?"

Mark says, "Yeah. Um . . . well, he got in trouble for snipping off some girl's pigtail. And I . . . well, I'm not gonna say—let's just say that I can relate." Mark and his classmates all laugh together.

"All right, we'll leave that alone," says Mr. Besenkopf. "Who else is willing to share a similarity?"

Allison raises her hand. "Even though he loved to have fun, he still took his talents very seriously and didn't think that just 'cause he was young, he couldn't do it. I mean, he had to be independent and support himself when he was sixteen. Like, we all have to practice a lot on our instruments while our friends are just messin' around, and it's not like we don't feel like just hanging out and whatever, but we got work to do, and if everyone else wants to just sit around and—"

"Whoa, whoa—okay, we get it," Mr. Besenkopf interrupts teasingly. "That's a great insight, Allison." Two others share similarities between Haydn's childhood and theirs.

Mr. Besenkopf comments, "You know, you have brought out some rich information about a man who seems to have known the dark side of life but still chose to be a little lighthearted about it. Now let's take a look at how this might help us approach his music. Let's hear from Maurie about the third prompt. What connection did you see between Haydn's life and the music we are playing from the Surprise Symphony?

"This was hard," Maurie admits, "but I guess now I see the whole second movement as kind of funny. Yes, there's the famous big chord that surprises people, but the rest of the movement carries that humor with it even though it is so gentle and soft on the surface."

"Great! Let's pursue this a bit. How would you play this if you thought of the whole movement as part of the joke and not just the one chord?" Maurie does not have an immediate response, but Jonnie's hand pops up.

"This piece is just so . . . [she hesitates, looking for the right word] . . . PROPER. It's simple, elegant, and very formal sounding. To have that joke in it gives it almost a silly lightness. It's like you want to exaggerate the lightness and make it overly clean and stuff to bring out the irony."

Mr. Besenkopf is smiling and nodding so hard that he looks like a bobblehead doll. "Yeah! Yeah! This stuff is happening in the late 1700s. It is fun for me to picture a room full of stuffy aristocrats listening to their composer's latest symphony, and then just jumping out of their seats, and then maybe laughing at themselves a little bit, and enjoying the humor of it for the rest of the movement, while the music continues to be so formal and, as Jonnie said, 'proper.' So how exactly will our playing be different with all of this in mind? Jonnie already mentioned light and clean. How do we make this happen?"

Marcie immediately lifts her bow to answer. "We need to keep the weight of the bow on the strings super light."

"Good," says Mr. Besenkopf.

Darla adds, "And we have to stay relaxed and not rushed, or it will all be messy and not clean."

Mr. Besenkopf responds, "These are great ideas. Let's try this."

They begin. Mr. Besenkopf conducts with a comically straight face and very detached, light movements. After several measures of playing, Mr. Besenkopf stops the group and says, "It is so fun to hear the lightness in your playing. I was noticing how Jake used super light bow strokes, but his wrist was still flexible and relaxed. Let's all do that." They play again. Mr. Besenkopf stops again. "Now check your bow hand for stiff fingers, and relax the tempo. I can hear Haydn saying, 'Loosen up.'"

After a few more measures, Mr. Besenkopf stops one more time. "Yes! Now I can hear how each of the separate notes almost vanishes as you start light and take the weight off of the strings. This is awesome. Let's play the whole piece now, and enjoy the joke the whole time." They play. "My gosh!" exclaims Mr. Besenkopf. "Our stylizations just absolutely transformed. It's almost like the joke is on US—that we just thought this was regular music before. Now we get it. Way to go!"

UNDERSTANDING THE MUSIC CONNECTING LITERACY EVENT

Connecting in music can be any kind of insight involving music and can take place during any activity. The event described above takes place in an orchestra ensemble, a setting where the teacher can have students make connections and then realize them through performance. While significant connecting is not necessarily demonstrated or demonstrable by any outward change of behavior, when the connecting process can come into the foreground while other processes are otherwise dominant (such as when students are performing), the connecting is more musical than at other times, such as when students are simply reading a language text.

Text

The primary text in this vignette is the second movement of the *Surprise Symphony*, even though students do not directly interact with it until the very end of the instructional event. The students interact with this text indirectly as they attend to the language texts found on Wikipedia, to their fellow students' comments, and to Mr. Besenkopf's gestures as he conducts. So although attention to these other texts is the direct activity for the students, they understand that all of these interactions will inform their negotiation of the piece they are performing.

One of the ways Mr. Besenkopf brings connecting processes to the foreground is to utilize traditional language texts such as the Wikipedia site and the written assignment prompts. It is fair to say that connecting is the only type of interaction with music that significantly involves such language texts.

The other students' comments comprise an important text in this activity. Witnessing (negotiating) the insights of others and contributing (creating) through comments stimulate the conceptual activity of the students as they compare their understandings with those of others. As mentioned, these interactions with text are given focus and purpose by the indirect presence of the symphony movement and the possible connections between it and the discussion.

Texts that are musical in nature include the instruments the students are playing and the musical score they are reading, but perhaps more significant are the conducting gestures of Mr. Besenkopf. He is able to execute gestures that to a large extent capture the insights of the students and convert them to musical form. Students complete the connection by combining their understanding of his conducting with their own insights, enacting the musical results on their instruments. These musical texts inform students' negotiations and creations within the central text of the symphony movement.

Processes

While this literacy event features instruction in which connecting is purposefully drawn into the foreground, it substantially involves performing and to an extent includes creating. During the initial foray into language texts (the assignment prompts and Wikipedia), connecting is essentially unaccompanied by the other processes. The connecting process remains dominant as students engage in discussion with Mr. Besenkopf.

Then as students are asked to analyze connections between Haydn's life and his music and to apply these insights to their performance, the performing process becomes dominant in the foreground. Still Mr. Besenkopf is determined to keep connecting near the foreground during the performance as he incorporates a constant string of visual reminders of the discussion into his facial expressions and light, detached conducting gestures.

Creating processes are subtly involved in this instruction as students must imagine what a joke might sound like in classical music. They have visual stimulation from Mr. Besenkopf's conducting, but their creativity is crucial even in interpreting the conducting, let alone incorporating the variety of insights they have gained from their reading and from the class discussion.

Literacies

The primary literacies addressed by Mr. Besenkopf in this instructional literacy event include (1) the ability to gather historical information and connect it to one's own life and (2) the ability to incorporate conceptual insights into creating and performing. The ability to make connections to students' personal lives is nurtured by Mr. Besenkopf's second prompt: "Identify at least one similarity between Haydn's childhood and your childhood." Mr. Besenkopf shows sensitivity to students' existing literacies by highlighting aspects of Haydn's life and work to which students may easily relate, given their life experiences outside of music.

The ability to incorporate insights into creating and performing is nurtured in two ways. First, Mr. Besenkopf requires students to engage in imagining as he includes the third assignment prompt: "Identify one connection you see between Haydn's personal characteristics and musical characteristics in the *Surprise Symphony*." Second, he immediately incorporates an opportunity for students to experiment musically with the task while providing support through conducting and feedback. This pattern of first imagining and then applying is a staple in Mr. Besenkopf's literacy strategies.

CONCLUSIONS

Music teachers are and should be interested in all kinds of meaning in students' lives—not just musical meanings. Musical experiences may connect to any kind of life meaning or musical meaning. It is not overstepping his/her boundaries for a music teacher to provide interactions with music that he/she predicts will have positive meaning in students' lives. However, I suggest that music teachers' training and expertise give them the mandate to guide musical interactions but not to predetermine and orchestrate extramusical meanings. Therefore, connecting-oriented instructional strategies should target music participation as the most common arena for the realization of connecting meanings, with the realization that there may be personal connections that are not naturally part of music participation but may be of equal value to the student. Thus we see gradations of the musical nature of connecting meaning. Students in Mr. Besenkopf's orchestra explore similarities between a composer's life and their lives; this is musical only in that Haydn was a composer and that one of his works is among their concert literature. Their connecting becomes clearly musical when these connections become part of their music performance and impact it. What Mr. Besenkopf models is (1) choosing rich texts for students to negotiate and create, (2) then guiding students to make a broad array of personal and musical connections, and (3) finally requiring students to apply connections during musical participation—in this case, performance.

REFERENCES

Minichiello, V. (2005). The meaning of music in the lives of older people: A qualitative study. *Psychology of Music, 33*(4), 437–451. Retrieved from http://search.proquest.com/docview/1339521?accountid=4488

NCCAS. (2014). *MU:Cn10,11-E.* Retrieved from http://musiced.nafme.org/files/2014/06/Core-Music-Standards-Ensemble-Strand1.pdf

20 Dance
Connecting
Pamela S. Musil

The National Core Arts Standards for Dance state, "To be literate in the arts, students need specific knowledge and skills . . . to a degree that allows for fluency and deep understanding. In dance, this means discovering the expressive elements of dance; knowing the terminology that is used to comprehend dance; having a clear sense of embodying dance; and being able to reflect, critique, and connect personal experience to dance" (2014, Introduction: Dance). In the preceding chapters, the first three of these fluencies have been explored and unpacked through specific lenses that have provided means for understanding and magnifying each artistic process of creating, performing and responding. In this chapter, the final anchor standard of connecting becomes central as we explore what it means "to reflect, critique, and connect personal experience to dance" in ways that consider "other contexts of meaning or knowledge" (NCCAS, 2014, Introduction: Dance).

One mode of connecting dance to other contexts is to explore and view dance through its social and cultural lenses. The ability to recognize, understand, discuss, and empathize with social and cultural experiences different than our own is an important social literacy that can be developed within the dance classroom, particularly when teachers make informed efforts to ensure diverse content within their curricular plans. This chapter explores the process of connecting through issues of diversity and the marginalization of diversity, namely, culture, race, and privilege. Though these issues permeate educational discourse and are important considerations within any classroom, they sometimes remain unquestioned in traditionalist dance classrooms despite abundant literature calling for critical examination and change (Dixon Gottschild, 2003, 2005; Kerr-Berry, 2004, 2010, 2012; West, 2005). Speaking of the systemic marginalization in American dance education that privileges Eurocentric dance forms such as ballet and modern dance, Kerr-Berry (2010) asserts that power thrives in institutional structures and "without a balance of power, inequities abound and the marginalization of people and their perspectives persist" (p. 3).

Dance educators need to ensure that the curricula they choose for the classroom avoids marginalization by exploring culturally diverse perspectives, but they also must be sensitive to the risks. For example, efforts toward diversity may risk superficiality and tokenism if not addressed with sensitivity to the individual. MacBean (2014) warns against relating the idea of diversity to groups of people with particular core identifiers (such as gender, race, socioeconomics, etc.) and promotes focusing instead on individuals, where diversity is viewed as a way of being rather than as a label.

Dance educators who make efforts to emphasize individuality as a central component of cultural identity do so partially by exploring dance through various lenses that promote contextual meanings. Context often is understood through social, political, cultural, historical, or community lenses, which serve to deepen and broaden understanding and empathy for individuals with backgrounds that are different than our own. The National Core Dance Standards assert that "[a]s dance is experienced, all personal experiences, knowledge, and contexts are integrated and synthesized to interpret meaning." Further, the essential question, "How does knowing about societal, cultural, historical and community experiences expand dance literacy?" (NCCAS, 2014, DA:Cn10.1) invites educators to consider the importance of these contexts in building dance literacies. Dance educators who neglect to do so risk the engenderment of contextually illiterate dancers—a condition that can happen in spite of an abundance of technical skill. That is, dancers with a lifetime of training are contextually illiterate if they remain ignorant of circumstantial factors that influence a work or a body of work within which they are immersed. Thus, it is the dance educator's responsibility to ensure that backgrounds and frameworks are addressed in culturally responsive curricula that engage students in experiencing and analyzing dance through lenses that consider the "perspectives of the peoples from which the dances originate" (NCCAS, 2014, DA:Cn11.1).

In the following vignette, Mrs. O'Hara, a middle-aged, middle-class, white dance educator, is trying to connect her middle-class, mostly white ninth graders to the street dance community in ways that transport them beyond mere performing skills. She wants her students to encounter diverse ideas to be more literate about the world they live in. Concerned particularly about issues of white privilege, Mrs. O'Hara recognizes how brown and black bodies are marginalized or even ignored in the traditional dance classroom and seeks to give credence to a dance form that has been created by people of color.

Mrs. O'Hara acknowledges that she lacks the knowledge, skills, or background to create a meaningful experience for her students and has sought to bridge this gap by inviting Jake, a guest artist from the community, to teach in residency with her class. A self-proclaimed *b-boy* (a slang term for *break-boy*, associated with break dancing, or breaking), Jake openly acknowledges the poverty that permeated his experience as a young Afro-Puerto Rican American growing up in inner-city Los Angeles and its influence on his dancing. In spite of these realities, he is a dance student at the local university, a recipient of a scholarship for inner-city youth.

We look in on Mrs. O'Hara's class at about the midway mark for Jake's three-week residency to find that students and Mrs. O'Hara—who has been taking class alongside the students—have learned a short sequence of top rock steps (a series of steps performed from a standing position) that they have been practicing. The environment is friendly as Jake encourages them to find ways to add their own hand embellishments and style—a reference to individuality—to the footwork they are practicing. The class warms up by reviewing each individual step they have learned to date, and Jake keeps them moving as he quizzes them: "Tell me what you understand and remember about breaking so far."

Students randomly call out, "It's informal," "Social," "Improvised," "Different moves and styles," "Born in the streets of the Bronx," and "Spread worldwide through the media."

Mrs. O'Hara, who Jake and students have begun referring to as MizO, interjects, "These are some pretty good descriptors, but I wonder if we could add some ideas about the movement itself." Jake keeps them moving in repetitive practice of one of the steps they have learned and asks, "How would you describe this movement?" Students think about how they would describe the movement from an embodied place as Jake probes further: "How does it feel inside your body? Does it feel light and delicate?"

Students keep moving as Carlos answers, "No—it feels heavy—sorta like I'm down in my body."

Jake nods encouragingly—"Yeah, in a more formal dance world, we call that being grounded, or feeling your weight. Remember when we talked about that and experimented with sensing our weight in those first few days?"

Jake moves on to another step as students continue following along. As they practice, MizO asks, "Why do you think street dancing evolved this way? Why doesn't it look more like ballet?" As they consider the question, MizO suggests, "Let's try putting the ballet back in our bodies for just a moment." She keeps the beat and tempo going as she leads them in a simple, repetitive ballet footwork sequence (learned earlier in the semester) that contrasts quite dramatically with the toprock footwork they have been practicing. "How does this feel?" Students indicate that it feels "lifted" and "light."

Jake continues, "So, how do these qualities reflect the culture that created ballet, and how do you think that compares to the culture that created breaking?"

Lisa remembers, "So, ballet came out of the court dances of royalty, so they were all stuffy and lifted, and it wasn't refined to have bad posture—like they wanted to defy gravity. But street dance seems like almost the opposite, like gravity is maybe a friend?"

Jake smiles at Lisa, nods in acknowledgement, and transitions into another step, but before he can get students moving with him, Andy raises his hand and asks, "Jake, didn't you say the breakers were dissin' somebody? Does that have anything to do with this discussion?"

Jake smiles and reminds him, "The term I used was disenfranchised. Can you remember what it means?"

Some students pull out smartphones to look it up; soon Matisse responds, "Feeling excluded and deprived."

"Yeah, that," says Andy sheepishly.

Jake adds, "But you know, Andy, the dissin' idea works too because breaking evolved as a sort of rebellion against the establishment: Young people in inner-city ghetto life were unhappy with the way they were excluded and marginalized—and street dancing was their way of claiming their own identities apart from the mainstream. So in a way, they were dissin' their disenfranchisement!"

Jake gets them moving again with a new step as Brooke gets an aha look on her face. "Sweet! You can totally see that in the way street dancing looks and feels—like it channels the weight of street life." James observes, "Even the posture is different than in ballet class, where we have to be all lifted and tall." Karen adds, "In breaking, it seems almost the opposite—like you want to get your center as low as you can. My hip-hop teacher in the studio where I take dance lessons always tells us to get down into our legs more."

Selma huffs and counters, "REAL breaking isn't learned in studios!"

Mrs. O'Hara interjects, "Tell us more about that, Selma.

"Okay—well, Jake said you don't learn it from a dance teacher—you learn by practicing with other b-boys and b-girls."

Jake motions for them to keep practicing as he walks among them and clarifies, "Breaking evolved and continues to evolve in the streets as an expression of community, but middle-class white suburbia now teaches it in studios because it's so popular. I personally think that's chill—I actually teach in a studio myself. The problem is when people with no background or understanding try to teach it and leave out the context. So then what you get is a perky, stylized cheerleader version without reference to origins or culture. Worse than that, they claim it as their own—like they invented it or something. That's what we call appropriation, and that ain't chill at all."

Mrs. O'Hara inserts, "Students, do you understand what Jake is saying here?" Students stop their practice as MizO writes appropriation on the board and asks students to look it up on their smartphones. "What is the dictionary meaning for this word?"

Students consult their smartphones, and Sam offers, "Taking something for one's own use?"

Mrs. O'Hara replies, "And, how do you think it might it apply here?"

Sarah, who has been silent until now, raises her hand. "So, are you saying I shouldn't use these dance moves because I'm a white girl from the suburbs?"

MizO responds, "This is a great question for us to consider. As artists, what do you think?

Karen offers, "I never really thought about it before, but maybe my blond Barbie doll teacher isn't the best authority on hip-hop, especially when she never says a word about where it came from."

Sarah counters, "But how else would we learn these moves? No one on my street corner is doing this stuff."

MizO smiles and says, "Another excellent question. We are asking hard questions about access, appropriation, and privilege. Who gets to appropriate these movements? Who has that privilege? And, who gets to call it art?" These are important questions, especially here in our community, where most of us are what we might consider privileged. Do you think people sometimes appropriate artistic content from other communities? I can think of other examples we could discuss."

Thoughtful, if somewhat uncomfortable, silence ensues. Students and MizO alike have a hard time relating to the street life they've been discussing, and this new conversation has raised issues many have never even considered. Jake intervenes, "I really appreciate the fact that we can bring this conversation into the open. I also think we need to be careful about creating stereotypes either way. I probably shouldn't have referred to cheerleaders in that way. And I mean I've got blonde b-girl friends who can kill it on the dance floor!" He winks playfully to let students know they are not being singled out or shamed and motions them into movement with another toprock step as he continues, "So it don't matter what color your hair or skin is. The main thing to remember here is that you can't just grab somebody's culture or identity and wear it like an old T-shirt. You can experience it, yeah—maybe even try it on through the dancing, music, and stuff like we're doing right now—but ya gotta acknowledge its origins. You also should not assume to understand b-boys and b-girls worldwide because of one or two experiences. I mean, my moves and my experiences don't represent or channel every breaker." He transitions to the final step they have learned in their sequence and keeps them moving as he summarizes, "Breaking is individual. We express our individuality through our dancing and our individual styles—just like some of you do in contemporary and jazz and ballet—we just don't go take class several times a week to study it like you do; we live and breathe it. It IS our identity and our culture, but as individuals—not as a stereotyped group of people."

As students continue in thoughtful practice, MizO summarizes, "This conversation we've been having today is so important, but guess what? We may not discover all the answers. I don't have all the answers to these questions, and Jake would probably tell you that he doesn't know all the answers either."

Jake nods and adds, "What's important is that we can feel safe talking about them, and we will continue talking about them together." Ending on a lighter note, he says, "And dang if these moves don't feel good!" He invites students to join him as they put together all the steps they've been practicing throughout class; he reminds them to add their own signature styles to express their individuality.

UNDERSTANDING THE CONNECTING LITERACY EVENT

Though it scratches only the surface of what might be addressed, this vignette introduces issues of diversity with particular emphasis on marginalization based on race, privilege, and socioeconomic status. Mrs. O'Hara's commitment to interacting with different dance modes and backgrounds in ways that avoid marginalization is a central part of this vignette and its unpacking. Importantly, her decision to bring a guest artist into her classroom affords Mrs. O'Hara and her students an opportunity to engage in conversation that likely would have been uninformed and lopsided without Jake's perspective.

What follows is an unpacking of texts, processes, and literacies that are in play as Mrs. O'Hara and Jake seek collaboratively to establish a culturally relevant and literate classroom where dance meaning is created and interpreted through the integration of "personal experience, knowledge, and contexts" and dance literacy is expanded through "societal, cultural . . . and community experiences" (NCCAS DA: Cn10.1 and DA: Cn 11.1, 2014).

Texts

The main text within this vignette is the mode of dance that Mrs. O'Hara's classroom is learning to read and understand. In this environment that Hanna (1986) termed the *soma* is an important conveyer of meaning as the quality and feel of street movement is one of the first texts students consider. According to Hanna, "The soma, being internally perceived, is categorically distinct from a body, not because the subject is different but because the mode of viewpoint is different: it is immediate proprioception—a sensory mode that provides unique data" (Fortin, 2002).

This initial exploration of how this movement is perceived inside the students' bodies provides personal data about the movement that then informs discussion, which leads to social and cultural decoding of the body in context. For example, the conversation that Jake and MizO facilitate about the differences between ballet and street dance postures, body attitudes, and weight sensing leads Lisa and Andy to consider contrasting statuses of privilege, which in turn, allows the unique context of breaking to be made more visible. This leads Brooke to compare the groundedness of breaking to the metaphorical weight of street life, which also sets the stage for critical conversations about privilege and appropriation as both Sarah and Karen begin to recognize how individuals—including themselves—sometimes appropriate content (such as break dancing) without regard for its origins or context.

This exchange opens the door to dialogue beyond the breaking community and subculture to society at-large and the injustices it sometimes perpetuates. The main importance of this text is that together, MizO and Jake have created a space where students can ask hard questions. Things don't get resolved, which is okay. Because these are ideas students are only just beginning to grapple with, this text will require further translation and decoding. Mrs. O'Hara's and Jake's comments indicate plans for follow-up discussion.

There is also a subtle but significant text that occurs between Jake and MizO as they work together as a team, not only in their efforts to situate street dancing in its proper context but to better understand one another as well. Their friendly interactions, their acceptance of one another as equals, and their ability to collaborate and learn from one another are texts that though not discussed and made apparent, are read and tacitly interpreted by their students. For example, Mrs. O'Hara's decision to allow Jake enough time in the classroom to establish relevance beyond the one-hit wonder model that prevails in many guest artist encounters creates text about the importance of the content. MizO further reinforces this text though her participation in class rather than observing from the sidelines or working in her office, which suggests a willingness to be vulnerable as she struggles equally alongside her students to learn the basics of a body language that differs significantly from her own. MizO's clear regard for Jake and the breaking content helps prevent the inadvertent labeling of street dance as other.

Kimmel's (2004) assertions about the social construction of gender relations might equally apply in this setting: "We respond to the world we encounter—shaping, modifying, and creating our identities through those encounters with other people and within social institutions" (p 193). And as West (2005) maintains, "In the fluid reservoir of text and language, body and movement, motion and message, dance educators have unique opportunities to transform, deconstruct, and create language that can dramatically shift attitudes and mindsets" (pp. 66–67). These various embodied and enacted texts between Jake and MizO allow students to see how dancers—and, by association, all people—can learn from, respect, and empathize with those whose experiences differ from ours.

Processes

The artistic processes in this vignette include not only the practice and embodied description of movement but also the simultaneous discussion that provides context. Coming to understand movement from an embodied place is always a powerful experience that connects us to our own physicality—so Jake's and MizO's efforts to keep students moving as they simultaneously process and discuss their experience is significant. Further connecting this embodied experience to cultural and social indicators establishes contextual literacy that informs student experience at a deeper level. For example, the ability to process issues of privilege and appropriation might not have been as potent had students not arrived at these ideas through their own embodied experience.

Literacies

In this classroom where students' lived and shared experiences encompass a very different world than that of the inner city, Mrs. O'Hara's decision to provide experiences with underrepresented communities is crucial. Mrs. O'Hara also aims to confront and combat illiteracies that are perpetuated in dance education through tacit, unquestioned acceptance of white privilege as the norm for what should be taught in the schools. She dares to consider Stinson's (2005) question, "But what about those dance educators who want to take a different stance, who want to use dance instruction not to reproduce the status quo, but to try to change the world?" (p. 56).

Though this one event would be insufficient for establishing depth of knowledge regarding street dancing and the various communities that created it, the conversation and experience still go far beyond what most students experience when they simply learn a fun hip-hop routine. The discussion, led equally by Mrs. O'Hara and Jake, is designed to create thoughtful reflection and conversation that leads students to confront difficult issues they have not considered previously. As students recognize how street dance has sometimes been appropriated by white privilege, they also begin to question the practice of society at-large. Mrs. O'Hara's purposeful comment about other examples of white appropriation hopefully will spark dialogue among students, their families, and friends and lead to follow-up conversation in the classroom. Mrs. O'Hara's and Jake's collaborative efforts to connect a simple experience with breaking to larger societal issues introduce life skills and literacies that take students well beyond the dance discipline, preparing them to live as productive and contributing members of a global society.

CONCLUSIONS

The ability to recognize, understand, and empathize with social and cultural experiences different than our own is a literacy that connects us to other human beings. In populations where students have limited experience with diverse people and ideas, the importance of infusing connecting literacies into the curriculum cannot be understated. Similarly, classrooms with broadly diverse students also need to be culturally relevant with diverse and underrepresented curricular content. Effective dance educators recognize that traditionalist dance classrooms where norms of white privilege reign unchecked and without examination have no place in the public schools. These educators work toward building culturally relevant and responsive classrooms where marginalization is recognized for what it is, and practice transforms tradition toward a future that includes and celebrates every diversely individual student.

As creators, consumers, performers, and connoisseurs of dance, the process of reflecting, critiquing, and connecting personal experience to dance through "other contexts of meaning or knowledge" (NCCAS, 2014) serves not only to enrich and enliven our experience and expertise but to make it whole or complete. Without connecting processes, dance becomes decontextualized and loses meaning. *With* connecting processes, dance retains its identity and, by association, its full potential for transforming and changing those who engage with it.

REFERENCES

Dixon Gottschild, B. (2003). *The black dancing body: A geography from coon to cool.* New York: Palgrave Macmillan.

Dixon Gottschild, B. (2005). Whoa! Whiteness in dance? *Dance Magazine, 79*(6): 46–47.

Fortin, S. (2002) Living in movement: Development of somatic practices in different cultures, *Journal of Dance Education, 2*(4), 128–136. doi: 10.1080/15290824.2002.10387221

Hanna, T. (1986). What is somatics? *Somatics, 5*(4), 4–9.

Kerr-Berry J. (2004). The skin we dance, the skin we teach: Appropriation of black content in dance education. *Journal of Dance Education, 4*(2), 45–47.

Kerr-Berry, J. (2010). Progress and complacency: A "post-racial" dance in higher education? *Journal of Dance Education, 10*(1), 3–5.

Kerr-Berry, J. (2012). Dance education in an era of racial backlash: Moving forward as we step backwards. *Journal of Dance Education, 12*(2), 48–53. doi: 10.1080/15290824.2011.653735

Kimmel, M. S. (2004). Inequality and difference: The social construction of gender relations. In L. Heldke & P. O'Connor (Eds.), *Oppression, privilege, & resistance: Theoretical perspectives on racism, sexism, and heterosexism* (p. 193). New York: McGraw-Hill Companies.

MacBean, A. (2014). Dancing into diversity: A curriculum for self-discovery, empathy, and creative leadership. *Journal of Dance Education, 14*(3), 117–121. doi: 10.1080/15290824.2014.922187

National Coalition for Core Arts Standards. (2014). National Core Arts Standards Dance, DA: Cn10.1 and DA: Cn 11.1: Connecting. Online at http://www.nationalartsstandards.org/

Stinson, S. (2005). The hidden curriculum of gender in dance education. *Journal of Dance Education, 5*(2), 51–57. doi: 10.1080/15290824.2005.10387285

West, C. S. (2005). Black bodies in dance education: Charting a new pedagogical paradigm to eliminate gendered and hypersexualized assumptions. *Journal of Dance Education, 5*(2), 64–69. doi: 10.1080/15290824.2005.10387287

21 Media Arts
Connecting

Benjamin Thevenin

Among the greatest strengths of media arts education is its emphasis on critical analysis and creative production as means of empowering students to discover their own voices and express themselves. However, perhaps the most commonly voiced critique of this tradition is that too often "media production [is] taught as a *decontextualized* set of tasks that teach students a narrow set of skills" (Hobbs, 1998, p. 20, emphasis added). For example, students may attend a film appreciation course or learn the latest editing software and thereby engage with *texts*—through analysis and production—but they have fewer opportunities to connect media art to *context*.

This is unfortunate. Because, as all of the chapters in this section are sure to demonstrate, the arts are such a rich resource when it comes to helping young people understand themselves as well as the people and the world around them. The National Standards discuss the potential of media arts education to encourage students to be able to connect the art they analyze and create "to various contexts, purposes and values, such as social trends, power, equality and personal/cultural identity" (MA: Cn11.1.I). Given the increasingly important role that media plays in contemporary culture and politics, it is especially important that educators prepare students to make these connections. The following example looks at a video game design project in a media arts classroom. I will demonstrate that video games—which are often presumed to inhibit social development—are actually an effective medium to discuss the potentially positive role that media art can play in helping young people connect with others and the world around them.

Ms. Sarkeesian's tenth-grade media arts class is unique. The students learn to shoot video, edit audio, even code a little bit. But because she is also a social studies teacher, Ms. Sarkeesian is careful to remind her students that their work's production value is only as good as its social conscience. Throughout the semester, students compose photo essays depicting the neighborhoods they live in, produce short documentaries about heroes in their communities, and even build a Web site where they compile audio recordings of personal histories they collect from their friends and families. Their current project is titled the "Game for Change," in which students will design a video game that raises awareness about a social issue that interests them.

"Now I know what you must be thinking," Ms. Sarkeesian says. "Play time! But I'm giving you a heads-up—while most often we just play games to veg or have fun, they also can be artful and thought provoking. Let me give you an example."

Ms. Sarkeesian demos the game Darfur is Dying (darfurisdying.com) for the students. The objective of the game is to maintain a small village in war-torn Darfur by directing characters across the desert to collect water from a well. Meanwhile, the player faces an endless barrage of obstacles—sickness, drought, and violent warlords who kidnap or kill the villagers. A few students sit and play the game on the computer, while the rest of the class watches and comments on the game play, suggesting to the students playing where to go and what to do.

After a few minutes of playing the game, Ms. Sarkeesian begins, "I don't think I've seen you all this engaged all semester. What is it about this game that makes it more fun or interesting than, say, a documentary about Darfur?"

"It's less boring," a student immediately responds.

"Okay," Ms. Sarkeesian responds with a smile. "What does this game do to make it less boring?"

"Well, you get to control the character," another student answers, "instead of just watching something."

"Alright," says Ms. Sarkeesian. "So, the interactivity of the game gets you more invested in the message of the media—the fact that you're able to experience this issue through the eyes of a character rather than simply viewing charts and graphs or listening to commentators. Why do you think that it's so important that our characters here are the villagers? Why not make this a game about giving aid to the people in Darfur—flying helicopters in and dropping supplies?"

The students are quiet. A girl then answers hesitantly, "Maybe because we need to see how hard it is for them."

"Good," responds Ms. Sarkeesian. "Go on."

"I mean, in the game, we're in someone else's shoes, dealing with things that they deal with—only not in real life, just virtually, or whatever."

Ms. Sarkeesian explains that games are unique in that they encourage a special type of identification between the audience and characters. Players are faced with obstacles and must figure out a way to overcome them. As a result, a growing number of developers are using games to inform, persuade, and raise awareness about serious issues in the world. Darfur is Dying gives players a chance to experience—in this very small way—the enormous challenges facing the people of Darfur in a way that literature, news reports, or documentaries are not able to.

After their discussion, Ms. Sarkeesian discusses their "Game for Change" project. First, students will find an issue that really matters to them. Then, they will do some research—reading news articles, watching documentaries, conducting interviews, and so on. Finally, having gained some sense of the issue, they will translate this perspective into their design of a game. The following day in class, Ms. Sarkeesian demos a few simple game-creation programs including Sploder, Twine, RPG Maker, and so on; introduces the students to a few different types of games (platform and role-playing games, hypertext-based interactive fiction, etc.); and then sets them loose. Over the next few days, students work in groups, exploring social issues that interest them—from air pollution to gender equality to political corruption. Ms. Sarkeesian visits with each group one by one and discusses their research together. One morning, Ms. Sarkeesian sits down with two girls, Mary and Sue, and inquires about their research.

Sue states, "Well, we just figured—look at us. There's no way around this. We have to research fat girls."

Ms. Sarkeesian is immediately impressed by Sue's courage and asks the girls to go on. Mary and Sue explain that they both struggled with the issue of body image, and it was something that they wanted to try to make sense of. In their research, they found that the debate was pretty divided. On one side, there was a big conversation about the rise of childhood obesity in America, unhealthy eating habits of teens, the lack of physical education in schools, and so on. And on the other side, there was a conversation about the dangers of fat shaming, the rising number of girls suffering from eating disorders, and the recent popularity of pop music that was reclaiming the booty as beauty.

"It's a big, fat mess, really," Sue adds with a smile.

Ms. Sarkeesian proposes that the following day in class, the girls solicit feedback from their classmates on how they might proceed in the development of their game. But in the meantime, she shares with them another game, Depression Quest—a choose-your-own-adventure-style, interactive, fiction game that addresses the experience of living with depression.

"Play the game tonight," Ms. Sarkeesian says, "and pay attention to how the game is able to tackle such a complicated issue. Then, we'll talk tomorrow."

The next day in class, Ms. Sarkeesian carefully introduces Mary and Sue's project to the class.

"Basically," interrupts Sue, "we want to make a game that shows how it's hard to be a fat girl, but we need some help."

The students are stunned.

"I'm fat. Sue's fat," Mary says. "We deal with it every day. We want a game that helps us make sense of it, that helps other people relate to our experiences, and that tries to address the different perspectives we found in our research—stuff about being healthy, about self-confidence, fat shaming, obesity, eating disorders, loving your body, hating your body. But it's hard."

"So, class," Ms. Sarkeesian steps in. "Help these girls out. How might they approach developing their game? What are some choices they might make about the type of game, the characters, the obstacles they face, the objectives they have?"

The class sits silently for what seems like a long while. The teacher follows up with another question, "Who should the protagonist be?"

"Well, the girl," responds a boy, somewhat timidly.

"Alright," Ms. Sarkeesian follows up. "So, if our character is a girl who feels like she's fat, what are some obstacles that she faces?"

"Well," Sue offers, "all of the competing messages—positive and negative about how girls should treat their bodies and feel about their bodies, I guess."

"But how do you show that in a game?" asks a student. "Usually, enemies in games are just monsters that you destroy. You're talking about enemies that are ideas and not just bad ideas but a bunch of confusing ideas that contradict each other."

"Well, actually," Mary responds, "Ms. Sarkeesian showed us this Twine game about depression yesterday to help us brainstorm. It was . . . depressing. But it gave us an idea to how to make our game."

"Because it's just words, it's able to have more descriptions and emotions than like a first-person shooter or something," adds Sue. "So, if our main character is a girl who thinks she's fat, maybe the game is her coming across friends and magazine articles and blog posts and stuff that are all telling her different things about her body. And then you have to help her figure out what to make of all of them."

"Okay," adds Ms. Sarkeesian. "I feel like we're getting somewhere now. Does anyone else have some ideas to help out Mary and Sue?"

"I have a question," asks a boy. "So, how do you win this game? Can you?"

"Good question," responds Sue. "We were thinking that making a perfect ending where the girl becomes prom queen and valedictorian would be pretty messed up. But the depression game gave us an idea on what to do about the end."

Mary pulls out her phone and reads some of the final lines from Depression Quest to the class: "Like depression itself, Depression Quest *does not have an end really. There is no neat resolution to depression, and it was important to us that* Depression Quest's *own resolution reflects that. Instead of a tidy ending, we want to provide a series of outlooks to take moving forward. After all, that's all we can really do with depression—just keep moving forward. And at the end of the day, it's our outlook and support from people just like you that make all the difference in the world.*"

"So," Sue concludes. "Maybe our game won't solve all the problems that fat girls face, but at least we can share some of our experiences and do some good."

UNDERSTANDING THE CONNECTING LITERACY EVENT

Texts

In the previous scenario, Ms. Sarkeesian uses the "Game for Change" assignment to encourage her students to identify and analyze with the connections between texts—namely, video games, the students' research sources, and the games they develop. First, by providing the example of *Darfur is Dying*, Ms. Sarkeesian introduces the students to something that defies conventional expectations of video games as well as establishes games' potential to address serious issues. And this is possible because Ms. Sarkeesian keeps up with her field by playing video games, exploring game-creation tools, and reading game-related research. In his *How to Do Things with Videogames* (2011), Ian Bogost discusses the game *Darfur is Dying* and the opportunity it allows players to empathize with the struggles of others. Having read this text, Ms. Sarkeesian includes the game in her lesson to introduce the students to serious games. Ms. Sarkeesian then demos a number of game-creation tools in class—further establishing her familiarity with the field and providing the students with other examples of how they might approach the project. And last, in her interactions with Mary and Sue, she recommends that the girls check out the game *Depression Quest*. She is evidently familiar enough with the game to see how it potentially correlates with Mary and Sue's project, and by assigning the students to play the game, she is able to help them make connections between this text and the text that they are creating for their assignment. The girls' commentary on *Depression Quest*'s ending and how it is influencing their own creative work demonstrate their developing *connecting literacy*.

Next, the students are encouraged to make connections among the texts they engage with in class and other sources that they find in their research. Ms. Sarkeesian prepares them to engage in this type of connecting by asking them in class about the affordances and limitations of video games at addressing serious issues—specifically in comparison to media like documentary and print journalism. In this conversation, students identify how a variety of media might be used to address a single issue or subject, and they continue to explore the connections among these different media texts as they research their chosen social issues. The students are encouraged to explore a variety of media texts in their research—that not only use different media (print journalism, documentary film, etc.) but also exhibit varied perspectives on the same issue. Mary and Sue discuss their effort to make sense of the competing ideas surrounding the fat girls they encountered in their research. And the fact that they are unable to come to an easy conclusion on the matter is significant as well. Students' development of connecting literacies is not just about identifying correlations among texts—in this case the ideological perspectives voiced in media related to fat girls—but also about identifying the contradictions among them. And again, the girls' understanding of the complexity of this issue is reflected in the conceptualization of their game. Rather than establishing a hero and a villain or structuring the game so that the player is able to achieve a single objective and win the battle against fat girl-ness, Mary and Sue design a game that acknowledges—and even attempts to navigate—the messy reality of the issue.

Processes

Throughout the literacy event, the students participate in a number of processes—viewing and analyzing media, discussing it as a class, selecting and researching social issues, developing perspectives on those issues, designing their game, and getting feedback from the teacher and other students—but particularly significant, especially given the subject of video games, is the students' process of *play*. First, the teacher invites the students to play a game—and, in so doing, introduces them to the subject matter by allowing them to participate in a fun, low-stakes activity that also prepares them for further learning. Within the field of critical pedagogy, scholars and educators have long extolled the important role of *pleasure* in learning. Kellner and Share (2007) write that among media arts education's greatest strengths is that it often allows teachers (and students) to "bring pleasure and popular culture into mainstream education thereby making school more motivating and relevant to students" (p. 61). And this ethic of beginning student learning by inviting them to participate on their own terms is further demonstrated by the way that Ms. Sarkeesian handles the class discussion. The first question she asks is about why the game is more fun or interesting than a documentary about Darfur. Students respond readily to this question because it involves their immediate, intuitive responses to the game. And then after the students have voiced some of these initial responses to the game, Ms. Sarkeesian asks follow-up questions that cause them to consider the nature of their enjoyment and to begin to engage more critically with the game.

It is critical to understand that the process of play does not stop when analysis, research, and creative production begin. Throughout this assignment, Ms. Sarkeesian encourages the students to play—not just as consumers or audiences of media but also as researchers and developers. First, she encourages the students to select a social issue that matters to them (as opposed to a predetermined issue she imposes upon them) and then to explore the various media representations of and information about this issue. The *agency* offered to students in the assignment—allowing them to select the subject matter and then direct their research efforts themselves—resembles a type of play. And then, as the National Standards for Media Arts Education note, play is often used to "discover and share ideas for media artworks" as well as to practice "experimentation skills ... and trial and error, within and through media arts productions" (MA: Cr1.1.K; MA: Pr5.1.2). Again, this is evident in Mary and Sue's brainstorming—bouncing ideas off of each other, their instructor, and the other class members. But while understanding student learning through the lens of this process of play, this is not to suggest that the instructor takes a backseat and allows the students wholly to determine the class's course of study. If anything, structuring the class so that students feel free to experiment with ideas, try and fail, brainstorm, and so on requires more concerted effort on the part of the teacher (as Ms. Sarkeesian's scaffolding of student learning throughout the assignment demonstrates).

Literacies

Because of common associations with video games and play in general as being, at best, enriching but ultimately inconsequential activities and, at worst, a diversion from more important matters, it might seem counterintuitive to use a game-design assignment as a means of discussing how we might facilitate students connecting with each other and the world around them. But as demonstrated in Ms. Sarkeesian's class discussion about *Darfur is Dying,* games hold a powerful potential to allow those who play them to experience vicariously the struggles and successes of others and in so doing develop *critical literacy*. Through their playing (as game players, researchers, and developers), Ms. Sarkeesian's students are learning more about themselves and their world, and are developing as not just *consumers* and *producers* of media but also as *citizens*. Jenkins (2006) discusses the benefit of these unconventional, even pleasurable, learning activities in preparing young people to participate critically in society, writing:

> Right now, we are learning how to apply these new participatory skills through our relation to commercial entertainment. These skills are being applied to popular culture first for two reasons: on the one hand, because the stakes are so low, and on the other, because playing with popular culture is a lot more fun than playing with more serious matters . . . (p. 246)

Creating a game about a social issue for a class, while arguably not effecting much change, is a fun first step in one's development as a citizen, and it is helping the students, through play, recognize the connection between their engagement with media and their civic engagement. Ideally, as educators (like Ms. Sarkeesian) foster their students' (like Mary and Sue) abilities to make connections among media, art, themselves, and the world around them, the students will go beyond simply constructing and deconstructing media texts and engage in the greater task of "deconstructing injustices, expressing their own voices, and struggling to create a better society" (Kellner & Share 2005, p. 382).

REFERENCES

Bogost, I. (2011). *How to do things with videogames.* Minneapolis, MN: University of Minnesota Press.

Hobbs, R. (1998). The seven great debates of the media literacy movement. *Journal of Communication,* 48(1), 16–32.

Jenkins, H. (2006). *Convergence culture: Where old and new media collide.* New York: New York University Press.

Kellner, D., & Share, J. (2005). Toward critical media literacy: Core concepts, debates, organizations, and policy. *Discourse: Studies in the Cultural Politics of Education,* 26(3), 369–386.

22 Theatre
Connecting

Amy Petersen Jensen

In quality theatre classrooms, students use connecting processes and the associated connecting literacies daily by "relating artistic ideas and work with personal meaning and external context" (NCCAS Framework, 2014, p. 12). Many theatre tasks present students with chances to further develop their own distinctive artistic identities while actively engaging with other artistic forms and collaborating with other artists.

Theatre-based creative collaboration frequently includes cooperative efforts in which teams of artists (actors, designers, directors, etc.) interact to envision, develop, and generate ideas about how themes, concepts, or even full-length plays might be staged or presented to an audience. For example, students preparing to mount a fully realized theatre work in a public setting often assume unique artistic roles (i.e., director, designers, dramaturge, etc.) and the accompanying responsibilities related to those roles. During these creative experiences, they also associate with other artists who have assumed different artistic roles and responsibilities to bring the theatre work to fruition.

In this chapter I work to expand this notion of collaboration by suggesting that students, participating together in theatre creation spaces (including theatre classrooms), can truly form communities of practice (Lave & Wenger, 1991; Wenger, 2006) in which artists explore a "dialectic between ideas" (Tierney, 1992) or a conversation in which every person's ideas are explored and interrogated. I propose that young theatre artists should inquire actively outside of their own experience as they prepare to be more experienced theatre artists. This type of study invites them to evaluate their own perspectives and life experience. It also allows them to explore the interrelationship between their own artistic choices and those of others. When they do this, they potentially develop new and necessary learning and innovation skills, which are described by the Partnership for 21st Century Skills (P21 Mission, online). Additionally, within settings where interrelational understanding is fostered, students practice making creative decisions, critical thinking, and problem solving as they make connections between their own creative work and others' creative work.

Theatre teachers can prepare students to participate in these collaborative, creative processes by introducing opportunities for them to make connections actively between their own ideas and those of others. The National Core Theatre Standards encourage teachers to introduce connecting skills and knowledge that support opportunities to make connections by (1) engaging students in inquiry processes that help them to consider how others have thought about and created art, (2) encouraging student artists to acknowledge and value the interrelationship between their own artistic ideas and those of other student artists, and (3) inviting student collaborators to make and communicate artistic choices while considering how those choices might be received by others, including fellow collaborators, audiences members, and so on (Theatre Standards Connecting, online).

Additionally, by teaching connecting skills and knowledge that encourage students to explore beyond their own understanding, the theatre teacher can introduce students specifically to important larger discourses within the theatre field. For example, this chapter will demonstrate how one teacher helped students to better understand themselves and others in their community by engaging with the ideas in a play. Like Ms. Koi in the example below, theatre teachers can facilitate opportunities for student artists to experiment with asserting their own nascent creative ideas into those larger disciplinary discussions. Most importantly, a learning space that values connecting processes provides students opportunities to take ownership of their individual and collective artistic decisions while considering the artistic choices of others.

The following vignette demonstrates one theatre teacher's efforts to engage her students in these connecting processes.

Megan Koi (who is fondly called the Fish by her students) and her advanced drama students are preparing to produce selections from Mary Zimmerman's play Arabian Nights. *They will be performing scenes from the original work in a local community festival devoted to exploring Persian art and its influence on contemporary culture at the end of the term.*

While studying Zimmerman's play, the class has talked extensively about how stories are translated and shared across time and space and through different mediums. In earlier classes they have explored the stories in the play, which are told by the character Scheherazade, a woman who prevents her own execution at the hands of her husband for 1,001 nights. She does this by telling him the beginning of a fantastical story each night and then promising to finish it on the following night—producing a cycle of stories that endear her to her difficult husband, eventually convincing him never to kill her. Ms. Koi has pointed out that Zimmerman's episodic play invites theatre practitioners to stage the story through a variety of aural languages (including music and sounds from actors' bodies) and a variety of visual languages (including lighting, set decorations, costumes, and the movement of bodies in space). She also notes that instead of being linear in nature, the play tells snippets of stories that Zimmerman pieces together like blocks placed together in a crazy quilt.

In addition to reading the play's script the class has studied a few excerpts from the original stories. Ms. Koi purposefully chose Malcolm and Ursula Lyons's English translation because it had examples of the original Persian, Indian, and Arabic stories from One Thousand and One Nights (2008). The whole class has examined visual artifacts related to the stories, including images from ancient Persian and Egyptian art that depict scenes from the stories. Ms. Koi also has shared other resources with individual groups as they investigated possible staging ideas. For example she shared digital images of Henri Matisse's famous 4.5-by-12-foot paper cut-out "The Thousand and One Nights" (1950) when one group was struggling to visualize the setting. She spurs their thoughts says, "I know this is a digital image, but you can still see Matisse's effort to layer color. Why do you think he did that?" When another group was thinking about the sounds they wanted to convey, she invited them to consider the breadth and reach of the original stories in music that was derived from the tales. In this instance, Ms. Koi invited students to listen to a portion of the Rimsky-Korsakov's symphonic poem "Scheherazade" (1888) and compare it to a steampunk song with the same title by the band Abney Park (2013). In this instance, she simply says, "Super different, huh?" She uses the work to remind the students that there is no set sonic way to communicate the dramatic emotions of these stories by simply adding, "You choose. You get to decide how your work sounds, but what choices did these artists make that interest you?"

Using various versions of the stories, Ms. Koi has invited students to consider how and why these core ancient stories are told again and again through different art forms and from different cultural mind-sets. She summons them to imagine how they can participate in this rich artistic conversation by envisioning and developing their own version of one of the stories Zimmerman shares in the play. She provides them with access to other examples of how the stories have been told and also assigns them to research several other ways the stories might be interpreted.

Today class members are participating in one of several play development workshops. In this workshop, they are utilizing the knowledge they have gathered over the last few weeks to determine how they want to stage the visual landscape of their selection from the play.

Students are participating in round-table discussions where they are sharing their work to make decisions about each selection from the play. Ms. Koi has assigned students to six production teams that each includes the following collaborators: a director, a dramaturge, a scenic designer, a lighting designer, and a costume and makeup designer.

As class begins she reminds them, "Today your job as a production team is to make creative choices about the scenic, costume, and lighting designs. I expect that you will be using all of that knowledge you gleaned from the playscript and from others' interpretations of these stories. Use your research hats, people! Help us to imagine what we see as the lights come up on your story, and help your teacher to see how your ideas relate to the cultural and historical information that you have studied."

Ms. Koi moves around getting people started and answering questions that arise as each group discusses their design ideas.

Fahima, who is acting as the director of a scene from the play called Azizah and Aziz, leads, saying, "Okay, people, let's do what the Fish says. Show me your research, and let's talk about how it might help us think about what our performance space looks like." She excitedly rubs her hands together, clearly looking forward to what her partners have found, "Reilly, let's start with you. What are you thinking about for the set?"

Reilly takes over, "So I really have been thinking about our conversation yesterday. One-sided love really sucks! I've been trying to imagine how we could show how desperate Azizah feels when her love is not returned. She seems kinda broken. I especially noticed this brokenness at the end, when she and the other women are chanting about her loss because Aziz is a total jerk. I want the audience to feel this in her surroundings, but I really don't know how to show it."

Jasper, who has taken on the role of the dramaturge responds to Reilly, "So I have an idea about that. I was reading about some of the original Persian stories on Wikipedia, and I saw this old Arabic manuscript of The Arabian Nights." He shares the image of the text and says, "Look how beautiful those lines and spaces are in the written language. I wondered if we might find some way to do an Arabic translation of the word unrequited, so I used translation software to figure it out. This is what unrequited looks like in Arabic." He writes, "غير متبادل."

Reilly really gets excited about this saying. "I like it! I wonder if this lettering might be some sort of backdrop for the scene.

Miles jumps in, "I like that idea especially as it connects to the lighting! The lettering makes me think of the Matisse paper cutout thing that Ms. Fish showed us last week. For my research assignment, I found an article in the Wall Street Journal that talked even more about Matisse's cutout. This art historian guy said that Matisse felt he actually was cutting into the color itself as he made the pictures. What if we stenciled the Arabic word onto super stiff fabric and then cut it out? I could project different-colored light through the empty space to help the audience see the impact of all the painful stuff Azizah experiences. The continually fading, colored light can represent how her strength diminishes throughout."

Shondree replies, "I like the way that this helps us show Azizah falling apart, but I wish that we really could focus on showing the audience what a horrible person Aziz is. As a feminist, I want to make sure we emphasize how disgusting he is and that his acts are heinous. I don't mean to be rude, Ari, but Arab guys generally seem like dominating jerks."

Ari obviously is frustrated and pointedly says, "Aziz is Persian, Shondree, and because you seem to be making this conversation about me, you should know that I am not a Persian or an Arab—I was born in the States just like you. My grandfather IS from Iran, and he never has said a mean thing to anyone!"

Ms. Koi has been listening and hurriedly jumps in at this point. She says, "Okay, people, let's cool off for a second. Put on your artist's hats and let's try to find a way to depict Aziz that makes sense to everyone. I heard some great ideas earlier in your conversation. I really appreciate the attention that you have given to conveying Azizah and her heartbreak, but remember, Zimmerman makes this a story about two people and their progression. Look back at the script, Ari. What does the character Aziz say at the end of the scene?"

Ari nods. "Okay, on page 108 of the script, Aziz says this about losing Azizah, 'I beat myself, gentlemen for shame' and then later on that same page he calls himself 'a fool who lost Azizah.'"

Ms. Koi says, "Shondree is right. Aziz is pretty awful at the beginning, but I wonder if there is room for this character to grow?"

Shondree says, "I don't know if he deserves to grow."

Ms. Koi laughs, puts a hand on Shondree's shoulder, and continues, "I love it that you are forming such strong opinions about these characters—especially you, Shondree. I do think it might be prudent to learn a little bit more about the world of these characters so that we can make some final decisions about their growth. For example, can someone find out what Persian law or custom led to the betrothal of Aziz and Azizah as children? That's a question I have, but I wonder what new research questions you might have after this conversation. Fahima why don't you lead out in helping the group develop a few new research questions. I believe these answers might help you to make some concrete decisions that relate to your visual design ideas but also more fully represent the cultures we are portraying."

Fahima responds, "Okay, guys, let's make the Fish proud. We will come back to the conversation about the visual landscape next time with more info. What are our next steps for the research?"

TEXTS

Ms. Koi's classroom is rich with texts and discussion about those texts. The primary text that students are investigating in this scenario is Mary Zimmerman's play *Arabian Nights*. Ms. Koi has invited the students to read multiple selections from this text even though each group will only prepare and present one scene from the play. Ms. Koi asks them to refer back to this as they make choices about the theatrical presentation during their production meeting. Ms. Koi also has introduced the students to a variety of supporting texts, including written and oral stories, ancient art objects, contemporary art, and a variety of music. By sharing these supporting texts, she provides a rich fabric of knowledge that the students can draw from as they formulate their own ideas about the scene they will eventually present. Prior to the production meeting that occurs in this vignette, Ms. Koi invites students to do their own text-based research. Following her model, students read about and consider a variety of print and visual texts in their presentation of ideas about the visual landscape of the play. She also provides opportunities for students to make inquiry into texts that they find on their own. Ultimately within their production groups, students "synthesize and relate knowledge and personal experiences [as they] make art" (NCCAS, Anchor Standard). They are able to reason together, drawing on a variety of texts because she has helped them see and value a multiplicity of texts that they would not have located or even understood without her help.

PROCESSES

Students participate in three connecting processes during the class period described. Initially the students primarily focus on gathering and comprehending historical, cultural, and social research. Ms. Koi points out that it is important for them to think about how others have thought about and re-created the original stories that Mary Zimmerman borrows from in her play *Arabian Nights*. Through her examples, she invites them to consider how others' work might inform their own creative decisions. This requires students to justify creative choices through their research of the play and its associated texts.

Later, when students form into production teams, they practice the positive inter-relational work that is required for successful theatre collaborations. Together they work to integrate and synthesize the new knowledge that they have gleaned from their research. While the vignette does not describe how Ms. Koi and her class established protocols for their work process, it is clear from Fahima's early leadership that structures the conversation as well as the presentation of ideas by other group members that decisions have been made by the students about group dynamics and the focus of their conversations, including what information should be shared and how the group should function as collaborators.

Finally, students practice empathy by learning to balance their own personal beliefs with the collective understandings of the group. They make efforts to analyze the play in relation to their own perceptions and how the themes and characters in the play may be perceived in the world at large. This is specifically evident when Jasper describes his effort to make Azizah's pain visual to audience by using ideas he found in his personal research. It is important to note that there is a point near the end of the vignette where the group dynamic breaks down for a minute. Shondree and Ari are in conflict over the depiction of the Aziz. Truthfully their conflict seems to go beyond the scope of the project. In this moment, Ms. Koi steps in to remind the students that theatre artists work to balance their own ideas and opinions with the collective knowledge they have gleaned. She importantly points out that when our own belief systems are challenged, we sometimes need to identify and answer new questions that grow out of the work itself and out of the collaborative inquiry.

LITERACIES

Theatre is a discourse community. Like other discourse communities, the theatre community has developed "ways of using language, other symbolic expressions, and artifacts, of thinking, feeling, believing, valuing and acting that can be used to identify oneself as a member of a socially meaningful group (Gee, 1996, p. 131). In this chapter, Ms. Koi invites her students to participate actively as theatre practitioners by asking them to prepare and perform scenes from Mary Zimmerman's work in a local community festival. By doing this, she purposefully includes them in the larger discourse of the field. In preparation for this event, she invites them to explore the language and symbolic expression within the play and also within other associated art forms. Once they are assigned to production teams, the students complete their own research and then share ideas about the design of the play with each other, which leads to connections and collaboration. For example, Miles is able to build on Jasper's idea of visually depicting Arabic words because of his own research into the Matisse cutouts of *Arabian Nights*. During this collaborative stage, they demonstrate what they think, feel, and value in relation to others' ideas. In this way, they justify their creative choices based on their genuine understanding of inter-relational theatre contexts (self to text, self to others, and self to a larger community). For instance Shondree identifies herself as a feminist and speaks confidently from a position she is learning to negotiate within. Conversely, Ari is articulate in defending against the stereotypes that he feels she supports. Ms. Koi does not resolve the conflict between these two (and maybe she could have engaged in better conflict resolution in this moment), but she does remind them that they are artists and asks them to solve the issue at hand by reminding them of their artistic responsibilities (as director, designer, dramaturge, etc., in this case). In these roles (and with her help), they begin to transfer those feelings, ideas, and beliefs into practical artistic solutions to convey the meaning they intend.

CONCLUSION

The National Coalition for Core Arts Standards states that "artistic literacy requires that [students] engage in artistic creation processes directly through the use of appropriate materials . . . and in appropriate spaces" (NCCAS Framework, 2014, p. 17). When teachers and students effectively practice connecting literacies, they move beyond their own experience. As demonstrated in the vignette above, students can do this by accessing new ideas through research, actively questioning their own assumptions, embracing or rejecting familiar ideas about art, and synthesizing these experiences to develop their own artistic choices. Most importantly they learn from working alongside each other as they actively make choices about staging a work of art.

REFERENCES

Gee, J. P. (1996). *Social linguistics and literacies: Ideology in discourses* (2nd ed.). London: Taylor & Francis.
Lave, J., & Wenger, E. (1991). *Situated learning: Legitimate peripheral participation*. New York: Cambridge University Press.
National Core Arts Standards. *Theatre: Connecting*. Retrieved November 30, 2014, from http://www.nationalartsstandards.org/
National Core Arts Standards. *National Core Arts Standards Framework*, p. 17. Retrieved from http://www.nationalartsstandards.org/sites/default/files/Theater_resources/Theatre%20at%20a%20Glance.pdf
Partnership for 21st Century Skills. (2010). *Mission statement*. Retrieved from November 15, 2014, http://www.p21.org/about-us/our-mission
Tierney, R. (1992). Ongoing research and new directions. In J. Irwin & M.A. Doyle (Eds.), *Reading/writing connections: learning from research* (pp. 246–259). Newark, DE: International Reading Association.
Wenger, E. (2006). Communities of practice: a brief introduction. Retrieved from http://www.ewenger.com/theory/communities_of_practice_intro.htm

23 Visual Art
Connecting

Daniel T. Barney

The National Core Art Standards describes connecting within all the arts as "relating artistic ideas and work with personal meaning and external context" (NCCAS, 2014, Cn). The connecting processes, therefore, are paramount in helping students gain literacy in the visual arts as meanings from external contexts are related or connected to individuals. Within the visual arts, the connecting process is further developed through two significant aspects of literacy. First, students are challenged to connect their own understandings and experiences to artistic practices, which include their own work and the work of others (NCCAS, 2014, VA: Cn10). Second, students are asked to connect artworks and the relevant ideas they evoke with broader societal, cultural, and historical contexts to deepen understanding (NCCAS, 2014, VA: Cn11).

To learn how visual artists, educators, historians, critics, and theorists not only make meaning from visual art texts but how those texts are connected through artistic discourse, including artistic production, takes time and experience with numerous works and cultural narratives. Such literacy requires an analysis of the methodologies of art practitioners. While not easy, students can and should be engaged in scrutinizing artistic disciplinary methodologies. The artistic processes of artists, how meaning is constructed and discussed within the field, are important to literacy instruction. This of course can be accomplished while students also are pursuing their own artistic investigations actively in relation to complex disciplinary conversations.

One way to increase one's literacy in this seemingly overwhelming process is by learning how different artists connect media, processes, and concepts with various sociocultural narratives and then playing with, perhaps through emulation or adaptation, such processes to explore germane personal and larger contextual connections. This is the pedagogical strategy described in this chapter, which emphasizes how literacy connections can be made as students engage in a contemporary art practice in relation to existing and emergent understandings in visual art. Making is not enough. Discussing is not enough. They must be connected, both being tied to personal experience and understandings, along with sociocultural contextualization.

Gaining literacy in the visual arts surely entails having deep and meaningful experiences in creating art, but solely making artistic-looking things, without serious attention to connection processes, does not increase literacy. Walker (2001), for instance, warns art teachers not to "yield to student pressure to move quickly to the artmaking process itself" because if students do not bring much "in the way of knowledge to inform their artmaking," then they "will soon lose interest" (p. 47). She asserts that artists can "sustain their interest in a single big idea because they probe the idea at deeper levels, asking new questions and acquiring more knowledge" (Walker, 2001, p. 47). We will see in the following vignette how Ms. Duran, a high school art teacher, does more than simply provide students "with information" to "build their knowledge base" (p. 39); she is teaching her students how to connect their current understandings with artistic discourses that will build new connections, thus increasing their literacy within the visual arts, and she starts this complex network of connections on the very first day of the semester.

Ms. Duran has been gathering postcard reproductions of various artworks for the last decade. Every time she visits a gallery or museum, she adds a few cards to her collection. Art schools, hoping to recruit students, also send postcards showing the work of faculty, visiting artists, and even highly regarded student work. Ms. Duran has several shoeboxes full of these postcards scattered around the room.

Ms. Duran's Art 1 class enters the classroom on the very first day of the new semester at Sierra High School. She welcomes her new students and asks each student to select a postcard he/she will use in an activity that will take place shortly. Ms. Duran knows that her classes are more successful when students build trust and respect for each other. She believes the sooner they start learning about each other as individuals, the sooner a culture of support can begin to emerge. In the past, Ms. Duran has taken time in class for students to introduce themselves. She noticed, however, that the same standard narratives were repeated over and over, with minor variations. Students shared very general information, and even when asked to "share an interesting fact about yourself with the class," these facts tended to be a bit silly rather than poignant. Because art often disrupts standard ways of perceiving and experiencing the world, Ms. Duran begins this first semester with an activity that attempts to encourage the access of personal lived experiences. She does this by challenging students to break from their standard narratives of self by asking them to make new connections.

"Please take the next thirty seconds to choose a postcard from the shoeboxes on the desks," instructs Ms. Duran. "These are just small reproductions of the originals they represent, but I thank you for taking care of them as you make your quick selection." After each student has a postcard, Ms. Duran asks the students to study the image and to read the information on the back of the card: the title of the piece, the artist's name, date the work was completed, medium, and size of the work, as well as any additional

contextual information, like who owns the work or where it was exhibited or performed. Ms. Duran wants to understand the reading needs of all learners and their current literacies with print texts as well as with artistic perceptive abilities, and this exercise acts as an informal pre-assessment. It also is designed to help students in their understandings of literacy connections and contexts within the visual arts (Barton, Hamilton, & Ivanic, 2000).

Ms. Duran waits a bit, answers any quick questions, and continues, "My name is Azucena Duran." Ms. Duran then makes an effort to show the class how she randomly selects a card from one of the shoeboxes. She holds up her postcard, which is an abstract image of blue-grays, with a few reddish marks, and one columnar shape, pale-yellow in hue, leaning in toward the center. "Let's see," contemplates Ms. Duran. "I am single, like this column shape. I rarely slow down or stand still. See how this shape is leaning? I hate bananas, and this pale yellow is the exact color of the inside of a banana. Has anyone ever been to the Oregon coast? I used to visit the beach when I was little, and this is how I remember seeing the overcast sky meeting the foggy horizon into the gray of the Pacific Ocean. See these three red streaks? I have three scars. I got one when I was twelve, playing soccer. I can't remember how I got the other two. From the information on the back of the card, I see the title of the piece is called, Rise 13, and when I was thirteen years old, I had to get out of bed at four in the morning to go berry picking in Oregon to make money. That was so early!"

Ms. Duran explains to the students that the artist did not create this painting as an homage to her life; in fact, she explains her process, "I had no idea what I would share with you until I tried to connect my life with the content in this work. And, of course, if I were to study more about this work—who painted it, when it was painted, where it was painted, and other contexts surrounding the work—then I would be able to make other connections to which I might not now have access. Right now, I only connect with what I see because I really don't know much about the other factors presented on the postcard."

Ms. Duran continues and asks, "Who would like to go first, introducing yourself using the postcard? I'm going to ask all of you to try it because it relates to what we will be learning this semester."

"Can I ask a question, Ms. Duran?" asks Brennan, a student Ms. Duran has yet to get to know on this first day of class.

"Of course!"

"Do I actually have to like the art in the postcard I chose?"

Ms. Duran laughs, which eases the first-day anxiety of some of the students, "No, in fact you bring up a great point we don't usually talk about on the first day of class. We can learn a lot, making new insights, even by engaging with art we don't necessarily like. Let's try it out. Do you mind going first?"

"Sure, I'll try it out. Hi, classmates, my name is Brennan, which rhymes with Vija Clemmin." He pauses. "Sort of." Brennan's classmates smile, eager to hear the next connection he will make to this reproduction of a much larger drawing. He holds up the postcard for all to see, but a few strain to view the piece. Ms. Duran helps by grabbing the card and walking around, so all can take a closer look, then passes it back to Brennan, so he can continue.

"As you can see," Brennan explains, "this is a drawing of waves, lots of waves, and I almost drowned last summer. Seriously, it was super intense. I was just at this lake with my family, and I was under the water for quite a while. I'm okay, but this image reminds me of that day right before that happened." There are a few follow-up questions as students want to know more details about Brennan's experience, but he moves on, sharing his continued love of water sports and spending time with his family.

"Do you all understand what we are doing with these postcards?" Ms. Duran asks. "If so," she continues, "then let's break up into smaller groups and introduce ourselves, connecting to the content invoked by our postcard."

The students shuffle into smaller groups of about six to eight students, taking a minute or two each to introduce themselves with their postcards.

"Okay, it looks like everyone is finished with introductions. Let's mix things up a little. Pass your postcard three people to the left."

There are some shocked and hesitant faces among the class, but everyone passes their selected postcards to the left, including Ms. Duran, as directed.

She explains the next task, "Now I'd like us to go around the entire room more quickly, stating your name and then sharing one or two personal connections about yourself, responding to this new postcard. I'll go first. Let's see. I am Azucena Duran, as I mentioned before, and you see this painting here?" She holds up her new postcard and glides it slowly across the air in the direction of each of the student's gaze. "The painting shown here portrays a still life of three dead fish on a table. I really dislike eating fish, but I really like salmon, including the color. It might just be one of my favorite colors of all time. That's all. Let's start with you." She indicates that the student on her left should address the entire class, and they all follow Ms. Duran's example, sharing a connection or two with this new postcard. Ms. Duran enjoys learning about each of the students.

A few of the students also indicate how they have made either a radically different or a similar connection with their new postcards as they overheard one of their classmate's introductions using that very same card. They discuss how this simple exercise disrupted the standard introductory narratives usually shared when meeting someone new.

For example, Charreese shares, "I never would have thought to talk about my obsession with trying out different kinds of fruit. I really don't share that with anyone. I just keep the photos and description about the fruit for myself, but my group really seemed interested in the process and what drives me to do this."

"Wow, we certainly are going to need to talk more about your project, Charreese. It is a project that we definitely can connect with current artistic practices!" Ms. Duran says excitedly.

"I am so glad you all are in this course with me. We will be learning a lot about how art really can help us make new connections and also how it challenges and even opens up standard ways of knowing and doing, just as we saw today with our simple postcard exercise. Okay," continues Ms. Duran, "we don't have a lot of time left, but I want to do a quick project that will get us right into the processes of creating used by contemporary artists. You will see that Charreese's fruit project really is in line with contemporary art making and inquiry."

Ms. Duran goes online and shows her class a few images by the conceptual artist Kenneth Josephson. The line of inquiry she shows her students is of Josephson's work that includes work such as New York State (Ship), 1970; New York State, 1970; Michigan, 1981, and Postcard Visit (67–35-8–32), 1967. All of these works are black and white, showing Josephson holding a postcard up in the air as he photographs it in a particular context.

"What do you notice about these images?" asks Ms. Duran.

Kyle immediately shares, "It's so meta!"

"What do you mean, Kyle?" asks Ms. Duran.

"You know, the photographer is holding a photograph that he didn't take in a landscape with his arm showing himself in his own photograph," Kyle adds.

"That's deep!" Candace says, smiling at Kyle. "It is meta."

"Well, check this artist out." Ms. Duran shows another artist's work who maintains a Flickr account called Looking Into the Past (see https://www.flickr.com/photos/jasonepowell/sets/72157613841045343/).

Jason Powell is a contemporary artist who finds a historic image from the Library of Congress, prints it out, and then holds it up while photographing it in the present-day scene.

"What?" There is a palpable gasp from many of the students.

Henrich is the first to ask, "So this artist finds old photographs and then searches out what the place looks like now?

"Well, he could have searched out the location first, then searched for the image, then gone back to photograph it. He holds the photographs up just like Josephson did, but the process seems really different," adds Lennie.

"You know what is really interesting to me?" shares Ms. Duran. "Powell says (in Hunsinger, 2009) that he actually was inspired not by the famous conceptual photographer Kenneth Josephson, as I thought, but by another photographer named Michael Hughes, who "takes photos of souvenirs superimposed on the tourist attraction that they represent" (Beale, 2008, n.p.).

"Who is interested in trying this type of process out?" Ms. Duran asks for a raise of hands. Almost everyone agrees this could be an interesting experience.

"When are we going to do this? Do we bring in souvenirs? Old photographs? Do we get digital cameras?" ask several students in quick succession.

"Actually, we are going to start right now. You will have fifteen minutes to take some pictures like we've just seen in class today. Here's the challenge: take your postcard out into the school or onto school grounds, without disrupting other classes, then take a photograph of you holding your postcard in a new context, just like we saw in the work of Josephson, Powell, and Hughes," explains Ms. Duran. "However, we are going to upload your photographs directly to an online image management and sharing application." She asks the class which applications they use the most; answers include Flickr, Tumblr, Photobucket, Pinterest, Instagram, as well as others, but Ms. Duran finds that the majority of her students use Instagram. Ms. Duran also sees that about half her students have phones that can be used to take photographs and run the Instagram application. She quickly passes out instructions to log into an account that she had previously set up, so students use a joint account for this activity. She also has searched for a new hashtag (#) that nobody else has used, so their images can be aggregated into an online exhibition.

"Remember, this is simply an exercise right now. We will talk about your experiences when you return." Ms. Duran has students working in small groups so that all can participate even if they do not have a camera phone with capabilities to download the application. "Before you search out your sites, each of you—even if you're working in groups—should upload at least one postcard photograph response. Also don't forget, add our hashtag (#) to each image you upload!"

The students are excited to try out this new strategy that they've discussed on their first day of art class. When the students return, they see Ms. Duran has used a Web site online that searches images by their hashtags, creating a digital exhibition of their responses. The students share their experiences concerning the perceived successes and difficulties encountered in selecting a site that connected with the postcard images in an interesting way and any technology issues that arose. Ms. Duran says class is almost over, but they can continue to post images using her postcards along with this hashtag as much as they want. "We will talk more about the artistic process of these three artists as well as your responses next time we meet," she informs them. "I'll see you all next class!"

UNDERSTANDING THE VISUAL ART LITERACY EVENT

Texts

Ms. Duran uses a postcard reproduction as a visual text that can incite meaning for viewers by connecting formal elements and subject matter to personal experience through visual analysis. However, the postcards also serve as content to create new texts and discourses as these are placed in new contexts in relation to contemporary discourses surrounding that art making. A reproduction of an original artwork most often may be used in a classroom to inspire visualization strategies or to talk about the specific historical importance of the work being represented, but in Ms. Duran's class, the postcard itself is being used as subject matter for art making.

The bodies of work created by the three artists shown by Ms. Duran act as conceptually bundled texts that are connected by style and technique. The students had to read and interpret the images as texts in relation to the process in which they were created. Ms. Duran shared how these three photographers created their images for these specific lines of inquiry as she shared her knowledge of these artists. Two of the artists actually created their work to be shown online, while Josephson's work was created for galleries.

The school and the grounds transformed into visual art texts as students juxtaposed their postcards in that space, selecting a potential image that included their extended arms to be uploaded on a public image-sharing platform.

Processes

There are many connecting processes utilized in Ms. Duran's class that supported literacy instruction in the visual arts. Gee (2007) describes how video game designers create literacy events in which cognitive connections are created as players overcome obstacles, develop a sense of identity, grasp new meanings, respond to challenges, and perceive the world. While Ms. Duran is not a video game designer, she designed a series of activities sensitive to connecting processes that encouraged students to build cognitions as art makers and interpreters in relation to a variety of negotiated variables (Flower, 1994). Her curriculum did not dictate uniformity of responses but acted as a structure emulating some of the key functions of an increased literacy within the visual arts. This includes disrupting repetitive or standard narratives, placing artistic work in conversation with various artists to emphasize similarities and differences, and investigating contexts for the creation and sharing of one's artistic work.

Ms. Duran's simple postcard introduction activity illustrates how connecting with artistic content encourages new narratives, but the process of connecting in this way is actually more significant as an art process than the artistic nature of the content itself. For example, perhaps students just as easily could have disrupted their standard introduction narratives if they were challenged to introduce themselves using a variety of candy bars as texts. Regardless, the process of connecting one's personal experiences to a material or image as text is an artistic process of meaning making; the postcard exercise happened to connect with the artist exemplars in a very apropos way, increasing certain cognitive connections.

Literacies

Walker (2001) suggests teachers not only should teach skills and art making strategies to their students but also teach how to connect students' own personal understandings to the ideas that matter to the field of visual art. Ms. Duran has a significant task to teach students to become literate in the visual arts. It is an ever-increasing field that shifts and changes like other disciplines. However, even on the first day of the class, students are engaging with artistic literacy practices that explore questions and issues addressed by artists. Of course, as time goes on, literacy will deepen as students make more disciplinary connections together, adding rich complexity to their learning in and through the visual arts collaboratively. This socially constructed literacy (Yandell, 2014) is highlighted in Ms. Duran's class in this vignette, nested in art as a larger community of practice.

CONCLUSION

Ms. Duran is attempting to make the pedagogical activities she selects in her class authentic to her discipline. There are many conversations about what the visual arts are, even among experts in the field. Ms. Duran celebrates these rich but varied points of view. In showing Josephson's work, which is much more a part of an institutional canon, alongside the more popular work of Powell and Hughes, she is presenting a range of philosophical approaches that later will be discussed as institutional and social theories of art. Right away, students are not simply learning about these artistic perspectives, but they are having embodied methodological experiences that are shared among a group of learners and are embedded in current artistic practice. They are connecting their own experiences with the work and processes with which artists use today. This is of course a nascent entering but is an engagement far different from simply reading about how artists work or what their practice might mean to individuals. Visual art is a discipline with a deep history of cultural production. Students are a part of this cultural production and, as we have seen in this short vignette, are certainly capable of becoming more literate by connecting with that discipline in ways that artists do.

REFERENCES

Barton, D., Hamilton, M., & Ivanic, R. (2000). *Situated literacies: Reading and writing in context*. New York, NY: Routledge.

Beale, S. (2008). Photos of souvenirs superimposed on tourist attractions. *Laughing Squid*. Retrieved from http://laughingsquid.com/photos-of-souvenirs-superimposed-on-tourist-attractions/

Flower, L. (1994). *The construction of negotiated meaning: A social cognitive theory of writing*. Carbondale, IL: Southern Illinois University Press.
Gee, J.P. (2007). *What video games have to teach us about learning and literacy*. New York, NY: Palgrave Macmillan.
Hunsinger, E. (2009). Looking into the past, old photos superimposed on present day scenes. *Laughing Squid*. Retrieved from http://laughingsquid.com/looking-into-the-past-old-photos-superimposed-on-present-day-scenes/
National Coalition for Core Arts Standards. (2014). *National Core Arts Standards Visual Arts: Connecting*. Online at http://www.nationalartsstandards.org/sites/default/files/Visual%20Arts%20at%20a%20Glance%20rev.pdf
Walker, S.R. (2001). *Teaching meaning in artmaking*. Worcester, MA: Davis.
Yandell, J. (2014). *The social construction of meaning: Reading literature in urban English classrooms*. New York, NY: Routledge.

24 Dance in the Elementary Classroom
Connecting

Jennifer J. Wimmer and
Kori Wakamatsu

Early childhood scholars continuously have called for teachers to attend to the needs of the whole child including the "physical, social, emotional, and cognitive domains" (Bredekamp, 2011, p. 124). Similarly, the National Association for the Education of Young Children (NAEYC and National Association of Early Childhood Specialists in State Departments of Education (NAECS/SDE), (2003), notes, "Children from babyhood through primary grades—and beyond—need to be cognitively, physically, socially, and artistically active" (p. 2). While increasingly mandated curriculum and state and federal standards direct teachers' focus to the cognitive needs of children alone, research suggests that it is not possible or helpful to separate the mind from the body. Indeed, studies of children in classrooms indicate that the body plays a crucial role in meaning making (see Rosborough, 2014; Roth, 2014). Specifically, Banovcanova and Slavik (2014) state, "The body is where learning begins and it is from the body that knowledge emerges" (p. 7). In this chapter we explore how dance provides teachers with opportunities to attend to the development of the whole child. Specifically, we share how one teacher integrates dance and literacy in an effort to provide students with opportunities to connect themselves to their worlds.

Elementary teachers are keenly aware that stillness and silence are not part of their classrooms. A glance into any elementary classroom reveals constant movement and motion. Young children rarely walk; rather, they skip, twirl, hop, and gallop about the classroom. From an artist's perspective, the classroom is a stage with children in a constant state of creating and performing—for themselves, each other, and the teacher. While they may not have a formal understanding of the elements of dance, which includes the body, space, time, and energy, they utilize each as they move about the classroom. Indeed, from the moment a child steps into the classroom, teachers are aware of the importance of the body and the role the body plays in all aspects of children's development. With budding artists in the classroom, teachers have opportunities to engage students in meaningful artistic learning opportunities.

Dance opens up space for students to connect their personal understandings with the world around them. Indeed, as Hong (2000) states, students "engage in a process of meaning-making which opens doors to new ways of seeing, new ways of thinking and therefore new ways of knowing the world" (para. 9). As students learn and develop, it essential that they are provided with opportunities to engage in connecting. Though it may seem that all four processes are described in this chapter, *connecting* requires the enactment of creating, performing, and responding for children to make art. For example, students demonstrate connecting as they "create and perform a dance that expresses personal meaning" (NCAS, 2014, DA: Cn10.1.2.a). Specifically, dance provides "a way of connecting up experience through the body . . . that helps students understand the materials, ideas, and information found in schooling" (Dils, 2007, p. 98).

As teachers provide spaces for students to make meaning, then students have opportunities to ask questions, seek information, and construct ideas. Indeed, this type of learning focuses on children making meaning of their worlds while connecting content to their personal experiences (NCAS, 2014, DA: Cn 10). Specifically, dance provides a means for students to use their bodies, time, space, and energy to communicate their thoughts, understandings, and emotions about the content they are learning. Thus, dance invites children to connect themselves to the world in an embodied, holistic way.

In the vignette below, a second-grade teacher engages her class in a learning activity that creates a space for her students to connect personal meanings and understandings of literature and art through their bodies.

Ms. Park has just finished leading her second-grade class through a dance warm-up in the gym. Today's lesson marks an important shift of focus. Because the students have acquired a strong knowledge base and emerging skill set regarding to the elements of dance (space, time, and energy), Ms. Park is launching a unit on choreographic process and artistic inspiration. It is a significant introductory lesson.

She reveals the book 600 Black Spots *by David A. Carter. It is a pop-up book, and the children literally ooh and ah over the majesty of the first page, which has cleverly fringed white strips straddling a vibrant, red background. Each section of fringe makes a subtle noise as the page opens and closes. "White grasses tip-tap and ninety black spots," she reads. She challenges the children to be quiet enough to hear quiet tip-tapping of that page.*

"Dancers, what are all the ways your body can tip-tap?"

Instantly, the children begin tapping their fingers. She reminds them to find new and interesting ways to tip-tap: "Can you tap an elbow? How can you use your spine? Can you tip-tap slower? Try to be on a different level than those around you." After this initial exploration, Ms. Park praises the students.

"Freeze!" She beats her drum to emphasize the freeze. "I saw and heard some great tapping! Over here, Owen was tapping his head while sliding into the splits! Over there, I saw Makenzie tapping just one finger very delicately. Then, there was a moment when Fernando was furiously tapping his feet while upside down!"

The next page creates a moment of magic. It reads, "Mondrian floats with shadows and sixty black spots." She tells them quickly about Piet Mondrian's art and how he experimented with stark, bright shapes on a white background. She asks the children to sit and face the only white wall in the space. She turns off the overhead fluorescent lights and flips on a halogen work light—the kind you might expect to see in a garage—resulting in more oohs and ahs. She steps in front of the bright, warm glow and begins designing geometric shapes with her body as vivid shadows are cast on the white wall. "Boys and girls, when it is your turn, can you create interesting shadows? When I tap you on the shoulder, you may begin creating shadows." About one-third of the class creates shadows as the others watch. Before the next set of students has a turn, she stops to help students make connections: "Students, what kinds of images do you see in the shadows?"

"When Janessa stepped in front of Claudia, their shadows looked like an octopus!" was one answer.

"It looked like an underwater adventure," another student responded.

The other groups have turns, and Ms. Park reminds the students to look for the intriguing images. Ms. Park then shows the students a one-minute shadow dance by the Pilobolus Dance Theatre that she has cued up on her electronic tablet. They watch intently; Ms. Park directs the students to notice how the dancers are using their bodies to create interesting shapes and movements. She further encourages the student to notice how the dancers' movements communicate ideas and emotions. Before the students have a final opportunity to dance in front of the halogen light, Ms. Park provides a time for students to ponder how they can connect their ideas about the image from the book, the video shown, and their movements to communicate an idea or feeling to the class.

As the lesson progresses, a page about "Blue Memphis arisin'" provides another opportunity to have students make rich, outside connections. She asks if students know where Memphis is and if they know anything about it. The students are quiet, not sure how to answer. Ms. Park explains that Memphis is a town in Tennessee where music flourished and a style known as the Memphis blues developed. "What does it mean to have the blues?"

"It means you're sad."

"Yeah, like you're so sad that you have blue tears, and so you're called blue."

"Good answers, dancers. I'm going to play a song by W. C. Handy—he is known as the Father of the Blues. Even though the blues might be sad, it also has a smooth quality—the kind that might help you find floating and rising movements like the image on this page. Listen to the music, think about this page, sense the sadness, and let your body react. When the music starts, you may begin." As the music begins, the students begin moving in diverse ways. Some swing and sway, others walk with heaviness, and others focus on rising and falling. The qualities in their movements are becoming more refined. It is likely that this is the first time these students have heard this style of music, and the sound certainly has informed their movement quality.

The class moves on to the next page, and the students explore mirroring—inspired by a hidden mirror on the page. The students then are asked to apply their most abstract thinking skills.

"Children, when I show you the next page, you decide how to let the image inspire your movement. Go with your first idea. Follow your instincts, and see how many different and interesting choices you can make." As Ms. Park turns the page, a treelike figure emerges, and she reads, "Yellow on red and nineteen black spots." This is an important opportunity for the students. Up to this point, Ms. Park has carefully guided them through the movement and directed their focus with words like tapping, twisting, and rising. This is the first time in which the children find the meaning, motivation, and movement vocabulary for themselves. Some children create fire-like movements with their arms, and others make tall shapes. A few are nervous and perhaps not sure what to do. Ms. Park skillfully rescues them: "If I tap you on the shoulder, sit down right where you are, and watch your friends' ideas about this page." She makes sure to tap the less-confident students while decidedly keeping the confident movers standing. As these students move, she asks those who are watching to be ready to report on what they see. After a few comments about fireworks and strong movements, it is the other groups' turn. The once apprehensive students move more securely this time. Ms. Park tries to match the beat of her drum with the movement choices of the students.

And so the lesson continues this way; students creatively respond to movement problems. They embody choices regarding tipsy, teetering tassels; entwining, spontaneous forms; and Fauve kabooms.

The students are getting physically tired at this point. Before they conclude the movement, though, Ms. Park engages them in a culminating activity. "Dancers, think of your favorite page and the way you moved today. Don't tell me; just think about it. Why was it your favorite? Maybe it was the way your shadow looked on the wall, or it could have been the feeling of momentum as you teetered. When I give you the signal, move out into the space, and show me your favorite moment from today." This quick assessment allows the students an opportunity to reflect and summarize the experience through movement. It gives Ms. Park a snapshot of the most impactful moment for each student. It also offers helpful information about skill, movement preferences, and comprehension for future lessons. "Dancers, find an ending in three, two, one. Excellent!"

Ms. Park gathers the students and finishes the class with a discussion. "Why do you think the author David A. Carter chose to create the pages he did in this book?" Some simple answers are shouted out.

"Because he likes shadows."

"And maybe he's from Memphis?"

"Do you know what, students? I think you're correct. This book doesn't have a story line or specific plot. I think the author created the pages based upon things from everyday life that inspired him. Do you know that some of the best art, dance, and music are created that way? We can find inspiration in the things that affect everyday life and work and play." As the lesson wraps up, Ms. Park encourages the students to think about things they see, experience, and learn about that inspire them. The next lesson will provide them with opportunities to create their own dances about their everyday lives.

UNDERSTANDING THE LITERACY EVENT

This vignette highlighted the importance of teacher decision making in both planning and teaching a lesson. Throughout the vignette Ms. Park attended to the needs of the individual students as she sought to create a space that opened opportunities for learning. While students were encouraged to be independent learners, there was also a great amount of support and guidance offered. Ms. Park used a variety of text, processes, and literacies in an effort to support students as meaning makers.

Texts

A variety of texts were present in this vignette; some of these included the pop-up book, the physical space, and the students' bodies. Children's literature is a common text found in an elementary classroom. Indeed, children's literature is a powerful tool for opening up worlds for students. It allows them access to vocabulary, ideas, and worlds that are unknown. While the book may be used in traditional ways to read, summarize, and respond; the book also can be used as a stepping stone to allow children to connect their experiences and understandings to the larger community. Recent research suggests that when given opportunities, students are able to respond and connect with the text in richer and more meaningful ways (Serafini & Ladd, 2008) when there is a focus on the visual components rather than simply the words. We were able to witness this connecting as Ms. Park asked the students to demonstrate their understanding of the words, pictures, and art through their bodies. The text was not simply a print-based book; rather, it was a launching pad for connecting the reader, the text, and the context.

Space and bodies were also key texts in the vignette. While the physical space was important, as it afforded opportunities for the students to move about, the learning space that Ms. Park created was critical. Alerby, Hagstrom, and Westman (2014) state, "A place for learning can thus create expectations and opportunities, be inviting to certain activities, and be inspiring. It may also be the opposite and thereby constrain learning"

(p. 12). As evidenced in this vignette, a space was created that allowed for exploration, creativity, and creation as the students connected through their bodies.

Ms. Park was acutely aware of the students' cognitive understandings of the text and the connections they were making as they danced—the students' bodies were a text for Ms. Park. As a result of her observations, during the lesson, she created a space for the students who were hesitant, a space that allowed them to observe, think, and then create. During this time classmates' bodies also became a text as they engaged in watching one another's interpretations of the pop-up book.

Processes

The students were engaged in connecting processes throughout this vignette. They were presented with new content about various art forms and then encouraged to embody these ideas and express them through dance. It is important to note again that connecting occurs through creating and responding in the early elementary grades. For example, Ms. Park introduced the students to shadows through the pop-up book and then again as she demonstrated shadows using a white wall and halogen light. The teacher was not the only model; she allowed the students to create and perform for one another, making the teacher–student roles fluid. The students explored and shared their personal understandings of Mondrian's art as they created interesting shapes with their bodies.

Another page of the pop-up book introduced students to the Memphis blues. Rather than simply telling the students about the blues, Ms. Park allowed them to listen to the music and then connect those feelings to movement. Ms. Park did not direct their movements but rather encouraged them by stating, "Let your body react." The Enduring Understanding for Standard 10 reads, "As dance is experienced, all personal experience, knowledge, and context are integrated and synthesized to interpret meaning" (NCAS, 2014, DA: Cn10). Throughout the vignette the students utilized their knowledge, abilities, understandings, and the space to connect to the music and art. They demonstrated their connections through individual movement; they participated in connecting through creating meaning.

Literacies

Throughout the vignette, Ms. Park provided opportunities for the students to use and develop specific dance literacies as they engaged in physical performance problem-solving tasks. Hong (2000) states, "The development of dance literacy involves the 'encoding' or expression and 'decoding' or interpretation of symbolic forms" (para. 16). Indeed, each page of the pop-up book provided opportunities for the students to decode or interpret the images and then encode or share their interpretation of the image through movement. The pop-up book, video, and music afforded students opportunities to make meaning and then share that meaning with one another.

As the students engaged in dance throughout the learning activity, they had opportunities to "explore, construct, communicate, interpret and negotiate" (Hong, 2000, para. 26) personal meanings through dance. Dance requires students to participate in powerful literacies, not only literacies that require more than rote answers but, rather, literacies that require embodiment. Serafini (2011/2012) suggests that teachers engage students in "intellection," which requires teachers to plan instructional practices that compel "readers to go beyond literal levels of meaning, reject the notion of a single main idea, and construct meanings for themselves rather than search for predetermined answers" (p. 241). Allowing students opportunities to share their understandings that extend beyond discussions and writing creates spaces for students' thinking and learning to expand. It also allows students of all abilities to engage in meaningful, embodied literacies.

CONCLUSION

The purpose of this chapter was to explore how dance and literacy can be integrated meaningfully in the curriculum to create opportunities for students to connect themselves to their worlds. The Essential Question for Standard 10 reads, "How does dance deepen our understanding of ourselves, other knowledge, and events around us?" It is important that students develop an understanding that movement has meaning and that their personal interpretations and expressions are valued; this key idea separates dance from general physical education. Indeed, dance has the ability to integrate the domains of the whole child in a unique way because it focuses on the embodiment of cognitive ideas and expressive emotions that often are presented and shared in their homes, schools, and communities.

The benefits of arts in the curriculum have been well researched (Bonbright, Bradley, & Dooling, 2013; Davis, 2008), with Heath (2014) strongly stating, "Art making affects memory, language, vision, auditory perception, emotional development, and mental health and well-being" (p. 358). Returning to the beginning of the chapter, we want again to remind elementary educators of the importance of teaching the whole child, not simply focusing on their cognitive needs and development.

REFERENCES

Alerby, E., Hagstrom, E., & Westman, S. (2014). The embodied classroom: A phenomenological discussion of the body and the room. *Journal of Pedagogy, 5,* 11–23.

Banovcanova, Z., and Slavik, J. (2014). Body in education. *Journal of Pedagogy, 5,* 5–8.

Bonbright, J., Bradley, K., and Dooling, S. (2013). *Evidence: A report on the impact of dance in K–12 settings*. Silver Spring, MD: National Dance Education Organization. Retrieved from http://arts.gov/sites/default/files/Research-Art-Works-NDEO.pdf

Bredekamp, S. (2011). *Effective practices in early childhood education: Building a foundation*. Boston, MA: Pearson.

Carter, D. A. (2007). *600 black spots*. New York, NY: Little Simon.

Davis, J. (2008). *Why Our Schools Need the Arts*. Teachers College Press: New York.

Dils, A. (2007). Why dance literacy? *Journal of the Canadian Association for Curriculum Studies, 5*(2), 95–113.

Heath, S. B. (2014). The foundational bases of learning with the arts. *The Educational Forum, 78*, 358–362. doi: 10.1080/00131725.2014.944078

Hong, T. (2000). Developing dance literacy in the postmodern: An approach to curriculum. Paper presented at Dancing in the Millennium: An international conference, Washington, DC. Retrieved from http://artsonline2.tki.org.nz/Teacher Learning/readings/danceliteracy.php

National Association for the Education of Young Children & National Association of Early Childhood specialists in State Departments of Education. (2003). Early childhood curriculum, assessment, and program evaluation: Building an effective, accountable system in programs for children birth through age 8. A joint position statement of the National Association for the Education of Young Children (NAEYC) and the National Association of Early Childhood Specialists in State Departments of Education. Retrieved April 23, 2015 from https://www.naeyc.org/files/naeyc/file/positions/pscape.pdf

National Core Arts Standards. (2014). *Dance standards*. Retrieved from http://www.nationalartsstandards.org/sites/default/files/Dance_resources/Dance%20at%20a%20Glance.pdf

Rosborough, A. (2014). Gesture, meaning-making, and embodiment: Second-language learning in an elementary classroom. *Journal of Pedagogy, 5*, 227–250.

Roth, W. M. (2014). On the pregnance of bodily movement and geometrical objects: A post-constructivist account of the origin of mathematical knowledge. *Journal of Pedagogy, 5*, 65–89.

Serafini, F. (2011/2012). When bad things happen to good books. *The Reading Teacher, 65*(7), 238–242. doi: 10.1002/TRTR.01039

Serafini, F., & Ladd, S. M. (2008). The challenge of moving beyond the literal in literature discussions. *Journal of Language and Literacy Education [Online], 4*(2), 6–20. Retrieved from http://www.coe.uga.edu/jolle/2008_2/challenge.pdf

25 Creating and Continuing the Conversation between Arts and Literacy Educators

*Roni Jo Draper and
Amy Petersen Jensen*

Throughout this book, arts educators have shared glimpses into classrooms where arts educators are working to create environments in which students are provided opportunities to engage in authentic arts practices. We acknowledge and hope it has been made clear throughout this book that there is no one set of arts practices or literacies central to creating, responding, connecting, and/or performing. Indeed, some readers may be frustrated by the lack of prescription we offer for how to create classrooms that support artistic literacies. However, this has been our intent. Rather than provide step-by-step prescriptions for how to address literacy in the arts, we invite arts educators and literacy educators to enter into conversations with one another and work together to create arts classrooms that foster in young people all the literacies required for engaging in the human conversation. For this last chapter, we will make recommendations for what arts and literacy educators can do to prepare young people to engage in the human conversation through the arts.

RECOMMENDATIONS FOR ARTS AND LITERACY EDUCATORS

Consider the work of textile artist Consuelo Jiménez Underwood as an example of an individual engaged in the human conversation. Underwood uses her experience growing up near the US/Mexico border as a child of a Chicana mother and an undocumented Mexican father, her understanding of border politics, and her reading of the environment to create pieces that inspire, question, and critique issues surrounding migration, immigration, and the environment. Through her work titled *Undocumented Border Flowers*, Underwood seeks to challenge the ecology of creating and maintaining a physical barrier between the United States and Mexico. As Underwood explains, "I'm here to talk about that border and what it is doing to us as caretakers of the earth. . . . The natural animals and plant life [are] going to be the true victims of this wall" (Underwood, n.d.). Underwood's work challenges the viewer to question the consequences—human and otherwise—of altering the landscape and restricting migration between nation-states. Clearly, Underwood participates in conversation with other artists as she both engages in and challenges the limits of textile work (Román-Odio, 2012). Moreover, through her work, Underwood is engaged in the human conversation wherein she uses her perspective and voice to participate in public deliberation around border politics.

As educators who seek to prepare young people to participate in the human conversation, we mustn't suppose that we know all the texts learners will confront or seek to create. Indeed, Underwood's literacies certainly include the ability to successfully interact with traditional print texts in ways familiar to language arts teachers. However, her literacies are much broader than that. Her literacies surrounding texture, color, space, scale, and textiles—how to weave, the limits of fiber, the possibilities of incorporating nonfibrous elements (e.g., barbed wire, safety pins, and warning signs)—allow her to express ideas impossible to express through print or even verbal language. The world would miss out if Underwood's education was limited to print literacies and ways with words. Simply put, literacy educators mustn't be complicit in limiting the literacy education of young people by promoting narrow literacies. Here, in our final chapter, we make suggestions for what literacy educators can do to promote artistic literacies and, thus, support a broad literacy education within schools.

First, educators need to **honor the arts**. This will require that literacy educators seek to promote arts classrooms as spaces where young people engage in art making rather than seeking to use arts classrooms as spaces in which to learn and practice traditional print literacies. Many literacy educators have not come to their position as literacy educators through the arts themselves. They may, in fact, hold misconceptions of the nature of the arts. For example, some literacy educators may believe that the arts is simply about perfecting techniques or understanding basic elements of a given art form. Literacy educators who often come to their positions via language arts classrooms (Blarney, Meyer, & Walpole, 2009) may draw upon their love and understanding of the language arts and work simply to translate those practices to arts education settings. As such, literacy educators, supposing that they are working to improve classroom instruction, may unwittingly promote practices appropriate for promoting literacy associated with traditional reading and writing of print texts. However, these practices (e.g., finding the main idea, summarizing, or making an argument) actually may thwart efforts to promote artistic literacies.

Certainly, artists such as Underwood must engage in what traditionally would be described as the language arts. She speaks about her art. She engages in written exchanges in which she describes her own artistic methods and decisions. She likely reads print material about her work and the work of other artists. No doubt she has made a careful study of print texts that describe the environment and ecology around the border. These traditional print literacies, therefore, play an important role in her life.

However, the work itself, which sprawls over an entire wall, does something that mere words cannot do. Literacy educators, therefore, must be mindful that any curricular advice they suggest work toward building arts literacies.

We are reminded of Barney's description of Ms. Baker (in the creating section of this volume) and the effort she made to help her students not only consider the work of an artist (in this case Jan Yager) but the methodology the artist undertakes to create his/her art. Furthermore, the focus of instruction was not on the finished pieces that the artist creates but rather on the way the artist is involved in creating even before he/she begins work on the final piece. Arts educators certainly understand that creating begins well before artists begin work on their finished piece. However, art educators may lose sight of the fact that engaging in the authentic processes surrounding art making is at the heart of arts education. Rather, Ms. Baker and her students could get so excited by Jan Yager's sculpture and jewelry work that they try simply to imitate Yager's work. Indeed, many arts educators may see their role as helping young people learn techniques and to guarantee that the finished pieces created in arts classrooms are well done.

To ensure that instruction in arts settings force on authentic practice, a literacy educator involved with an arts educator might ask, "What are the authentic practices related to this artist or this art form?" This question shifts the focus of instruction away from the finished product and toward the processes involved in art making. In this way, the work of an artist like Underwood or Yager still remains a useful study for arts students. However, rather than focus solely on the art pieces themselves, the literacy educator can converse with the arts educator about the processes involved in investigating one's environment or engaging in method as part of arts practices. These processes, then, can become the focus of instruction designed to support art creation like that typified in Ms. Baker's classroom.

Second, literacy educators as well as arts educators would do well to *familiarize themselves with the National Core Arts Standards*. In fact, reading the National Core Arts Standards together and discussing them may serve to forward the conversation between arts and literacy educators. Again, because literacy educators may be unfamiliar with the texts, processes, and literacies central to the arts, they must take the time to familiarize themselves with the National Core Arts Standards. Meanwhile, arts educators may feel that they understand their subject areas and needn't study or discuss the National Core Arts Standards. However, these standards, like all standards documents, impose upon educators and other stakeholders (e.g., policy makers and parents) a particular vision of classrooms (Popkewitz, 2004). It would serve educators well to read and discuss the standards as part of conversations of how educators might go about improving instruction in the disciplines—especially discussion that include how to support authentic disciplinary literacies.

Indeed, the National Core Arts Standards seek to help young people engage in the kind of art making found in the arts world—Underwood exemplifies these activities. Underwood is not engaged, for example, in creating art through relying on media and methods used by other artists. Rather, she is engaged in using her own voice. However, literacy educators may not be familiar with the aims of arts education. They may unwittingly believe that arts education is about helping young people make frameworthy drawings or paintings or perform a pitch-perfect concert or dance with exactness and precision. Instead, when literacy educators acknowledge their own limited understanding of the arts, they can read the NCCAS Framework (2014) to understand that "fundamental creating practices of imagination, investigation, construction, and reflection" (p. 19) are central to creating in the arts. Moreover, these creative practices are not consistent with mimicking the work of others. This is an important distinction that those who wish to promote the arts must understand and support. Familiarity with the National Core Arts Standards would be helpful to anyone seeking to support all the practices, processes, and literacies related to the arts.

We recognize that while the standards address the processes individually, the processes involved in art making never really are isolated. Thus, we understand that artists engage simultaneously in creating, performing, responding, and connecting when they are participating in authentic arts practices. Indeed, this is clear from even the cursory description of Underwood's work on *Undocumented Border Flowers*. The challenge is for arts educators to be mindful of necessity to engage learners in all the processes.

For example, let us return to the music chapter on performing written by Broomhead (in the performing section of this volume). In the chapter, Broomhead describes the work of Ms. Yarn, who is interested in helping her students gain and sharpen their performance literacies. In fact, arts educators can become overly concerned with one aspect of their art. Music educators, for instance, can place most of their attention on ensuring that an impending musical performance is well done (because that is ultimately what the audience and the performers would enjoy) so that they may not attend to the other arts processes.

Arts and literacy educators familiar with the National Core Arts Standards can use the standards to discuss how instruction in arts classrooms might attend to all the processes rather than give undue attention to only one. The arts educator may ask, "What is the process you are making the focus of your instruction?" and "How might instruction focused on the other processes help learners progress in the desired process?" For example, Ms. Yarn created instruction that allowed learners to connect to musical selections by analyzing them and describing key components of the various music genres. Learners also had a chance to respond to one another in their ensembles and to the feedback (response) to their work provided by

Ms. Yarn. In this way, Ms. Yarn doesn't compromise instruction in the other processes (creating, responding, and connecting) to focus on performance. Instead, she understands that instruction that attends to all the processes enhances students' overall art knowledge and experience.

Third, arts and literacy educators must *focus their conversations on the texts, processes, and literacies central to the arts.* This may seem redundant to the previous two points, but that is simply because it builds from the recommendations we have already made. Certainly arts educators are in an ideal position to identify the texts, processes, and literacies central to their disciplines. However, inviting an outsider interested in supporting artistic literacies to engage in conversation about arts literacies may help arts educators notice challenges for learners in arts settings. To be of help to arts educators, literacy educators must enter conversations with arts educators curious about the arts. This begins with asking questions like these: What are the texts that are important here and now? What are the literacies required to negotiate and create those texts? How can instruction be created to help learners confront and create those texts in meaningful ways? Note that entering the conversation with questions is very different than entering the conversation with answers (something that we worry far too many literacy educators do).

Again, looking to the art and work of Underwood, a literacy educator may be of tremendous help to an arts educator by asking questions about the pieces created by Underwood and the possible literacies needed to create and appreciate or read them. These conversations are helpful for arts educators who may take for granted their own abilities to negotiate and create texts or who may not understand the need to make the processes and literacies used to engage with the texts visible to their students. These conversations, therefore, have the potential to make clear to arts educators what they can do to strengthen their own instruction and make the arts more accessible to more young people.

It may be tempting for literacy educators to focus on the possibilities of print literacies in arts settings. For example, in Thevenin's discussion of media arts (in the responding section of this volume), a literacy educator may be tempted to suggest that Ms. Cage augment her instruction with opportunities for the students to create written responses to the film that they viewed or to the pieces that their classmates created. While we would not argue that engaging learners in composing traditional print texts is never appropriate for arts classrooms, we would argue that serious consideration must be given to any curricular decision made in an arts setting to ensure that the instruction will advance students' understanding and ability to participate in arts practices. In the case of the example that Thevenin shared, Ms. Cage provided instruction that focused squarely on students' understanding of the affordances and limitations of texts. Naturally the texts under consideration were appropriate for a media arts setting (e.g., film and drawings). Instruction around texts ought to take place in other classrooms (e.g., language arts, science, or mathematics); however, arts classrooms offer ideal settings for young people to discuss how to choose particular texts for particular purposes.

CONCLUSION

These three recommendations are simple, but we believe that when arts and literacy educators approach their work together by first valuing the place of arts education as part of a complete education for all young people, familiarize themselves with the National Core Arts Standards, and focus on the texts, processes, and literacies central to the arts, they are in a position to be of tremendous help to each other.

Arts education has a history of being extracurricular, and all too often people obtain the bulk of their arts education outside of public-school settings (e.g., private dance or music instruction, community theatre, and recreational filmmaking). However, to continue to relegate arts education to the private sector is to continue to allow access to the arts to those individuals with the economic advantage to obtain such education outside of public-schools settings. Indeed, the human conversation is too important and must include the arts.

All of the contributors to this book have described arts classrooms that provide support for young people to learn the skills necessary to participate in the human conversation. Oakeshott (1959) explained that the excellence of conversation "springs from a tension between seriousness and playfulness" (p. 14). Indeed, the arts offer individuals an opportunity to experience that tension. Musil's description (in the connecting section of this volume) of a dance classroom wherein the teacher uses the space to discuss issues of race as they relate to dance is an excellent example of working within the tension of seriousness and playfulness. Indeed, Ms. O'Hara could have focused her instruction only on the playfulness of dance and even the joy and beauty of hip-hop. Instead, she seized the opportunity to engage her students in confronting serious issues surrounding race, racism, and privilege. And while students did not reach conclusions, they were better prepared to enter the conversation, to use their voices—their bodies—to understand themselves and build relationships with others. Indeed, it is perhaps because art finds itself affixed squarely between seriousness and playfulness that an arts education is crucial for all young people and not just a select few.

We believe that access to the human conversation requires access to the multiplicity of texts and literacies used to sustain the conversation. When we look at the world our students meet outside of schools, we see a wide range of texts (print, film, drawings, sounds, and bodies) and an even wider range of literacies needed to make sense of those texts. Certainly, education in the arts offers access to those texts and literacies that cannot be found in other subject areas. We, as educators, must not be complicit in limiting access to the arts for many of our students; to do so ultimately limits their literacy education. Rather, let's work together as educators to support a broad literacy education, one that promotes facility with print-based literacies and one that promotes facility in other literacies like those found in the arts. And let's do this by creating classrooms that look more like the worlds we are preparing young people to enter.

REFERENCES

Blarney, K.L., Meyer, C.K., & Walpole, S. (2009). Middle and high school literacy coaches: A national survey. *Journal of Adolescent and Adult Literacy, 52*(4), 310–323.

National Coalition for Core Arts Standards. (2014). National Core Arts Standards Framework. Online at http://www.nationalartsstandards.org/sites/default/files/NCCAS%20%20Conceptual%20Framework_4.pdf

Oakeshott, M. (1959). *The voice of poetry in the conversation of mankind*. London, England: Bowes and Bowes.

Popkewitz, T.S. (2004). Educational standards: Mapping who we are and are to become. *The Journal of the Learning Sciences, 13*(2), 243–256.

Román-Odio, C. (2012). Colonial legacies and the politics of weaving in Consuelo Jiménez Underwood's fiber arts. *American Tapestry Alliance*. Retrieved December 18, 2014, from http://americantapestryalliance.org/education/educational-articles/political-strings-tapestry-seen-and-unseen/colonial-legacies-and-the-politics-of-weaving-in-consuelo-jimenez-underwoods-fiber-art/

Underwood, C. (n.d.). *Video*. Retrieved December 18, 2014, http://www.consuelojimenezunderwood.com/cju-speaks-on-undocumented-flower.html

Contributors

Julia Ashworth, MA, is an assistant teaching professor of theatre education in the Department of Theatre and Media Arts at Brigham Young University (BYU). She has worked in the field of arts education—as an artist, administrator and K–12 teacher—for more than fifteen years. Her duties in the Department of Theatre and Media Arts at BYU include serving as artistic director for The Young Company and acting as program director for the Theatre Education Program. Her work focuses primarily on theatre for young audiences and applied theatre practices.

Daniel T. Barney, PhD, is an associate professor of art education in the Department of Visual Arts at BYU, where he teaches courses on qualitative research and analysis, curriculum theory and development, and issues in contemporary art. His research focuses on the intersection of pedagogy and arts-based research methodologies. His work is published in journals such as *Visual Arts Research, Mentoring & Tutoring: Partnership in Learning, International Journal of Education through Art,* and *Journal for Artistic Research.* He currently serves as assistant editor of arts-based research for the *Journal of Curriculum & Pedagogy,* is on the international review board of both *Studies in Arts Based Educational Research Series* and *Springer Briefs in Arts Based Educational Research Series,* and he serves on the editorial review boards of the journals *Art Education* and *Journal of Cultural Research in Art Education.* Dr. Barney was the 2011 recipient of the Pacific Region Art Educator of the Year Award for the National Art Education Association (NAEA) and the 2012 recipient of the Pacific Region Higher Education Educator of the Year Award (NAEA).

Paul Broomhead, PhD, is a professor of music education in the BYU School of Music, where he serves as choral education coordinator. His publications have appeared in the *Journal of Research in Music Education, Music Educators Journal, Bulletin of the Council for Research in Music Education, Journal of Music Teacher Education, Teaching Music, Update, Contributions to Music Education, Reading Psychology,* and

Teacher Development. He was coeditor and participating author of the book *(Re)imagining Content-Area Literacy Instruction*. He has served the National Association for Music Education (NAfME) as national chair of the Instructional Strategies SRIG and as collegiate chair for the Western Division.

Roni Jo Draper, PhD, is a professor in the Department of Teacher Education in the David O. McKay School of Education at BYU. She teaches courses in literacy education, multicultural education, and research methods. Most of Dr. Draper's scholarship in teacher education focuses on preparing teachers to support the literacy development of young people within the disciplines (e.g., mathematics, science, engineering, and the arts). Her work has appeared in the *American Educational Research Journal*, the *Journal of Teacher Education*, the *Journal of Literacy Research*, and the *Journal of Adolescent and Adult Literacy*. She also has contributed to books focusing on disciplinary literacy including *(Re)imagining Content-Area Literacy Instruction*, which she edited and authored with members of the BYU Literacy Study Group.

Amy Petersen Jensen, PhD, is a professor and chair of the Theatre and Media Arts Department in the College of Fine Arts and Communications at BYU. Amy teaches in the Media Education Master's Degree and in the undergraduate theatre education program at BYU, where she prepares arts educators to teach theatre and media in secondary schools. She currently is the editor of the *Youth Theatre Journal* and has served as the coeditor of the *Journal of Media Literacy Education*. She currently serves on the leadership team for the National Coalition for Core Arts Standards, the advisory board of the *Arts Education Policy Review*, and is the advocacy director for the American Alliance for Theatre in Education's board of directors. Recent book publications include *Theatre in a Media Culture: Production, Performance and Perception Since 1970* (McFarland, 2007) and the coedited volume *(Re)imagining Literacies for Content Literacy Instruction* (Teachers College Press, 2010).

Pamela S. Musil, MA, is a professor in the Department of Dance at BYU, where she teaches dance education, dance science, and technique courses and serves as the contemporary dance administrator. Research interests include gender-related issues of dancers in adolescence, young adulthood, and various career stages, with particular focus on matters pertaining to women. Musil has served on the board of directors for the National Dance Education Organization (NDEO) and currently serves on the editorial boards for the *Journal of Dance Education* and *Arts Education Policy Review*. She is the current president of the Utah Dance Education Organization.

Benjamin Thevenin, PhD, is an assistant professor of Media Arts at BYU. His research focuses on the intersection of youth, media, education, and politics. He is the director of BYU's Hands on a Camera program in which undergraduate students teach media analysis and production to youth as a means of helping them engage with and improve their communities. Dr. Thevenin currently is developing his dissertation "Critical Media Literacy in Action: Uniting Theory, Practice and Politics in Media Education" into a new project. He lives with his wife and two children in the beautiful Wasatch Mountains of Utah.

Kori Wakamatsu is an assistant teaching professor at BYU in the Contemporary Dance Area. Before entering higher education, she taught both junior high and high school. She received her MA in dance from California State University, Long Beach, and a Theatre Endorsement from the University of Utah. Her research interests include pop culture, curriculum development, and collaboration. She has been honored to work on many collaborative projects such as the *Thought of You* animation, *The Nightingale* play, *Provo Sites* mobile dance series, and the *Theatre Engine* project.

Jennifer J. Wimmer, PhD, is an assistant professor in the Department of Teacher Education at Brigham Young University. Her research focuses on the intersection of disciplinary literacy, new literacies, and teacher professional development. She teaches courses in the elementary education program focused on foundations of literacy development and elementary literacy methods. Prior to her work at BYU, she taught first grade in the public schools.

Index

Abramovic, Marina 94–6
access 7, 50, 59, 61, 63, 99, 104–5, 113–14, 116, 128–9, 138, 148–54, 169, 188, 190, 202, 210–12
adaptation 29–33
aesthetic 26, 29, 42, 46, 48, 79, 91, 94, 97, 100, 103–4, 116, 120, 122, 130, 132, 134, 137–8, 145–7, 153
aesthetic choices 137
affordances 32, 128–30, 178
alternative media 29
analysis/analytical 22, 25, 27, 29, 32–5, 62, 70, 91–2, 95, 99–100, 103–4, 109, 117–22, 124, 128–30, 140, 144–6, 148, 152–3, 158, 162, 166, 174, 177–9, 186, 189, 194, 209, 213
Antigone 37–40
Arabian Nights 182–5
art texts 8, 22, 43, 48–9, 145, 152, 189, 195
artistic intent 20, 23, 69, 73, 75, 137
artistic process 3, 7–8, 23, 39–41, 47–50, 57, 103, 110, 142–3, 150, 165, 171, 189–90, 194–5, 208–9
artistic response 152–3
audience 20, 25–6, 32, 35–9, 41, 66, 69–71, 73–6, 84, 88, 91–2, 94–7, 104, 124, 129–34, 136–7, 151, 153, 175, 179, 181–2, 184, 186, 209, 213
Audubon, John James 140–6
Aufderheide, Patricia 129
authenticity iii, 3, 6–9, 14, 19–21, 23–5, 27, 36, 42–50, 69, 79, 87, 91, 122, 141, 146, 196, 206–9
authentic theatre participation 36
author 131

balance 111
Barney, D.T. 49, 144
Barthes, R. 43
blend 111
body/bodies/embody 6, 8, 20–2, 26, 38–40, 53, 56, 58, 63–4, 71–3, 77, 84, 85–7, 88, 93–4, 96–8, 100, 112, 117–19, 121–2, 150, 165–71, 173, 176–7, 194, 198–201, 203–4
body language 100, 117, 171
Bogost, Ian 178
Bolton, G. 84
Borstel, J 116
break-dancing, breaking, b-boying 76, 166–9
bricole 49
Broomhead, P. 61

Carter, D.A. 199, 201
Castro, J.C., & Barney, D.T. 49
Chang, C. 149–53
character 30–1, 34, 77–80, 82, 126–7, 175–7
character objectives 37, 38
choice 2–3, 23–4, 30, 34, 39, 52–5, 67, 69, 71, 73–4, 78, 81, 83, 85–8, 103, 130, 132–4, 136–8, 151, 176, 181–3, 185–8, 194, 201
choral blend, or unity 111–2
choreographer 21, 23, 25, 69, 74
choreography 8, 21, 22–7, 69, 116, 119–22
citizenship 180
Clemente, K 75
collaboration, collaborative 2, 35, 82, 170, 172
College Board 3, 20, 25, 27

218 *Index*

Common Core State Standards 1, 57–8, 103
communities of practice 43, 48, 92, 97, 181, 196
community 2, 5, 27, 29, 37, 44, 48, 52, 70, 83, 94, 122, 133, 149–51, 153, 166, 168–70, 182, 187, 196, 202, 211
complex/complexity 13–15, 43, 48, 52, 56–7, 65, 74–5, 103–5, 113, 117, 121–2, 144, 148, 153–4, 178, 189–90, 196
composing 13, 19, 100, 103, 174, 210
conceptual investigation/insights 34, 48–9, 57, 81, 91, 101, 141–2, 157, 162–3, 178
conducting 61, 113, 162, 163
context 5, 8, 13–14, 17, 24–5, 31, 33, 36–7, 40–4, 48–9, 51, 57, 62, 67, 73–8, 80–2, 84, 89, 92, 94–7, 110, 117, 121–2, 124, 128, 131–3, 136–8, 140, 144–5, 149–50, 153, 157, 165–6, 168, 170–1, 173–5, 181, 187, 189, 191, 193–5, 202–3
contextual research 137
conventions 32
conversation 1, 206
Cope & Kalantsis 109
costume 76–80
creating processes 13–14, 18, 44, 52, 163
creative process 133
Crista, Heloise 21, 25, 26
critical awareness, 139
critical literacy 82, 148–9, 153–4, 180
critical pedagogy 70, 74, 179
critical reflection 34, 70
culture 31, 34–5, 80, 124, 165–70, 175

dance texts 21
dance vocabulary 116, 120–1
Depression Quest 176–8
Deren, Maya 125–30
design 33, 35, 79, 80, 82, 127, 174–6
digital media 34
Dils, Ann 20, 199
discourse community 187
discussion 5, 15, 34, 37–8, 41, 44–5, 47–8, 62, 71, 74, 79, 82, 94–7, 100–2, 104, 121–2, 124, 126–7, 129–30, 147–50, 152–3, 162, 170–2, 178, 183, 185, 189, 201, 204, 208
Dixon-Gottschild 165

documentary 29, 81, 175, 178–9
drama text 58
dramatic conventions 41
dramaturgical choices 134
dramaturgical lens 136
Draper & Siebert 13
Duncum, P. 7, 97, 140

editing 35, 75, 81–2, 126–8
educational reform 1–4
Elements of Dance 118–21, 165, 198–9
emotions 53–5, 57
empowerment 175
ensemble setting 110, 114
Ericsson, Krampe, & Tesch-Romer 61
Esperanza Rising 133–9
evaluate 128–9
experience/experiential 48, 63, 91, 95, 97, 146, 148, 157, 165–6, 170, 173, 187, 189–90, 194–5, 199, 203
expression 29, 35, 76, 175

feedback 16, 21, 25, 62, 119, 128, 163
film 29, 35, 82, 125–6, 128, 174
Ford, Walton 140
foreground 18, 62, 66, 109, 110, 113, 158, 161, 162
Fortin, S. 170
foundational literacies 52, 57, 104
Friere, Paulo 79
frozen images, 85

Gallagher, K. 132
Gee, J.P. 4–5, 9, 37, 187, 195
general music 61, 68, 110
Gonzalez, J. 132
graffiti board 38, 40
Grand Staircase Project 70
Green, J. 116
Gude, O. 44, 154

Hagood, T. 20
Hall, Stuart 130
Hanna, Thomas 170
Haydn, Franz Joseph 159
Henley, M 116
hip-hop 76
historical information 138, 142–4, 163, 183, 195
Hobbs, Renee 104, 124, 130, 175
Hong, Tina 20, 24
Hughes, Michael 193
Hunter, V. 69

identity/identification 77, 82, 155, 169, 174–5
ideology 34, 178
illustration 126–8
imagination 2, 8, 13–18, 22, 26–7, 54–5, 57–8, 78, 84, 89, 101, 163, 183–4, 209
improvise/improvisation 13–14, 19, 20, 22–3, 76, 79, 81, 92, 119, 122
inferences and observations 138
inflection 14–15
information 2–3, 22, 31, 33, 45, 56–7, 65–6, 74, 86, 94, 99, 103, 133–4, 137–8, 140, 144–5, 157, 160, 179, 186, 190–1, 199, 201
inquiry i, xv, 3, 40, 43–4, 47–50, 84, 88, 89, 124, 132, 141, 143, 145, 158, 182, 186–7, 190, 193, 195
inquiry processes 182
interactivity 175
interpretation 17–19, 2–23, 25, 35, 43, 48, 53, 63, 70, 73, 75, 85, 87, 94–5, 109, 116, 121–2, 124–5, 127–30, 132–3, 136–8, 140, 144–5, 148–9, 163, 166, 170–1, 183, 195, 203–4
investigation 8, 40, 45–9, 137, 189, 209

Jenkins, Henry 180
Josephson, Kenneth 193
justice/injustice 148, 170, 180

Kalin, N.M, & Barney, D.T. 49
Kellner & Share 29, 179–80
Kerr-Berry, Julie 74, 165
Kimmel, M. S. 171
kinesthetic 20, 116–22
Kopplowitz, Stephan 70
Krasnow, D 70
Kress, Gunther 42, 130

Lamont, Hargreaves, Marshall, & Tarrant 61
Lavender, Larry 116
Lazarus, J 132
lens 5, 82, 116, 121, 136, 165–6, 179
Lerman, Liz 116
limitations 32, 128–30, 178
literature 30–3, 35
Lynne Alvarez 133, 136, 139

MacBean, Arianne 166
Mainwaring, L. 70
making 43–6, 49–50, 91–3, 99, 141, 145–6, 189–90, 194–6, 207–9
marginalization 165
Marshall, J. 44
mass communication 29, 35
meaning: extramusical 157–8, 163; musical 61, 62, 163
meaning making 5, 27, 43, 48–9, 52, 61–2, 91–2, 102, 121–2, 131, 139–40, 158, 195, 198–9, 204
media literacies 104
medium specificity 126–9
Meltzoff, Andrew 116
methods/methodology/methodological 43–4, 46–8, 71, 122, 140, 142–4, 149, 151–3, 189, 196, 207–9
Minichiello, V. 158
Moffett, A. 70
movement 20–6, 74–5, 96, 116–22, 125–6, 128, 167, 204; movement decoding 116; movement motif 22–4; movement potential 21, 22, 24, 26; movement texts 25, 120, 170; movement vocabulary 201
multimedia 32, 35
multimodality 82
multimodal literacies, 36
multimodal texts, 21, 40, 42, 56, 102–3
music context 13–14, 17
music notation: embellishing 13–15, 19; as text, 61, 65; score, 162
music texts 13–14, 16–17
musical instruments 61, 62, 65, 67, 162
musical models 14, 17, 61, 62, 65

National Association for the Education of Young Children 198
National Core Arts Standards 2–3, 208–9
National Core Arts Theatre Standards 36, 83; Core Theatre Standards, 132, 181, 187
National Core Dance Standards 69, 165, 166
National Core Music Standards 13, 62, 109, 157
Needlands, J. 84
New London Group 58–9, 152
No Child Left Behind 1
Nokes, J. 145
Non-print texts 36

Oakeshott 1, 4, 211
O'Neill, C. 84
Ottey, S. 74

participation 2–3, 8, 97, 104, 148, 151–4, 157, 163–4
Partnership for 21st Century Skills 83, 181
performance art 77
performing technique 67
photography 174–5
phrase shaping 14–17
physical movements 88
picture book 56
pitch 67, 111, 114
play 25, 39, 49, 54–5, 62, 89, 97, 119, 140, 178–80, 189, 195, 202, 211
play contexts 136
play texts 87
points of view 52
politics 124, 175–6
polysemy 130
popular culture 78, 179
postmodernism 34
Powell, Jason 193
presentation 47, 91–2, 96–7, 150
privilege 133, 148, 153, 165–72, 211
print texts 40, 87
process drama 52, 84, 87
production elements 69, 73, 75, 137

questioning 24–5, 71, 74–5, 92, 95, 97, 103–4, 152, 187

radio 31
recorded performances 62, 66, 67, 110
reflection 33–34, 74, 124, 129–31
remix 34, 77
research 31, 33–4, 44, 46–7, 50, 70, 74, 94, 96, 133–7, 140–1, 143, 145, 158, 175–80, 183–7
responding critically 132
Risner, Doug 74
Ryan, Pam Munoz 133

scaffold 32
Sehgal, Tino 94
semiotics 43, 140, 144
sharing 44, 47, 97, 142, 152–3, 192, 194–5

site as text 47–50, 69–73, 92, 96–7, 150–4, 202–3
slide show 39
social engagement/socially engaged/social literacies/social practice 4–5, 43, 56, 72–5, 91–2, 94–9, 116, 138, 148–9, 151–4, 196
social media 29–35, 77
soma, somatic 116, 170
speech prosody 14–17
Sterbak, Jana 94
Stinson, Sue 172
storyboard 101, 103
Surprise Symphony 158
surrounding ensemble sounds 61, 65, 67, 110, 113, 114

technology 31
theatre creation spaces 181
theatre literacies 40, 87
theatre literate 89
theatre practice 83
theatre processes 40, 41, 87
theatre texts 40, 87
theme 32, 79
theory 35
timing 67, 111, 114
Titze 109
tone color 67, 111, 114
tuning chords 111
Turrell, James 94
Twelfth Night 84

Underwood, Consuelo Jimenez, 206

vertical alignment 111
video games 29, 175–80
visual culture 140, 144
volume 111, 114
vowel shape 67, 111

Walker, S.R. 190, 196
Weintraub, L. 146
West, S'thembile 165, 171
whole child 198, 204
Willems, M. 53, 56
Wilson, Fred 144
writing as art making 43–4, 48

Yager, Jan 44

Zimmerman, Mary 182–5